Seasons of a Refractive Mind

Seasons of a Refractive Mind

Selected poems, aphorisms, and photographs

Glenn Alan Daley

Empty Rock™ *LLC*
Redondo Beach
2016

Seasons of a Refractive Mind:
Selected poems, aphorisms, and photographs
by Glenn Alan Daley

First edition

ISBN 978-0-692-75321-7

Photographs are by the author except those of the author. The child who appears in these photos is Serena Sakura Daley. The photograph of the author on the back cover is by Serena Sakura Daley.

The photograph referred to in "Drivers pose before the start of the British Grand Prix 1964" is by Michael R. Hewett, and may be seen on page 204 of *The Power and the Glory: A Century of Motor Racing*, by Ivan Rendell, BBC Books, London, 1991.

"Variations on a theme by Joshua Slocum" is an adaptation of public domain passages in *Sailing Alone Around the World*, by Joshua Slocum, 1909.

Published by Empty Rock™ LLC
PO Box 4270, Redondo Beach, California 90277

EmptyRock.com

In memory of

Ellen Wilshire, teacher

and

Bill Daley, brother

Contents

Preface

Minds tend to reflect the world around them. What we call a reflective mind, though, is one that looks in a mirror and sees itself, sometimes magnified or diminished as in a carnival funhouse, sometimes echoed between mirrors receding into the distance. Poetry can be that way.

But the mind of poetry may be more a lens than a mirror. A refractive mind allows light waves from outside to pass through, but reshapes that light to create previously unseen images, new views of large things far away and tiny things very close. The refractive mind inevitably contributes its unique optical distortions and color aberrations. Sometimes it blossoms with interior flowers, as in a kaleidoscope. Sometimes, though, it points at a mirror and catches itself in the act, which can be startling and amusing, often humbling.

I was born a week shy of spring. The seasons of life and of the spirit are bound to planetary rhythms of equinox and solstice, not tightly but loosely. I claim the privilege of counting by the season I choose. W. H. Auden anticipated walking through the woods fifty springs from his twentieth, and came up short by four. I am now in my fiftieth spring from my thirteenth. That was about the age I started writing poetry. Students today are encouraged to create poetry from the time they start writing, but it was not always so.

I was severely scolded by my first grade teacher for ending sentences at the edge of the page instead of wrapping them around to let the periods fall inside the lines, a rebellion that still infects some of my work. I have been scolded for other violations, such as writing paragraphs without five sentences or calling a thing *haiku* without the requisite seventeen English syllables. I've spent some three score years liberating myself from definitions imposed by others, a work that remains unfinished. Feel free to disagree with me about what makes a poem or a life. You won't be the first.

I over-pruned my lemon tree a couple of years ago, and it seemed it might never flower again. This year I watched the bees having their pleasure with the blossoms, and now there are tiny green lemons promising a pitcher of fresh lemonade to share with friends this summer.

The poems in this collection are overdue if not delinquent. They represent fifty springs, as well as other seasons named and unnamed. This spring feels like the right time to share them.

When the light is right and a camera is walking with me, we collaborate to borrow a little light from the universe. The camera reserves the right to get it all wrong; I reserve the right to add words or subtract colors later. The fault in this arrangement is my own, as I often get in too much of a hurry to bring the camera on its leash or to stop and play when the camera wants to. Words are lighter to carry but easier to misplace. Like you, I have had many especially good ideas while driving or washing dishes, ideas that evaporated with no written residue. The angels may claim their share.

The world on the other side of the lens can be stunningly beautiful and deeply troubling at the same time. We are often taught that action beats contemplation, though contemplatives teach the opposite. I may have found the worst of both worlds—ineffective action and disturbed contemplation. No, that's putting it too harshly. Writing is a kind of action that calls on the reader to come along.

I am a living witness to certain systematic injustices in American history, and have stories to tell and analyses to offer that don't fit the format of this book. As a parent, teacher, and citizen, I think I have contributed to the good fight, but I have made many mistakes, and wasn't always paying attention. On occasion I have become lost in the opacity of conflicting obligations. The study of quantitative methods while wrestling with bosses, creditors, doctors, and weeds gave me some new languages but also drained my reserves of creativity at times. The meanings of words have shifted too. Neither my camera nor my language is the same as what I started with decades ago.

Minds are subject to fevers and chills at least as much as are muscles and joints. My own struggle for mental health has sometimes yielded edible fruit, but for many seasons at a time has left me detached from storms without or distracted by entertainments within. I am currently spelunking my memory and boxes of notes for connected chambers with traces of those times. Some of the poems here emerged from that effort; I think there are still more to be found.

Finally, there are the poems and images that might have been born had I lived a different life, made different choices, encountered different people, obtained different rolls of the dice, or had different ancestors. But in that case everything about this volume, including its title and byline, would be different. These might be your pages and I might be in your chair reading them right now. Sounds like fun.

Imagining such a life—or lives—is both a waste of time and a wonderful source of entertainment and insight through seasons light and dark. I think a few poems like that have infiltrated this collection after all. Leakage remains an unsolved problem in constructing parallel universes. On the other hand, mind sharing is the point of the exercise, isn't it?

What these pages fail to express well is my gratitude to you for sharing them with me. In that, you give me life, and honor the dead and not yet born I seek to speak for.

June 2016

Warning: Some content may be unsuitable for young children or may activate stress responses for some readers.

I.

PSALMS OF A HERETIC

The news

Hors d'oeuvres
Tidbits of rare poison fish and endangered game
brought by satellite right to your table

Salad
Teaser greens with exaggeration dressing
tossed in front of your eyes

Soup
Peppery cream of negativity
stirred with garden-fresh kernels of hypocrisy
served in a shallow bowl

Bread
Freshly baked loaves of sourdough gossip
dripping with spicy political butter

Wine
The house label—a crackling blush *rosé*
that goes well with any embarrassment

Entrée
Barbecued ribs of avoidance and denial
tasty sound bites with crunchy nuggets of scandal
savory pre-digested slices of pseudo-wisdom
a half-baked *soufflé* of issues without substance
and plenty of video relish on the side

Dessert
Your choice of mudslinging pie or provocative cheesecake
served with human interest berries in a sweet syrup

Coffee
Brought to you compliments of our sponsors
a rich blend of mountain-grown fantasies
freshly ground and brewed onscreen
poured with splashing sounds and rising curls of steam
for your imaginary sense of smell

Bon appétit

§

The dance of the inarticulate god

A divinity dances through my already dying bones
forbids me to whisper ancient names
or claim prophetic promises
gives no reply to my questions
no exegesis of moldy scripture
no explanations but the logic of life
working its sensual syllogisms
a miracle in a single breath
redemption in each heartbeat
exquisite pleasures – oceanic joys
baptisms of blue-tongued fire
unspeakable gospels to my electric soul
rivers of unprovable truth in full flood
without meaning – without sense
enigma without end

Twirling worlds within worlds
commune in the wild eucharist of all being
molecular ecstasies – organic raptures
sunsets and seasons in pulsing succession
dogwood trees leaping up to breathe like whales
impatient cry of an expanding child
slow fire of coals inside my hips
voices of angels in pummeling rain
cockroaches announcing visions of bliss
wheels within wheels – seeds within seeds
orders and species of immingled delight
blown as stained glass from nova-fired starstuff
in the divine glow of time beyond time
beyond measure – beyond words – beyond reach
beyond my talent to grasp and turn

No – I cannot dance
cannot pray with mute feet
but sometimes my hands unbidden take wing
to sing in the silent multicolored music of the air
what my dry mouth cannot begin to express
the dance of the inarticulate god

§

Living in the wreck

Chains of ancient writings
anchor the missionary caravel to her final reef
christened for eternity
but now encrusted with the barnacles of time
ballasted with cannon and crucifixes
peopled by schools of easily terrified fish
and me the excommunicated paralytic bosun

Tourists dive down Sundays to see the wreck
but I have lived here all my life
I drown in holy water every night
and resurrect myself by morning for temporal affairs
a diurnal baptism that remains untold
when the proctors ask why I come in late—wet
moving slowly and counting prayers on seashell beads
while gasping for inspiration in the secular air

I cannot abide this dry world and soon return below
where I bless with sodden incense
the ragged fishing fleet at work overhead
and curse lighthearted souls in their pleasure craft
soaring through quicksilver emptiness above
while I earn my salvation deep in the dark
one wet heresy at a time

Communion is difficult alone
and with such elements as these
kneeling on a fallen t'gallant yard
while seahorses bow quietly around
and sharks loiter in the distance
no doubt reciting prayers of their own

The holy flesh rebodied
as hardtack wafers kept dry till needed
in iron-hooped drums crawling with maggots
now crumbling away in the current
go ye into all the world
soggy morsels of divinity

And the sacred blood
tapped from casks of native rum
raised in a chalice of stolen gold
the spirit now diluted by sea
but still throat-burning as it goes down
do this in remembrance
how could I forget?

What fails me is not memory
but faith and bones
crushed by gravity
seeking solace in a weightless world
unable to return to the old truths
yet unfit to reside in the new
I labor alone with the tools at hand
sowing seeds of outrageous doubt
among the coral rows
tending the sprouts of a new gospel
and someday in the fullness of time
the drifting continents will quake
at the sweetness of the fruit
born from such briny beds

§

Avascular necrosis

Without bone flesh cannot stand
bone without blood is strong enough
unless it seeks to be born again
a grand designer's practical joke
femoral sponge-cakes
leached of strength by the pyrrhic miracle
of natural regrowth from within
cratered by the rhythmic shock
of marching to an indifferent drummer
on a hardshore naval parade ground
near the shadow of a whitewashed chapel spire

Thirty years of consecrated pain
and nights burning on the altar within
finally redeemed by neither miracle nor oil
nor the laying on of hands alone
but simply sterile gloved fingers
and the cutting edge sacraments
of medicine and metallurgy
the curious vanity of science
ready to play god with the dying pieces
of a living human body
replacing parts from a catalog

I seldom display my piercings
the sword-wounds in my sides
sewn together by the surgeons
with my bright metal beneath
to be revealed only at airport gates
I walk with more vigor now
but pain still plays hide-and-seek
with moods and stray ideas
friends and strangers

After all I lack a prosthesis
for collapsed faith leached of strength
by natural regrowth from within
and cratered by marching for others

§

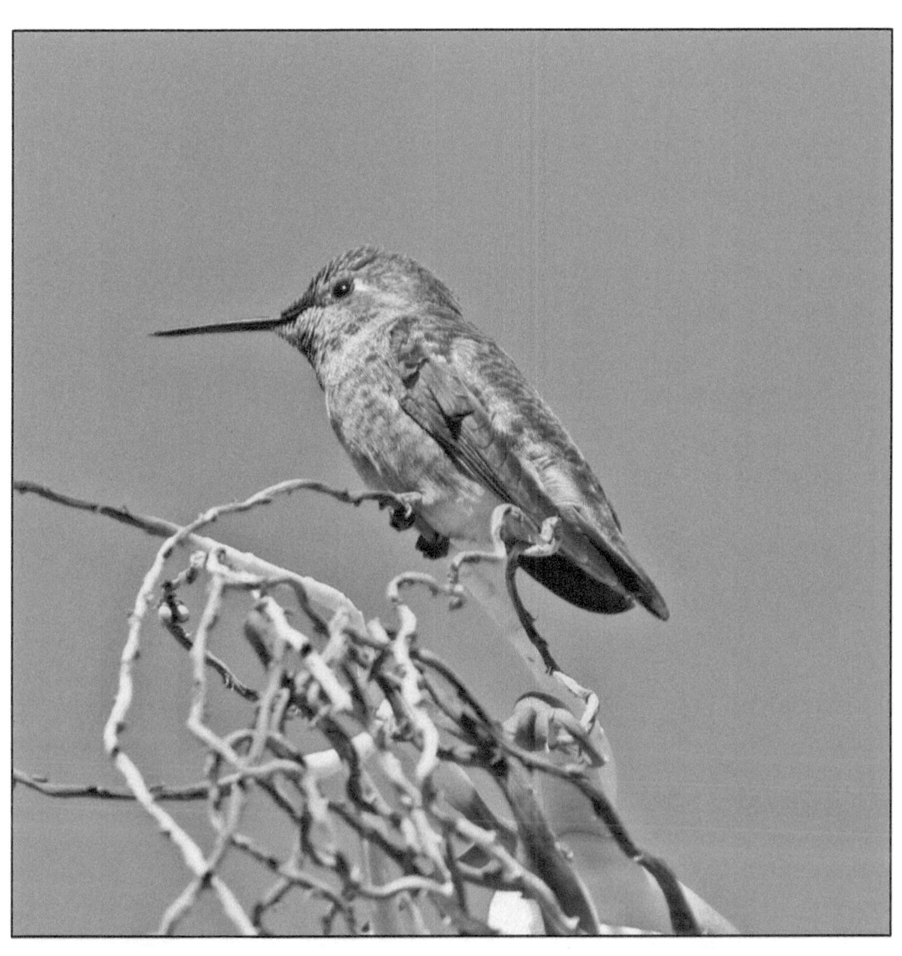

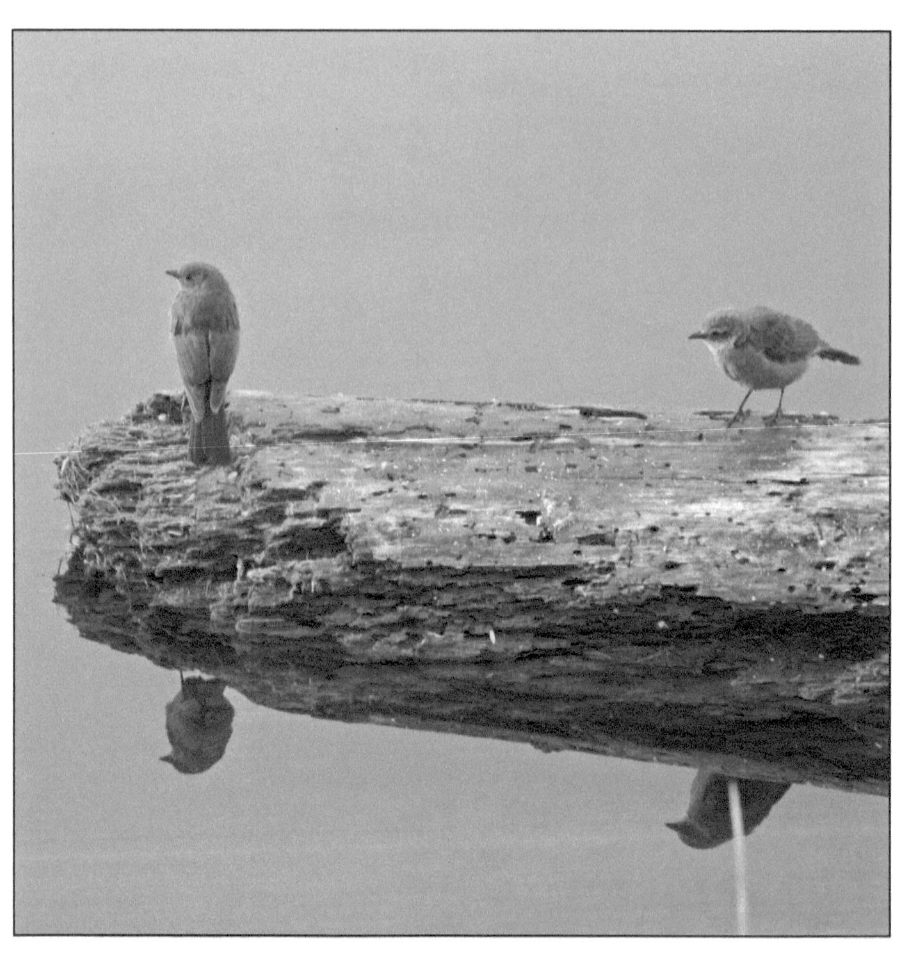

Iris and butterfly

Orange wings lined with black
flutter in the languid air
amid yellow-dabbed purple petals

My mind says *iris* and *butterfly*
and I stop my wandering walk
to watch and catch my breath

But the breath is not mine to keep
the iris is in my eye
the purple is in my mind
and the butterfly resumes its languid walk
while I wander and flutter
among the airy blossoms

§

Whether or not

After the rain
a solitary sway-backed gray horse grazes slowly
through the white-flowered clover meadow
around a single maple tree afire with dripping bright jewels
that catch the evening sunlight prying under clouds
against a backdrop of deeply shaded tall firs
the horse looks up at the sound of dogs barking

I watch through Pentax binoculars from the back deck
south of Salem where I house-sit
and help my daughter animal-sit
while the owners fly Lufthansa to Europe
and rent a big Mercedes to tour in
and my father walks along the sandy Lincoln City beach
remembering the beaches of Oahu
that he guarded with a Thompson submachine gun
in 1942

The horse grazes whether I watch or not
the tree drips sunlight whether the owners go to Munich or not
Venus shines as the evening star behind those clouds
whether I see it tonight from this deck or not
whether they saw it tonight from the Bayerischer Hof
whether my father sees it tonight from the Oregon sands
whether he survived the war
met my mother and fathered me
or not

§

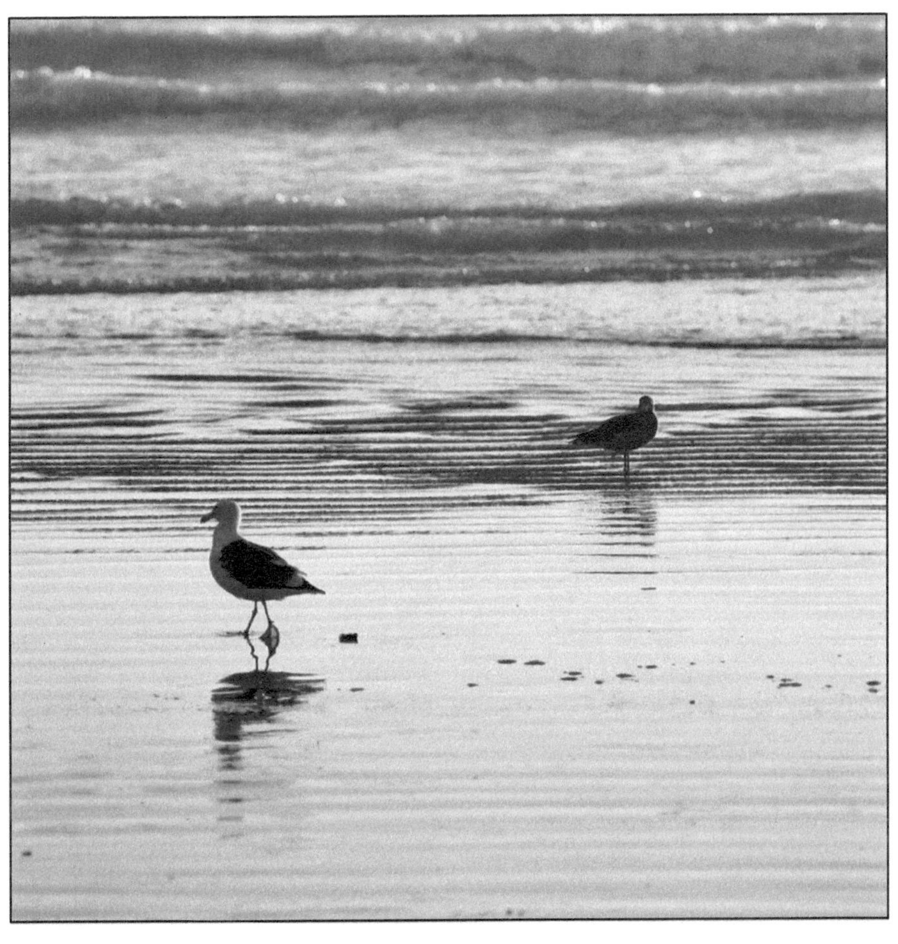

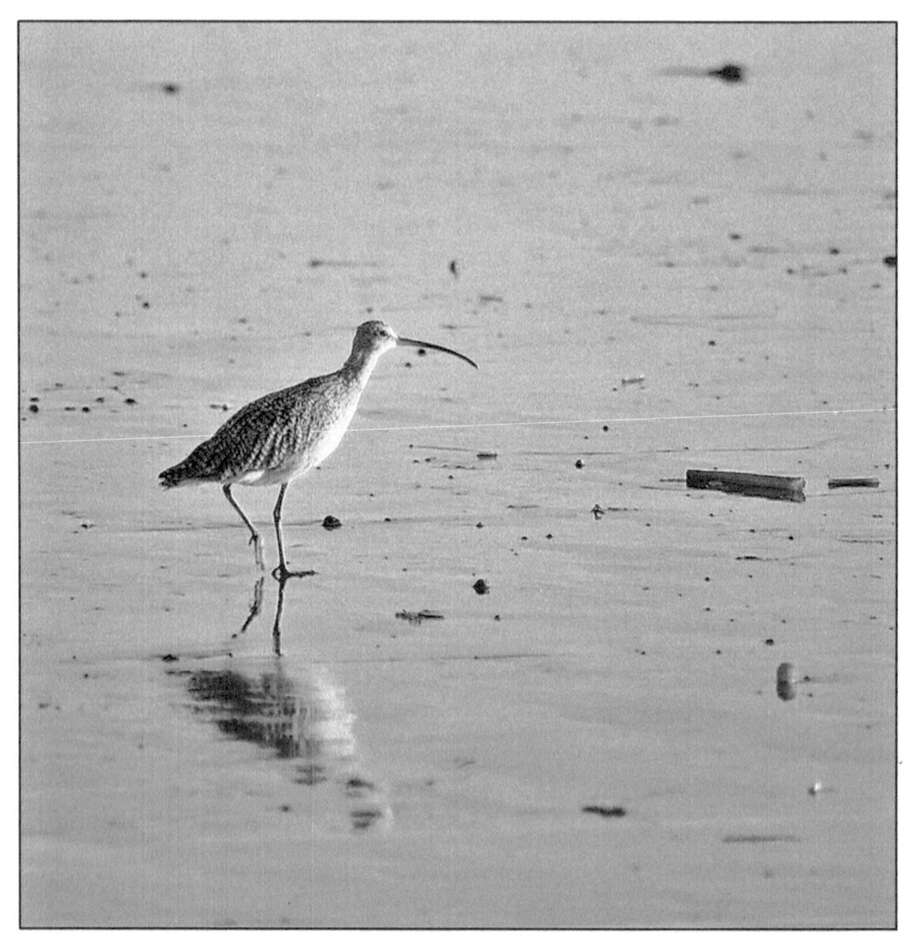

Argument

I am not quick to respond
and so I forfeit the match
but your pointed question conceives
a growth within me
that in its own full time
emerges living testimony
to my position
the fruit of my labor
I proudly love but you ignore
having long since won your title
my answer will outlive you

§

Corkscrew

Yes that's a corkscrew through my heart
it's just the handle you see
the tip is buried pretty deep
been that way a long time
don't like to talk about it
no I'd rather you didn't pull on it
others have tried and there's just no use
sure—someday it'll pop right out
damn right it hurts

So
in private silent nights
softly moaning
shuddering
with exquisite care
I twist and tug
in lifelong labor
to uncork and pour out
this well-aged bloody wine
and only
when I am done
may all you eager thirsty ones
crowding around
take
drink
remember

§

Exploratory

You brag how well you know me
then plunge the blade of your tongue
to part my reticent layers for exhibition
ripping out liver and intestines large and small
arranging them on your desktop
raw meat for your augury

I clutch my own naked spinal column
with both hands in the cavern of my gut
to still my bewildered vertigo
it's all I can do to moan without fainting
as you mistell my fortunes and my character
from the rendered entrails

I have a problem with anger you remark
and teamwork and leaving messes on the carpet
as I grab what I can and crawl toward the door
dragging the slippery spoils of your conquest
wondering where I can find needle and thread
to suture the rest of my life

§

Different rules

You said you were only there to support me
and then cross-examined me with questions
preloaded with your silver bullet strategy
plus a bit of evidence gossip
you had saved as a pocket ace for over a year
to draw and fire at the right moment
and then you took as proof
my tongue-tied bafflement

We simply played by different rules
you landed several swift groin kicks
before I made it through
the first bar of *Kumbayah*
and cheerfully helped roll my gurney
to the already waiting ambulance

§

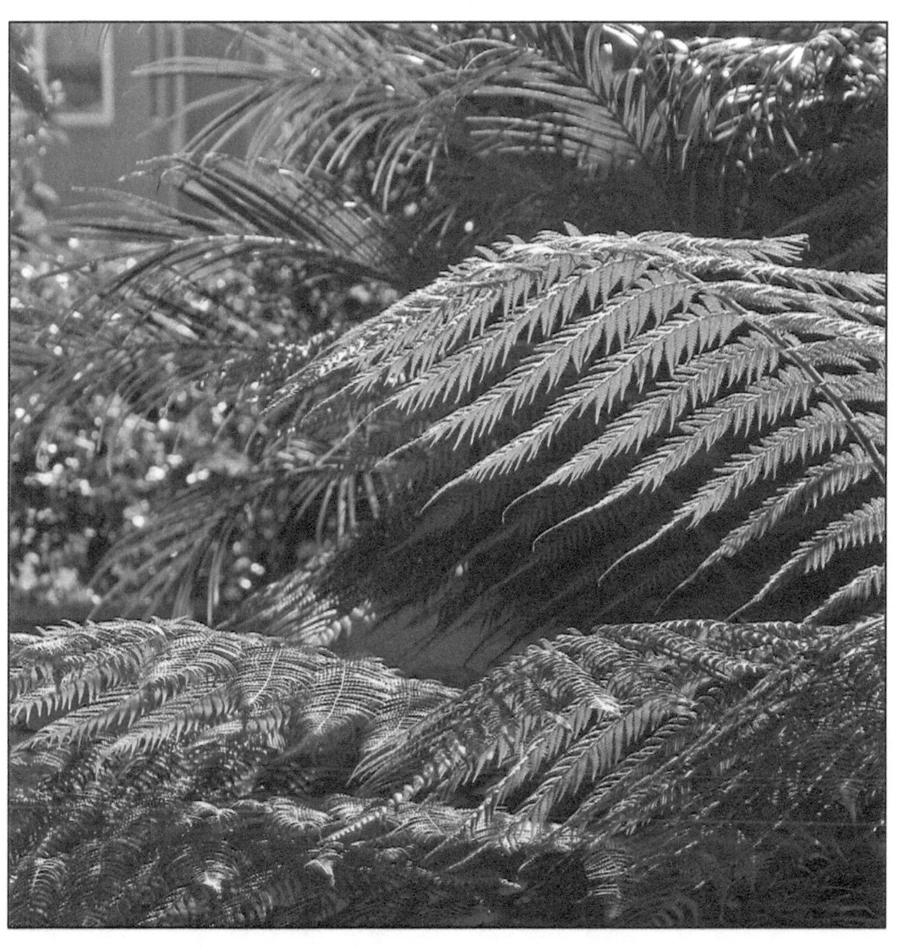

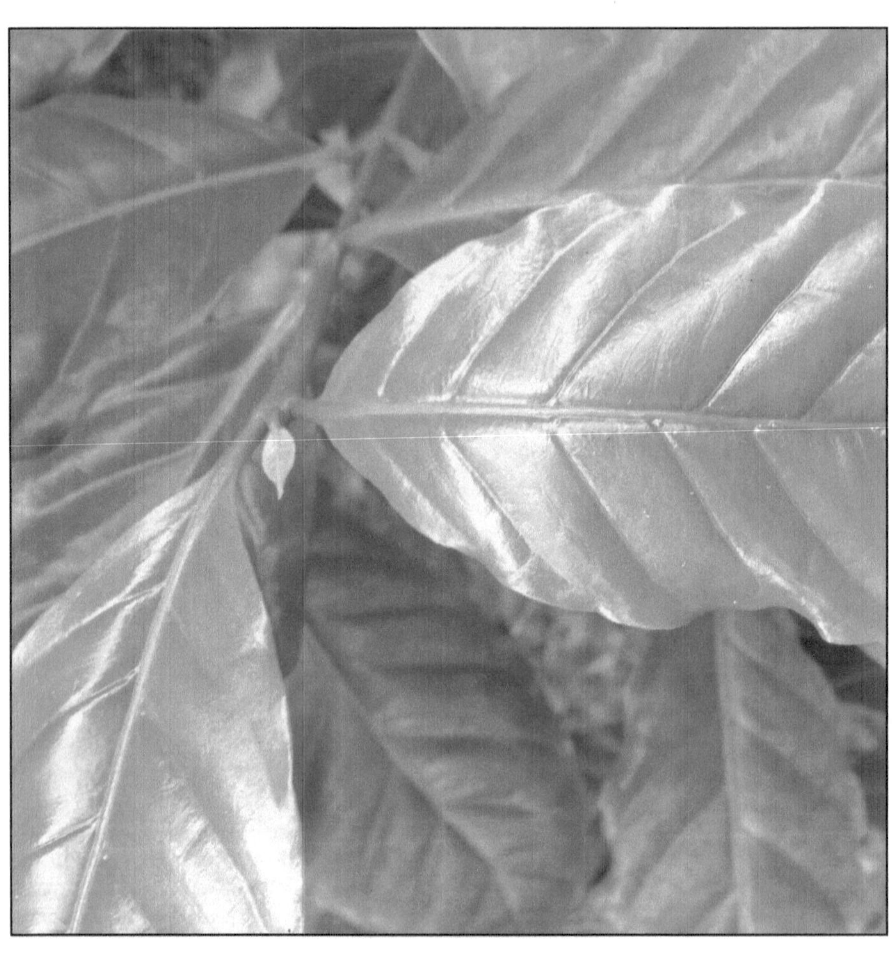

Another world

How did it feel
you twelve
to walk upon another world
plant bootprints
in the untouched dust
of the universe
leap lightly
across barren lunar plains
by Earthlight?

How does it feel
you twelve
to have walked upon another world
is Earth a stranger now
does any leap now tempt you
to compare
with that fire-sprung voyage
does the gravity of Earth's affairs
weigh you down
do tears spring to your moonstruck eyes
more readily
in the salty moon-tugged tides of this world?

And those now buried as dust
who no longer leap nor answer
what other world have you found
do gravity and memory pull you back toward us
does airless fire now breathe in you
or does the vacuum of the universe
suck you into its expanding emptiness?

§

The limit of adhesion

Wings carve solid air into downforce
that grips pavement by bare rubber fingertips
propelled by eight hundred hungry screaming horses
and your own fierce will

Every second devours a hundred yards
as you plunge feet first into the curved tilting depths
where multiple gravities suck you toward the wall
and thousandths of a second count your margin

Pull out of your dive a heartbeat too late
ask too much bite from rubber
and your multicolored chariot may fly into debris
shedding carbon fiber and kinetic energy
to protect your own fragile self tumbling through
in its tiny monocoque cocoon

Or lift your speed-foot a blink too soon
keep rubber in reserve
and you may forfeit the chase and the podium
the silver cup for the trophy room of old age
the permanent entry in the record books
the knowledge of what you might have done

You cannot refute the law of physics
binding lateral force to radius of curvature
as a function of speed
indeed you depend upon it
hanging from it as you swing through the apex
hunting for a line to pull you through
a fraction of a thought faster than ever before
and a quantum quicker than anyone else

So you try the grooves and changes
to seek out that sweet spot
where you carefully caress the limit of adhesion
and ride hot rubber for all the grip it can give
and your ground-bound missile misses the wall
by mere inches
turn after turn—lap after lap
in hyper-drive
alert—concentrated—pure
flat-out feedback fusion
mind body machine body mind body machine body mind
around and around and around
and getting it right every time

Wishbones drum the rhythm of the road
helmet buffeted by the storm of your passage
both hands grip the very rim of control
nerve endings extending beyond firesuit and gloves
to sense the pulse of the onrushing world
tiger-stalk your victims ahead
and twitch at threats from behind
slice off stragglers left and right
flooring every state of the art and
stretching every sinew of yourself
to get in front and stay there

You've never been more alive
as you dive into the valley of history
side-by-side with champions
knowing that only one of you
will come out first to take the flag
you make it look easy
but the secret you keep
is just how close you come
turn after turn—lap after lap
how close if we dared we all might come
to that invisible limit at the edge of the world
where existence and glory
hang by friction alone

§

Drivers pose before the start of the British Grand Prix 1964

These ghosts among the quick
in the gray photograph
grin like boys skipping school
or gaze off distant and cool
to belie their cocky youth
and rehearse their starting trick

Nine of eighteen will perish in race cars
within a decade of this moment
Jimmy Clark—dry-witted Scot
Jo Bonnier—founder of the driver's union
an early voice for driver safety
Bruce McLaren—youngest then to win a Grand Prix
Bob Anderson—Lorenzo Bandini—Peter Revson
Mike Spence—John Taylor—Jo Siffert
not counting Mike Hailwood in a public road accident
Graham Hill in an airplane—others of natural causes

Other shades not gridded for that event
were also taken in the era
as the sorcery of speed outraced by far
its poor apprentice safety
until drivers got organized
got more forgiving tracks
made safety rules less lax
grew less cavalier to recognize
strapping in was no indignity
while designers created a tougher car
to save their precious hero
despite the inevitable shunt

Yet still the dead come round from time to time
to wave the flag for their own
and names we look for fondly in the standings
become the names of ghosts when least expected

McLaren wrote his own epitaph
unknowingly—meaning it for a late friend
long before passing as his own car tester
that to do a thing well is so worthwhile
to die attempting to do it better
cannot be as much a waste in the end
as to live long and do nothing with one's gift

Gazing at ghosts like these we own
life richer for having seen them drive
and grieve for ourselves not having known
what we could have done while we were alive

§

Flying

The wax is melting
and I'll splashdown hard
which I think I knew all along
I simply misjudged
the fragility of these wings
and the heat

Yet the same fire that has killed me
has filled me with light
my dream of flight is who I am
and who I have become
in these last moments
of my escape from captivity
my joy in my last breath
it holds me up even as I fall

After all I do not regret
what I have seen from up here
that I could not from behind the wall
I know some have seen more
but I rather think
that few have dared
and many never had a chance

No one but me has seen what I've seen
I wish I could have shared more with you
and you with me
of whatever it is
that you see from your own brief height
I know it is different
I'm sure it's amazing
and I'm glad

§

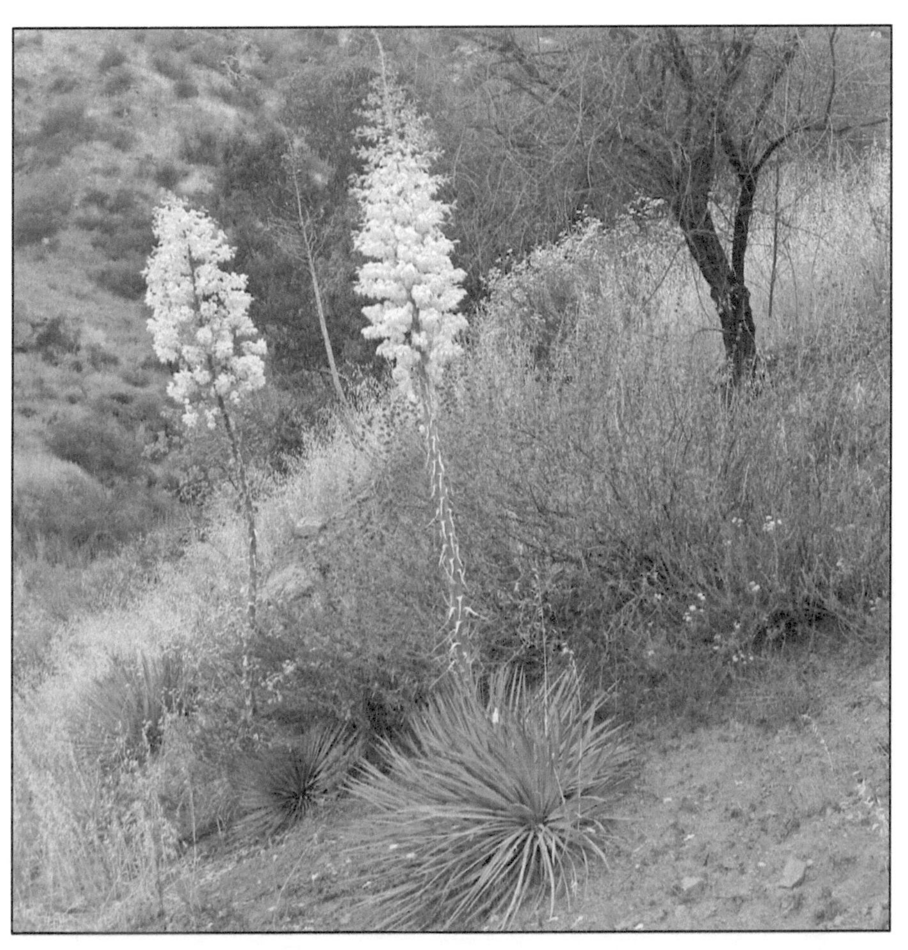

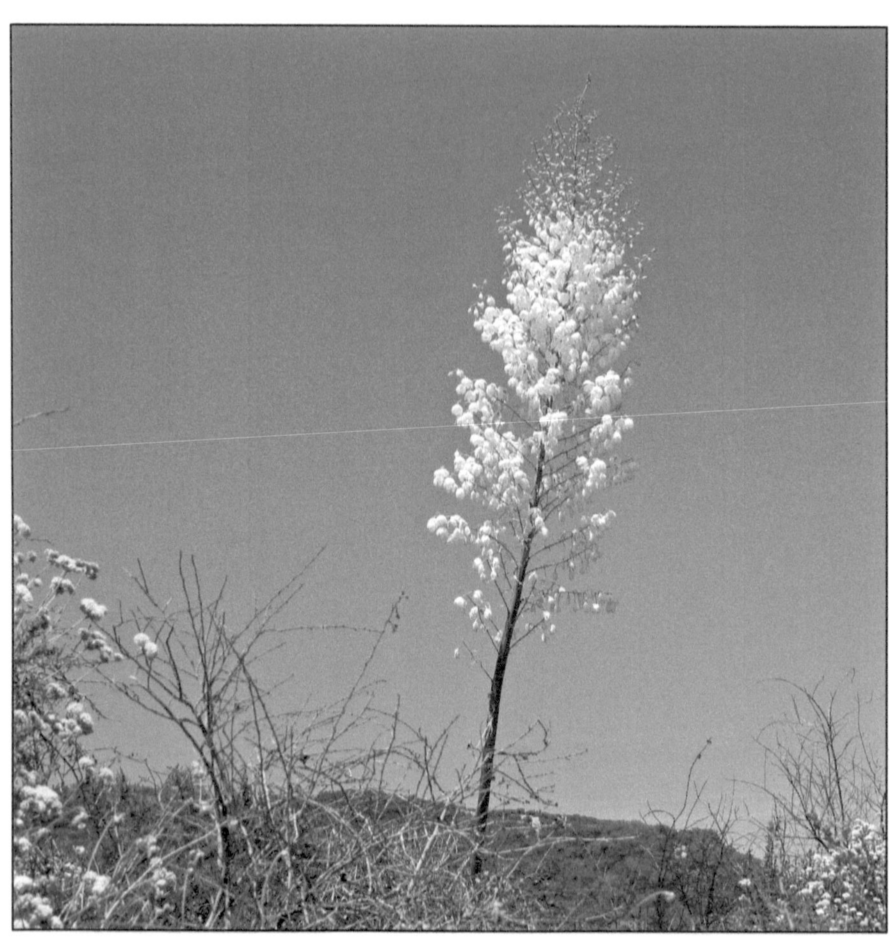

A very old couple

Throwing back the heavy gray blanket
of clouds from his bed
he stands up stretching
in his high blue house

He brings travelling bits of white cloud
and a flood of sunlight on steaming grass
then another cool storm
that leans into the afternoon
as cool rain blows across his face

She welcomes him home
with glad moist arms
wearing the dark smell of mud
the richness of earth air
she asks him where he's been
and tucks him in
and turns out the light
before going out to tend her wet gardens
of ancient roots and herbs

Then she wanders under the fog-shrouded moon
and prowls the shadowy world alone
creeping on all fours through dew-soaked grass
to stalk her careless prey

§

Trees being trees

These two leafy trees
if human
would chat
about the sunshine
and the breeze
and touch and smile and nod
but trees being trees
they bend and touch and straighten
in the breeze
branches wave
leaves flutter
roots dig in
trees being trees

§

Storm

Darkening sky
rolling seas rising
crescendo of howling wind
crests and hollows of water in motion
steep waves cresting
breaking into white madness
salty needles of hard-driven spray
blown by the screaming wind
impossible confusion
chaos

But deep below the surface
untouched by any wind
beneath the turmoil of the waves
under thermal water layers
below the flowing global currents
in the cold still depths
down deeper
deeper still
profound oceanic calm

§

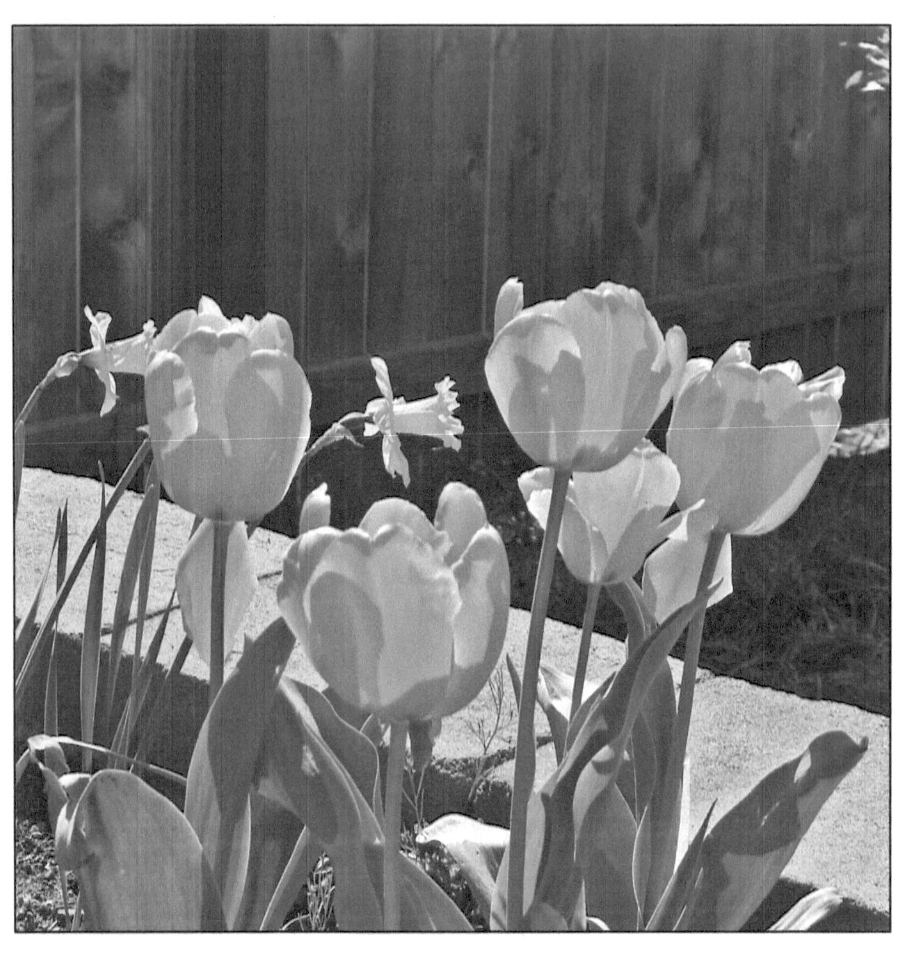

Traveling companions

Sail on then Yeats
to your fantastic Byzantium
and Coleridge dream of Xanadu
may you Wordsworth on forever
intimations of immortality
and shantih shantih weave and tangle
images of a dying culture
multilayered multilingual
Ezra-Pounded Eliot

But your gentle paths my Robert Frost
through rocky fields and snowy woods
in outdoor chores and conversations
give my feet more firm foundation
than those poets' wordy tricks
I consider you a brother spirit
from the city of hills

And even you dear Dylan Thomas
with your lovely leaping language
as you paint the shore of Wales
in swirls of deepest sense and non
mean more to me than any Grecian urn
the year of your death sang my birth

What I long for over rhymed exotic cities
is to walk the open road with you
my bearded friend Walt Whitman
and to join you Señor Neruda
in your fierce revolutionary march
amid the crying blossoms of springtime
in residence on the ever marvelous
but unfantastic and not immortal Earth

§

To William Stafford 1914-1993

You are misplaced in all the anthologies
by birth before Dylan Thomas
I read him in school before I knew you existed
but your mellow words are as far from his
as my mature age from those schoolboy days
he taught me obsession – unneeded lesson
you teach serenity – using imperfection
to learn to live in the world as it is
you seem unworried by the jeweler's craft
but delight to find a rough stone where it sits
and coax out the ancient message within

A more gentle mind is hard to imagine
or a man who fought more wars – I mean against
you arrived in a vintage year of births and deaths
but were too small to see the carnage then
and maybe there just wasn't enough meanness
to meet the demand that year and you missed out

At Powell's you made me work to get it
leaning forward on my folding chair
to hear your unpresumptuous voice
and catch the moment the sly twinkle in your eye
leaped suddenly into your lines
betrayed by only a hint of a laugh and a raised brow
expressing your own fresh surprise
to this day I cannot read your work
without hearing that reedy voice
and seeing that old soul smile

§

Poetry sucks mostly

I really don't get what it is I don't get about poetry
like it's an in-joke with me left out in seventh grade
when everybody and his brother knew about sex except me
and whatever I said that was so stupid and funny to the other boys
hell I don't read poetry because I like most of it I really don't
but because inside big books of it between the silly word games
lurks an occasional sudden mainline fix of pure uncut clarity
like the whole damn planet falling on your head at once
and I need it oh god do I need another hit of it

§

Poetry and pi

Poetry day comes around
a week after pi day
first digestion then inspiration
the mind's diameter expanding
with the belt's circumference
doesn't work with cobbler
which as everyone knows
are squared

§

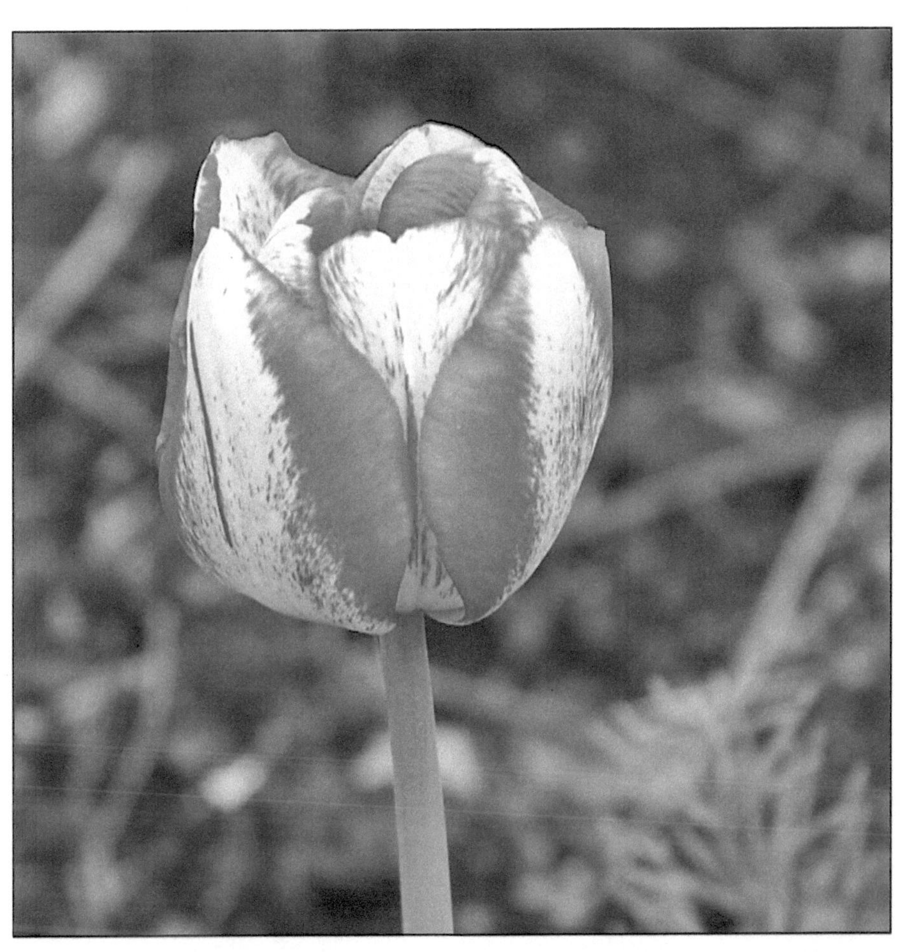

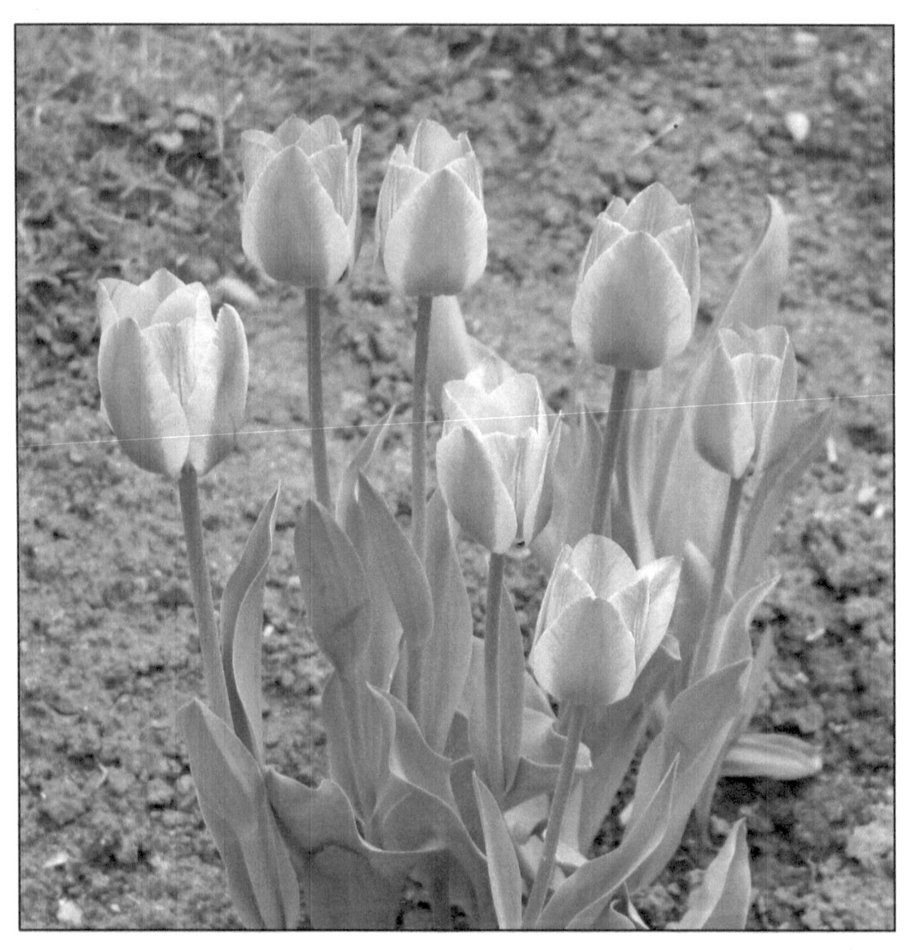

Anger

Matchhead
sulfuric
hissing out
at the slightest friction
no hesitation
no deliberation
a flare of light
quickly gone
forgotten
but for that other fire it started

Coal
hard
black anthracite
after much attention
and many patient strokes
glows with deliberate intensity
inexorable radiance
slow deep heat
long lasting
unforgiving

§

What happened

Trekking to lunch
a sweet colleague
elementary school ex-principal
hails me for a chat
I never asked
why you walk with a limp she says
it's my hips I shrug
they've been messed up for nearly thirty years
I don't say the Latin words
too long to explain
it happened in basic training I add
when I was in the Navy
you were in the Navy?
she asks with her eyebrows
why were you in the Navy?
well I volunteered I offer
almost prepared to say more
too long to explain
you volunteered?
then it's your own damn fault
she says and walks away
so I order lunch
my order comes out wrong
and I have to stand and wait
while the server explains
and explains again
the difference between what I paid for
and what I thought I ordered
so I finally sigh and take it
on its tray to the table
saved by a friend
what happened? he asks
it's my own damn fault I say

§

The language of the skin

I have learned to read the language of the skin

I have seen the life-force throb
in the seamless flesh
of a newborn child
the hormones swell in the red cheeks of an eager teen
the powder caked on the face of a lovely woman
who wanted to seem younger than she was
and the nimble lines in the laughter
of a one-legged three-war veteran growing contentedly old

I have seen cracks extend across a widowed grandmother's face
and the mask of death in the hardened gray pores
of a man whose very breath was smoke
the stretch marks of a woman whose labor created love
and the many scars of a man whose battles were unending

I have known the tenderness of caring touch
the hot slap of anger
the healing thrust of a deep massage
the rugged firmness of a handshake
and the lameness of a phony hug
I can trace the paths of my own mortality
as they creep across the back of my hand

Yes I have learned to read the language of the skin
and the translation thereof is this
that the ancient boundary
between ourselves and all that is other
is priceless
and exceedingly thin

§

God's voice

God's voice is faint
red-shifted from far away and long ago
it might have seared the night sky of the prophets
but now is virtually indistinguishable
from the background noise
during a total eclipse of eternity

I have listened for that voice
and what I heard were crickets outside
the birds that consume them
my own heartbeat and creaking joints
the laughter and sobs of children
brags of bloody fight winners wearing crosses
the race of contradictory words around my head
and the surprisingly lucid thought
that either God is completely inconsistent
or those are not God's words I hear

I have read every verse of the Bible
which is more than most believers
and enough to assure me
that the scriptures quoted the most
by hearers of God's voice
contradict God's words in other places
that don't get quoted so much
but they still make great cudgels
or small talk on folding chairs

By definition we're all atheists
not believing in all gods at once
we just disagree
about which gods we don't believe in
and which voices belong to gods
believed or not
and whose hearing is better
by the grace of God or not

§

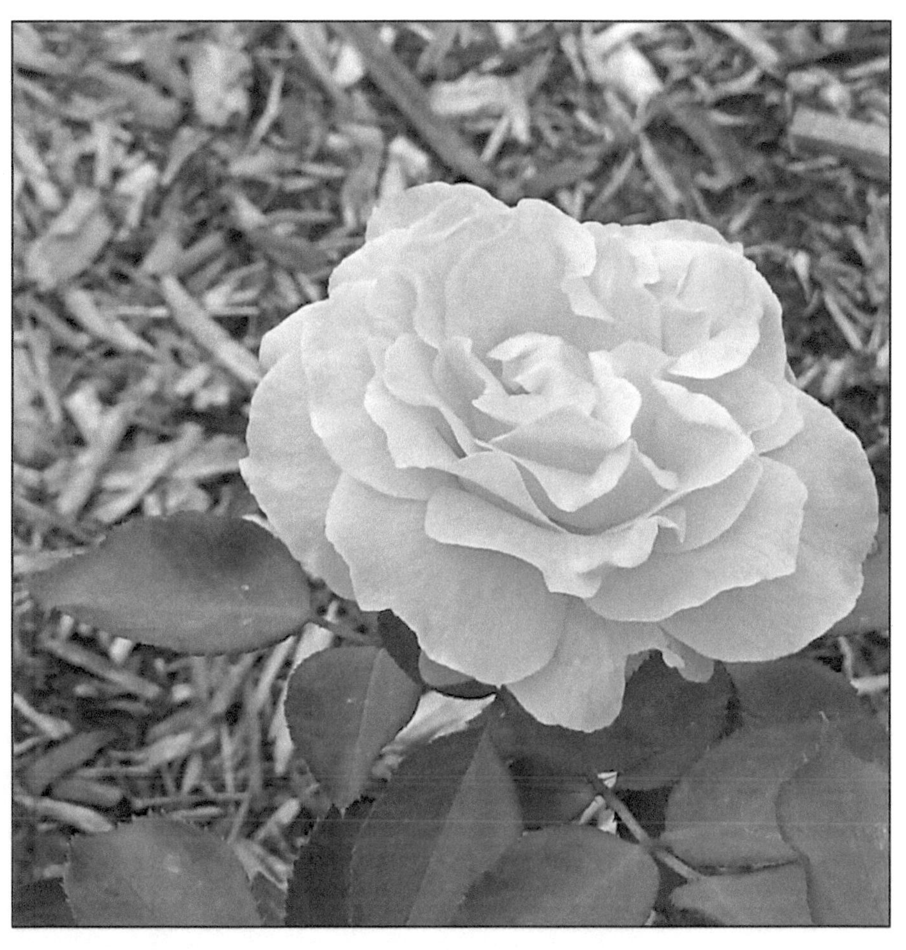

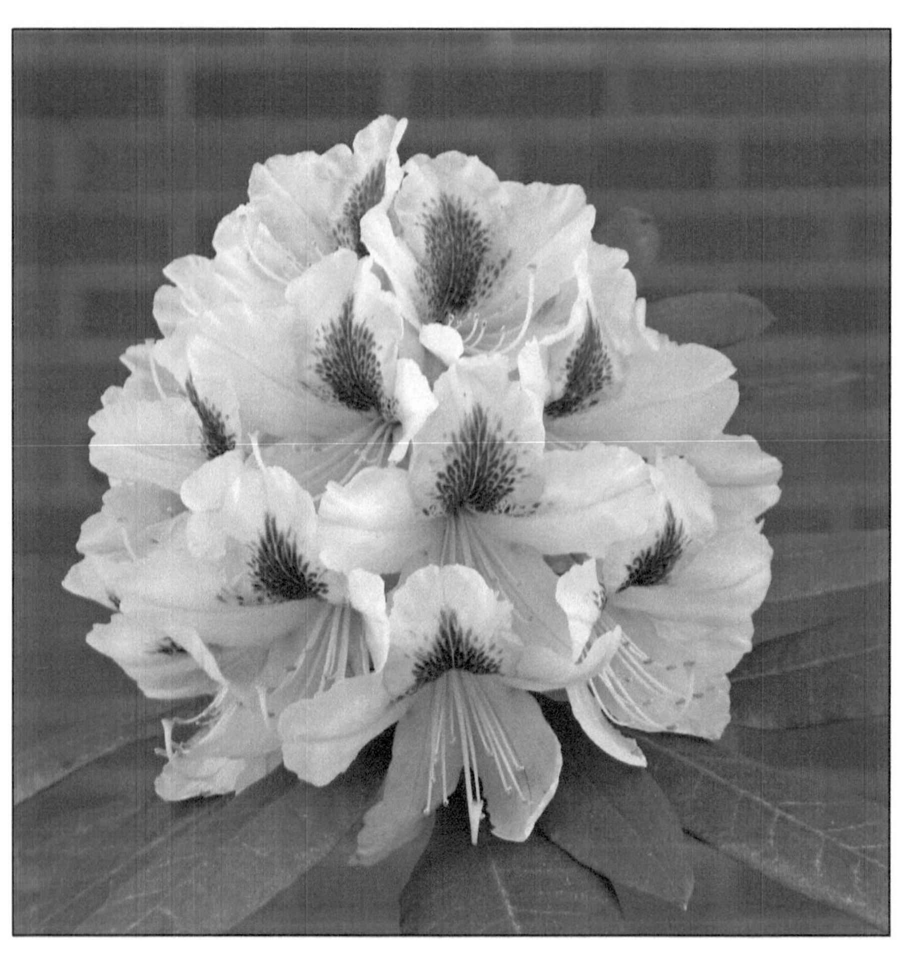

Books and friends

I have packed these books carefully
as many as fifteen times
to take with me to new homes
friends don't pack so easily
and I have lost the ones I moved away from
come with me so I don't lose you
or invite me to stay books and all

§

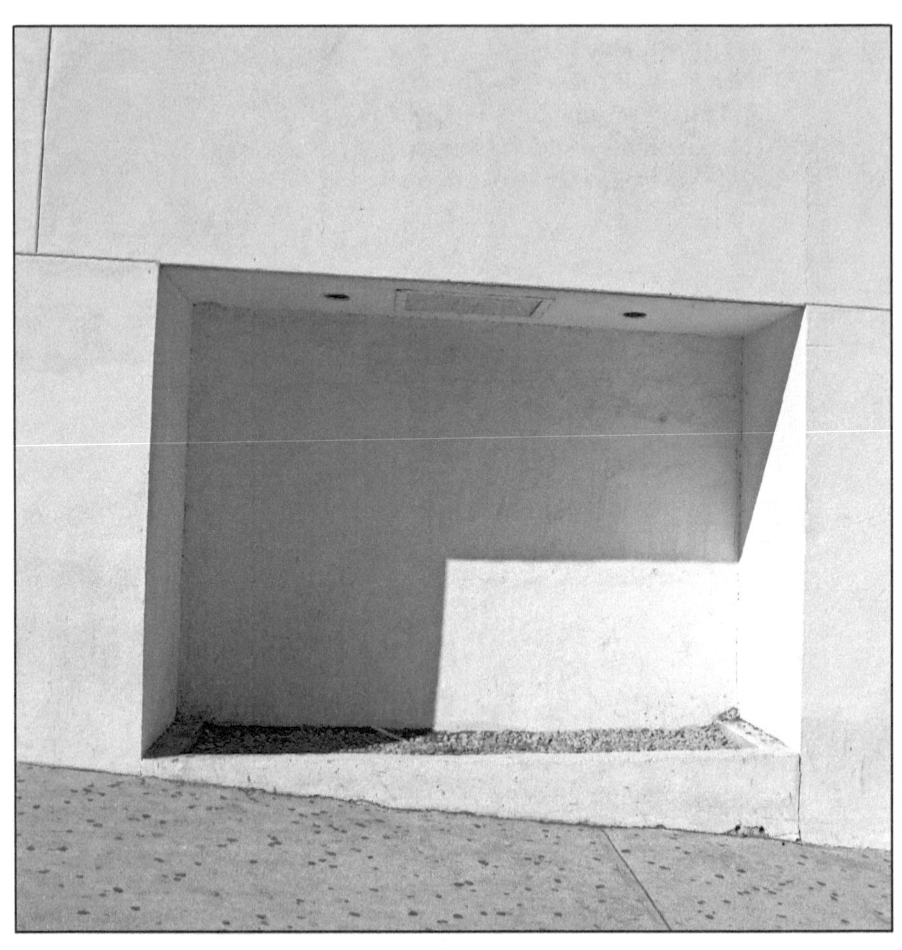

II.

UNBEARABLE QUESTIONS

Restroom doors

Rolling through humidity and pine trees
station wagon windows rolled down
my sister and brother and I
in the back seat
supposed to sit down
stop arguing
get arms back inside the car

We stop for stinky quarter-dollar gas
ice cold dime-bottle sodas from the red fridge
and stubby canned sausages to eat on crackers
but first we have to use the restroom

Clean door in the front of the station
says *whites only* naturally meaning us
but Dad tells us to go around back
to see the other toilet
the outhouse door with the word on it
we're not supposed to use
for people we're supposed to love as God loves us

But we're also supposed to call white grownups
where we go to church three or four times a week
brother and *sister*
even though they use that other word
and turn away when Dad drives the station wagon
leading the Bible school parade
down a street where people live
whose children
would never be welcome in that Bible school
or on that shiny white toilet
and I don't understand

§

The shoes

Shoes
thousands of cloth and leather shoes and boots
standing proxy for millions of bones without flesh
stripped of gold teeth and striped clothing
so all you can see now are bleeding
black and white photos and films
and a dusty heap of real shoes
without feet

Chanting
the film of young men with armbands
marching around outside the two-story house
taunting the inhabitants for being strangers
in the land where they too were born
booted feet cut circles in the land
mockery cuts holes in the soul
as the chanting youth in playground uniforms
pretend to be strong and just
to crank up their own souls
to the point of breakage
into hatred ready to break glass
and cook humans like themselves
just for being different

Stacks
faces stacked on the museum walls
the stacks of books on fire
smokestacks of the ovens
consuming authors of books written and unwritten
and wood frame stacks of beds
to store people in while they wait
to join stacks of bodies in trenches in the woods outside
I can no longer stack firewood
without thinking of
those stacks of people
in the woods

§

The art of dying

Some may die in a nuclear instant
not knowing what killed
with no time for art
or appreciation

Others may die in atomic agony
as ever so slowly roentgens kill
a lingering half-life with time to recall
beautiful visions of the white flash
and distant orange sunburst blossoms
bitter memories of fireball majesty
haunting prolonged moments of living
death that escaped immolation
drawing out lives of painful yearning
learning the art of living
as dying

Then there are the underground warriors
missile minders in shielded caves
submarine crews full fathom fifty
who may yet get their chance at natural causes
cancer pneumonia falling down stairs
who having fired away their fatal charges
may then face their own remaindered lives
in the long solitude of survivors
ever torn between gratitude and guilt
who struggle to master
the art of dying
as perfectly as they had
the science of killing

In the end we are all dead anyway
I heard a wise man say
but it still seems to be an art
it seems somehow to matter

§

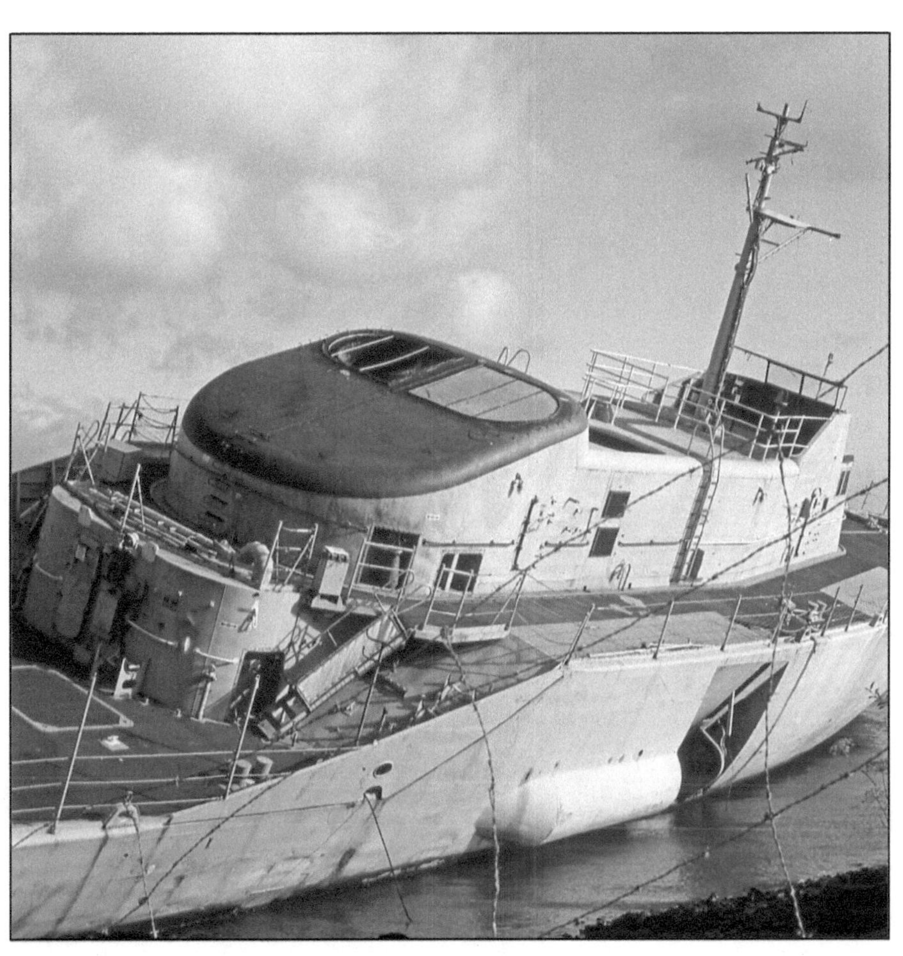

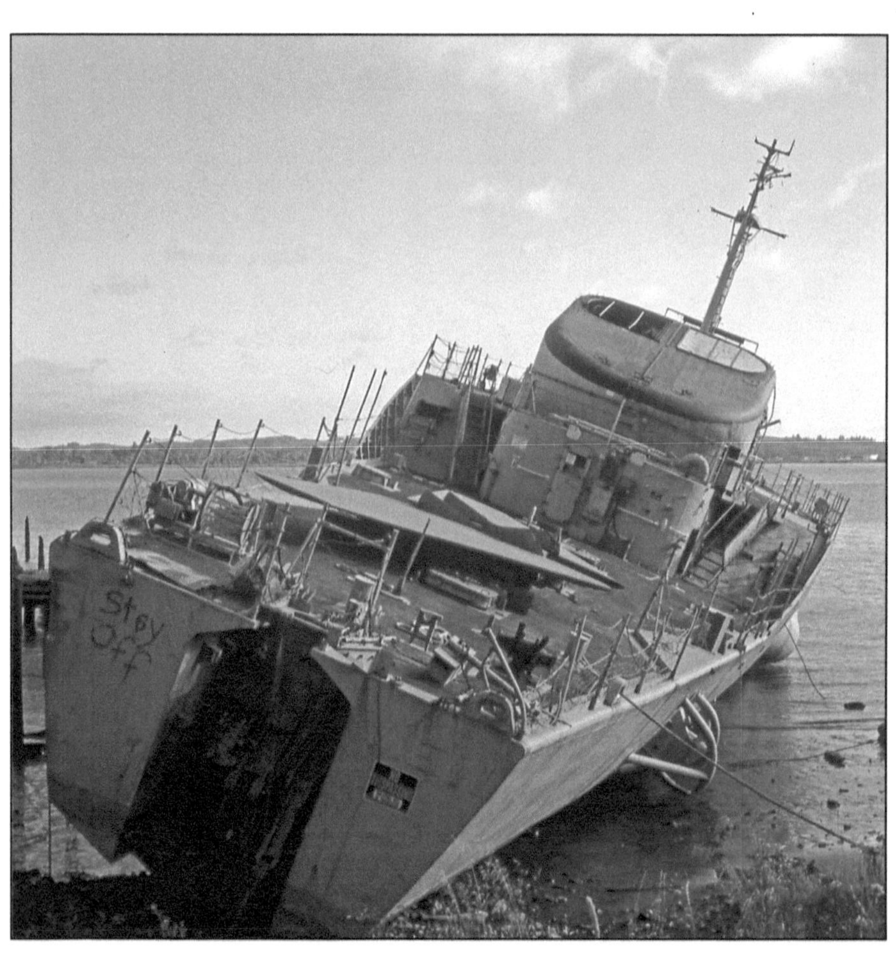
Stay Off

Conjugation

Beauty is
people are
life should be

Fear is
understanding is not
aggression has always been
deterrence doesn't
missiles do
mistakes are

Mistakes were
people didn't
the impossible did
humanity was
peace will be
forever

§

The thing I cannot grasp

Sunday in August
breakfast of *udon* and green tea
then standing on the bridge
T-shaped for "target"
staring down into the shallow river
and over at the skeleton dome
left by the *pika-don*
half a mile overhead and fifty-four years this week
crowds of people line up
at the stadium across the boulevard
to watch the Carp play the Giants

And yet I cannot get hold of this thing
tears mingle with sweat
cooked out of me by the fusing sun
yes I know most of the history and a lot of the physics
and I once met a broken old man
living off TV dinners in a trailer
who could no longer claim coherently
but whose family claimed from his own story
he had led the team that conducted the analysis
that selected this city
as the target
for all the right reasons

And yet I still cannot comprehend this thing
a young girl inside the museum
decomposes into loud sobs
at photos of irradiated bodies
my own lips bleed from being bit
as I hold my face in a mask
not to feel too much

Other Americans shoot each other
with Canons and Nikons in front of the cenotaph
where colored paper cranes multiply
I cannot do this thing
it is not a place to mark my presence
but to think of others in their absence

Later I ride a streetcar and ferry
out to the famous island
with my *Nihonjin fiancée*
and place coins before the orange *torii*
walk in the quiet woods
stand on an arching wooden bridge
over a clear stream
among the wildflowers and deer
not so far away
from the epicenter

And instead of trying to master
the meaning of death *en masse*
I listen to the water
the bare breeze through the trees
the voices of spirits even older
than nearby horrific history
though tomorrow I shall have to respond
thoughtfully
to her father the *sensei*
the country doctor
and his sincere questions
about the thing I cannot

§

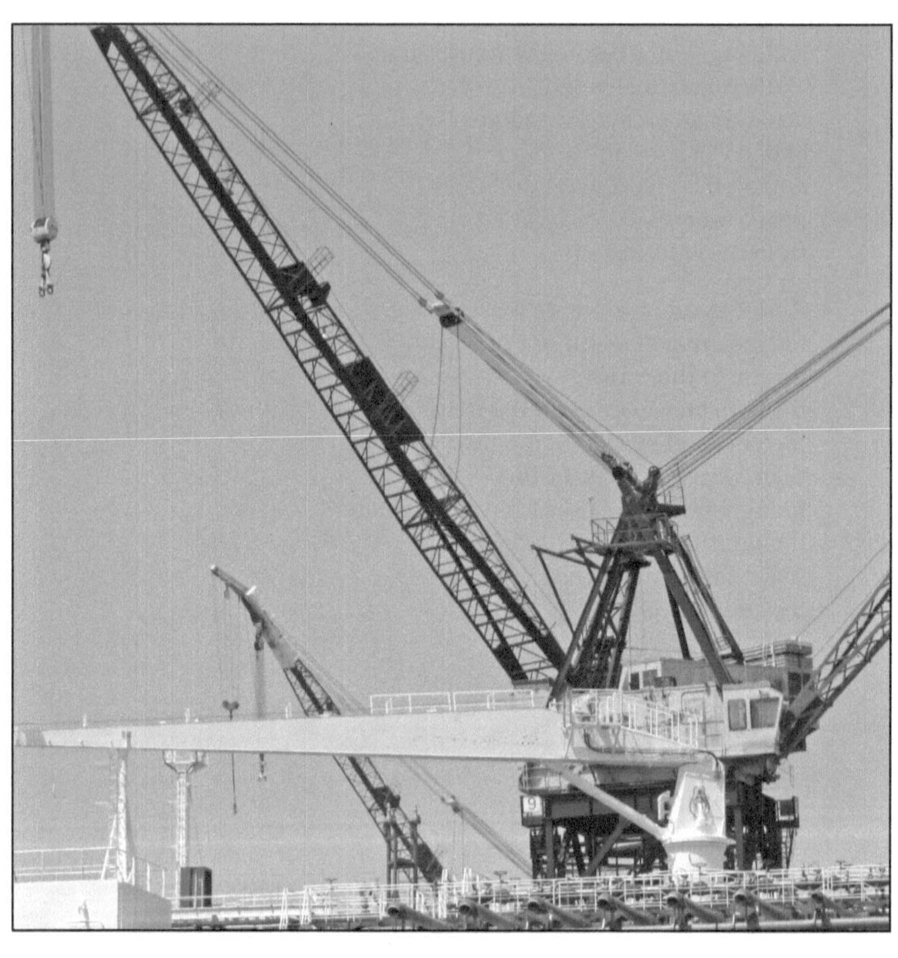

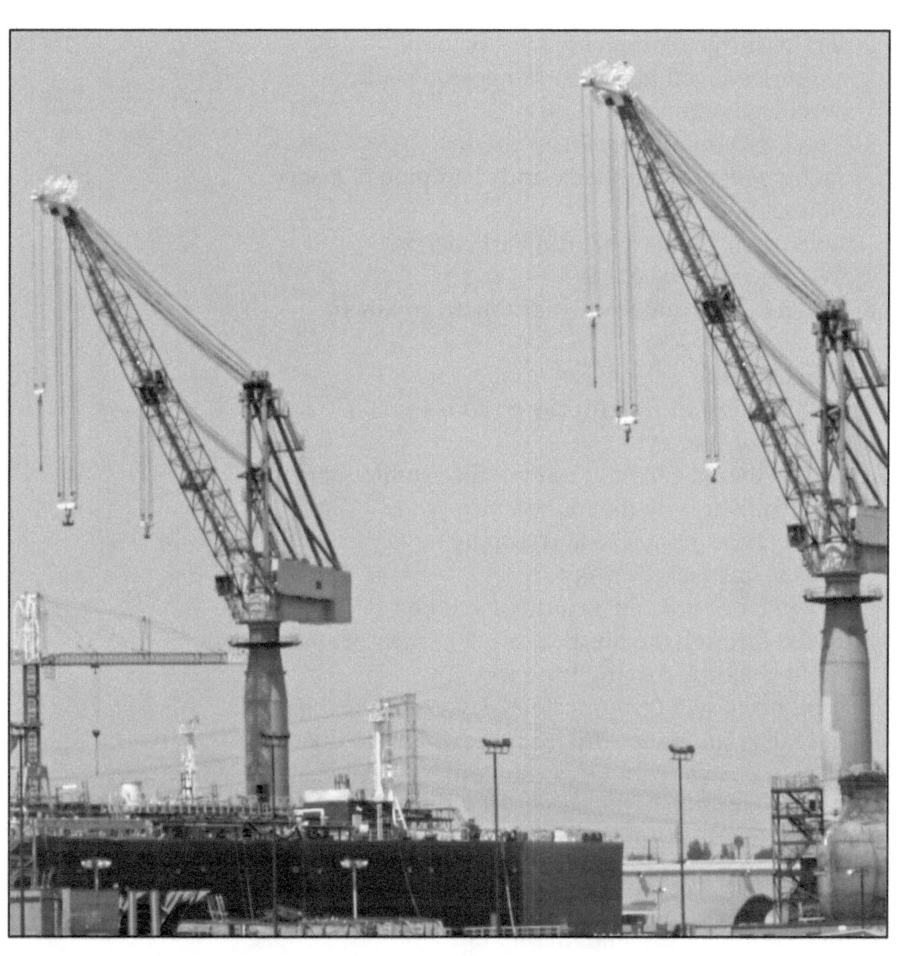

Peacemaker

Slender silver cylinder of death
erect in thy buried cement cell
fiery birthright compressed in thy loins
sun-furies caged in thy multimegaton skull
sweet navigational wisdom
coursing through thy silicon circuits
mighty defender of liberty and champion of justice
thou art hope to us
thou art joy thou art life thou art energy
oh sheer potential energy
locked in thy propellant yearning to go kinetic

Cold and still
thou standest in wait for the go codes
the turn of the keys
the "let there be light" granting thee sudden sanction
to go ballistic with the human race
to ascend from thy silo and leap up
into the unsuspecting sky
on a pillar of fire and a cloud of smoke
to soar through the mystical black infinity of space
on thy majestic curving trajectory
to plunge down through cloud-layered atmosphere
and fall as judgment-fire from heaven upon thy target
there to burn a glorious fused-atom moment
more brightly than the sun in all its grandeur
and in that one triumphant blow to slay more millions
than history's warriors ever conceived

Endowed with thy solemn mission
and blessed with ardent inexorable resolve
incapable of second thoughts or human-like worries
of bystanders or collateral damage
the ultimate in brute unconditioned power
fever dream of the ancients

Thou standest in silent wait for the triggering command
to terminate with prejudice
any nation bold enough to threaten us
to strike down their tyrants' belligerent arrogance
slaughter their workers in factories and peasants in fields
evaporate their nursing mothers and crying infants
consume the flesh upon their very limbs
and grind their bones to fine radioactive powder
that you scatter through the stratosphere
make hot gravel rubble of their homes and cities
ashes of their farms and their green forests
cancerous poison of their mountain streams
and night-glowing fireflows of their rivers

All this and more art thou capable of doing
for in thy powerful missile heart
beats the pure heart of thy makers
who through their mathematical particle-splitting craft
brought forth in thy isotopes
a device of awesome energy
and named thee *Peacekeeper*
thou art a credit also to thy noble caretakers
their well-groomed elite military discipline
thy discipline
their valor also thine
anyone who criticizes thee dishonors them
the price of thy purchase and maintenance
well worth every sweat-drop on every taxpayer brow

Holy holy holy art thou
oh instrument of terrible vengeance
oh noble mystical technology
of national security through human sacrifice
in the thrice-blessed name
of the Fathers of our Nation
the Sons of the Revolution
and the Spirit of Declared Independence
baptized in the blood of freedom's martyrs
consecrated by just cause
mandated by election
validated by constitutional inerrancy
funded by taxation and inflation
and served by generation upon generation
of those who distrust the enemy
and make enemies of those they distrust

While thou standest ready to kill
we shall fear no evil

And the teacher said
blessed are the peacemakers
for they shall be called
the children of God

§

The pirate

There is a parasite that gets into brains
and turns rational creatures into monsters
big loud leaders and little mean followers
or the other way around
bringing visions of threats where none exists
and fantasies of glory
earthly eternal or best of all both
it knows how to turn a song of freedom into hatred
of anyone who doesn't sing with enough feeling
it tricks people who would otherwise get along
into killing for self-defense
or killing first and then calling it self-defense
or being killed without knowing why
leaving others to carry out
the cycle of vengeance
that can never be satisfied

This pathogen reproduces and evolves
it changes colors and names
it has learned to outlive its hosts
how to inhabit inked symbols on paper
and ride vibrations in the air
how to transmit itself around the globe in seconds
and around again with greater potency
how to get invited into living rooms and stay the night
how to disguise itself righteously
and translate itself into new languages
before the old ones die out
the only way to get rid of it
is to take up arms against all those who carry it
or so it whispers with a smirk
as it leaps aboard a new vessel

§

Wonder

Our curved mirrors have cut apart light
from stars exploding and galaxies birthing
on the edge of the distant young universe
we count the coded blinks in signals
from planets circling nearby stars

Our robots have interrogated
seven other planets in our own neighborhood
about their mountains craters clouds and storms
rocky icy volcanic and oceanic moons
elegant white rings

Our cameras have fallen into methane lakes
and greenhouse pressure cookers
or crawled across cold Martian deserts looking for water
our sun-circling spies have crept up behind
dwarf planets asteroids and comets
for a look a sniff and a grab
while twelve of our own kind have walked
on one shining dusty moon

Yet no greater wonder have we found
than eight minute old sunlight
entwined in the limbs of a forest
maybe a million years old
warming the fallen trunk
of a five-hundred-year-old tree
that nurses new saplings in its giant soft bed
of needles and rotting wood
luxuriant with ferns mosses lichens and fungi
in the quiet inner space of a native grove
where goshawks and owls hunt shrews and voles
that thrive on ants and beetles and worms
in the warm comfort of the dead tree
a spontaneous opera of birth death and rebirth
unmatched in the distant spheres
as far as we so far know

But who among us can tell me
why of all known forms of life
the one that seems most able to wonder
at each new distant old world it finds
is the one most driven to consume sell and destroy
what it discovers
closer to home?

§

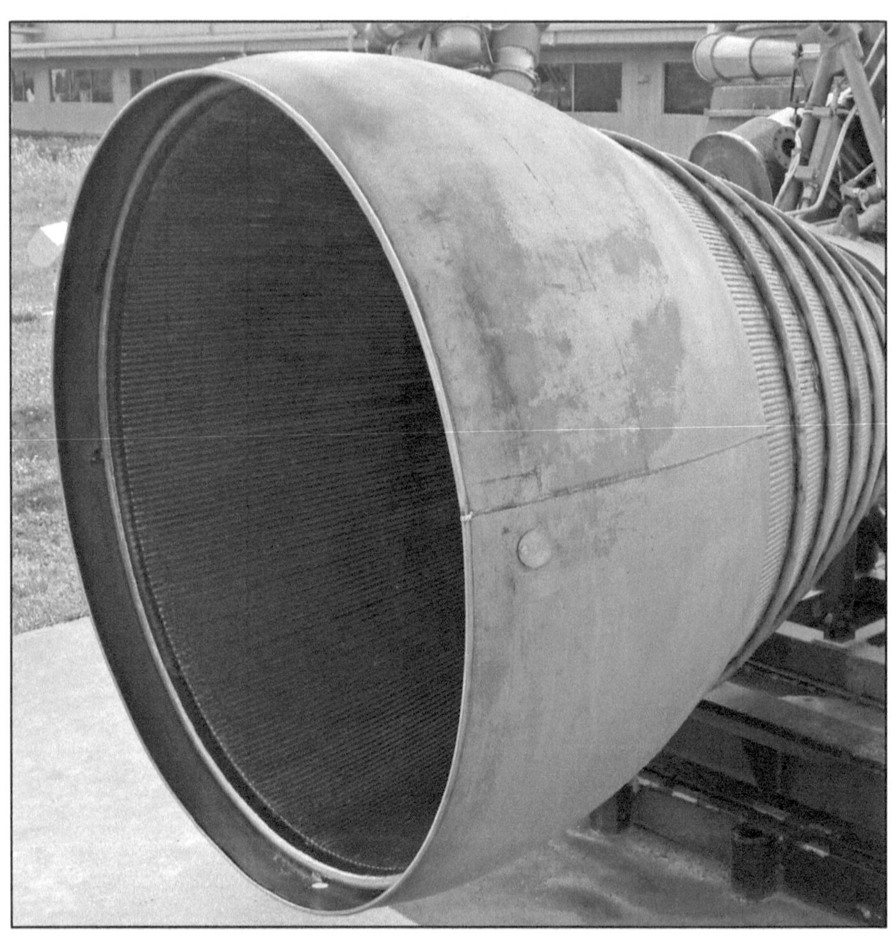

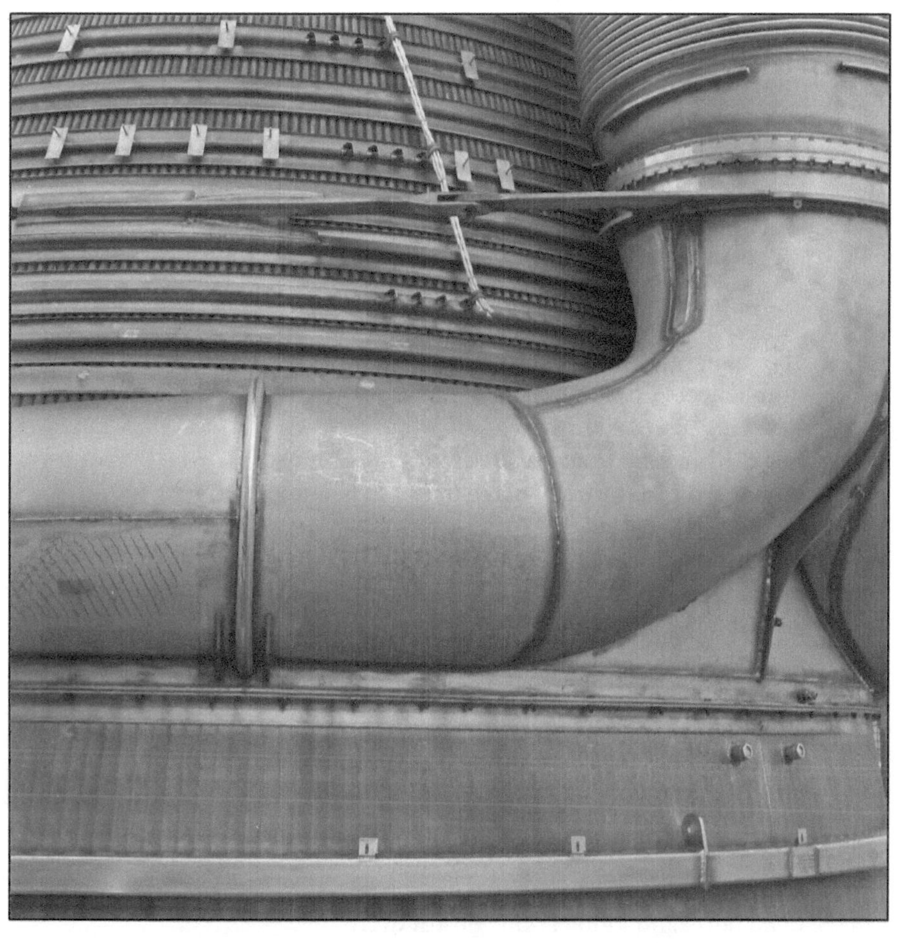

Intelligent life

Plasticoated ocean rises
over tarballed cigarette-butted sunscreened beaches
colorless coral reefs abandoned by fish
and handbuilt foundations of indigenous island homes

Old growth clearcut expands like tear gas
to occupy the space available
between parking towers and strip malls here
and antenna-lined gentrified ghettos there
under the vapor trails of executive ecotourists

Megachurches command the heights
above merging and diverging stagnant blacktop rivers
four-wheeled petroleum burners
hurrying at a walking pace
to get from here to there or there to here
or just out for a Sunday drive if they don't get killed first

Billions of similar sapient brains dot the globe
many clench hungry mouths and fists
and hold out stretched-clay figures
of dying children to journalist cameras
with more humanity than emoted in a binge-watched miniseries
somewhere else where high-def noisemakers
cover rattling dishes and chip-crunching jawbones
attached to satisfied guts
gym-hardened or sugar-softened

Arguments explode to kill and maim
in airports and along scenic desert drives
infantile avatars insult each other
about every problem's cause
too much government too little or just the wrong one
the wrong flavor *de jour*
the wrong flag planted in the illiterate manure
of competing poorly learned wrong doctrines
someone's parents and their whiplashed skin color
or simply the wrong chromosomes and body parts
on the bathroom floor

§

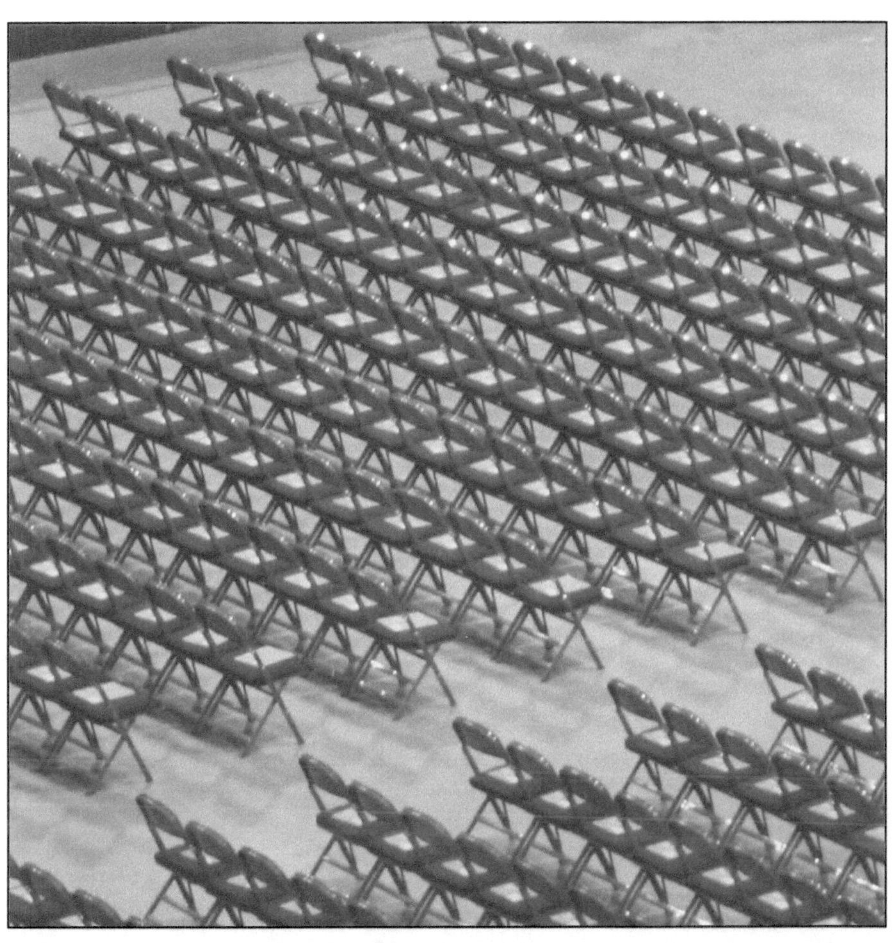

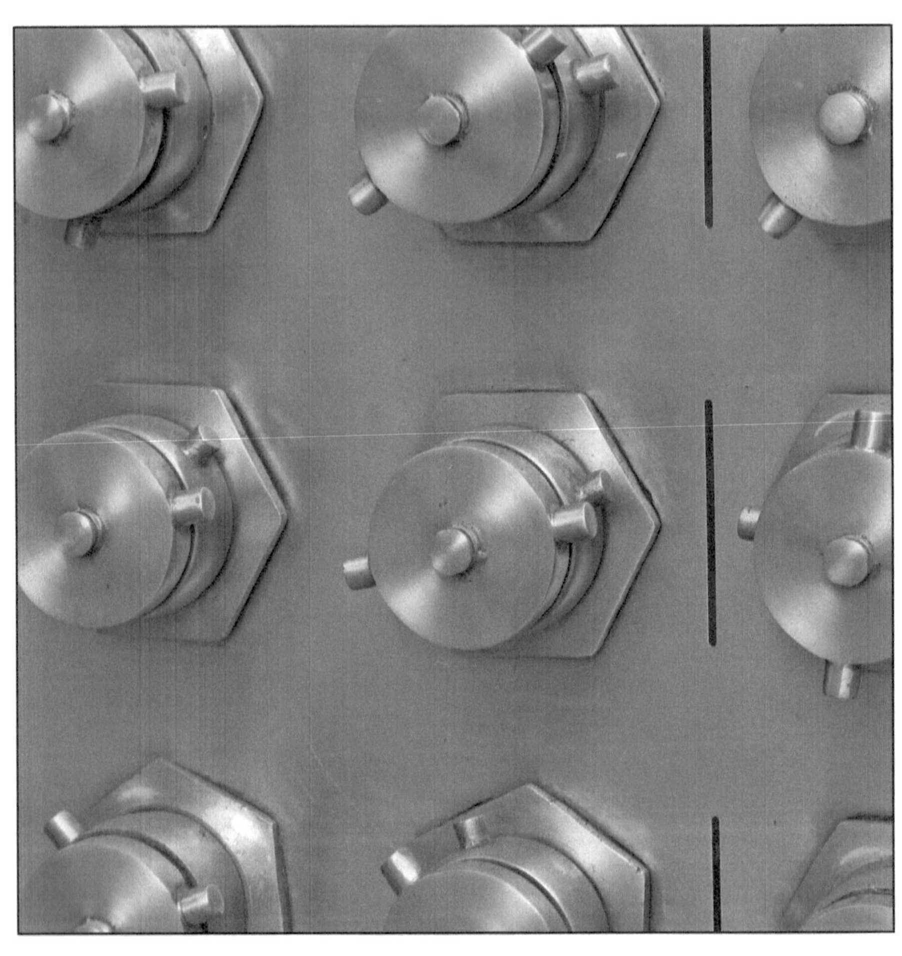

What I know

My species has long since
surpassed critical mass
yet I feel compelled to pick up
the fast food wrappers on the ground
around the orange ranger station trash can
without stopping to explain why

I know where I am
this bizarre place
where beauty and pain
poxes and smiles
necrosis and vitality
are so tightly bound
I struggle to say
what I know
when asked
and tell you where I am
on your maps

Write what you know they say
and critique us when we do
write what you know
but we all
do what we know
I know how to rejoice
I know how to wonder
I know how to comfort
and I know how to mourn

§

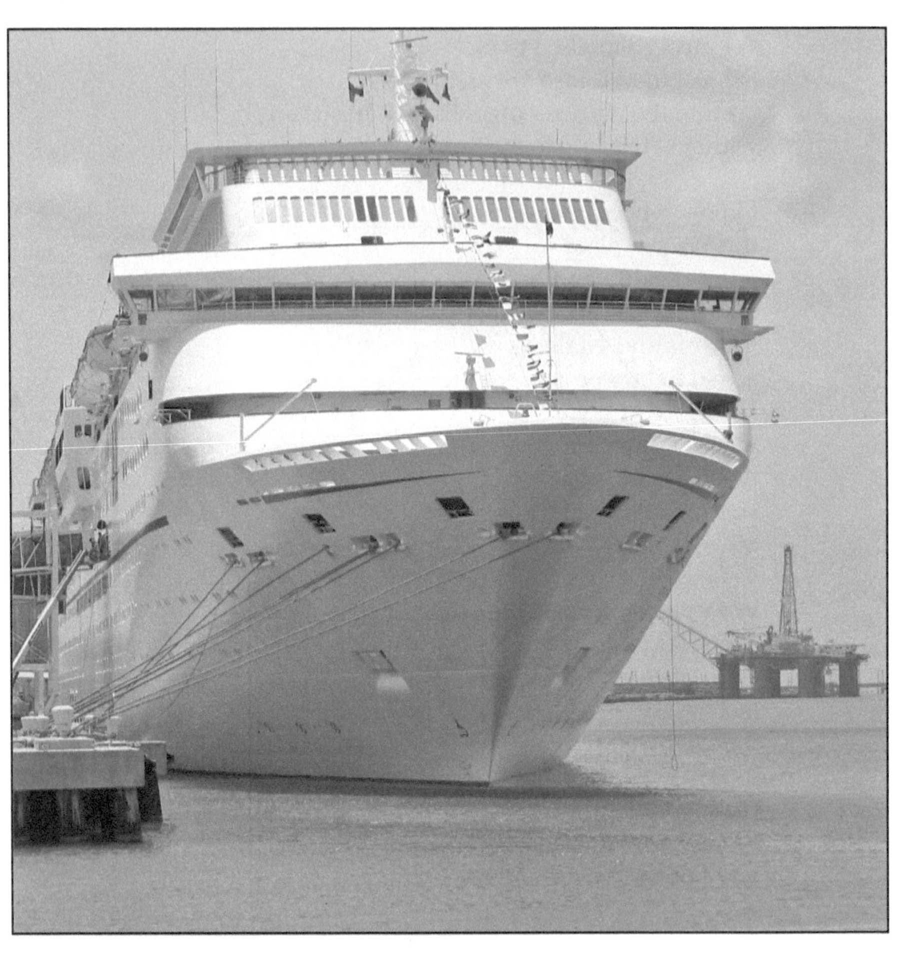

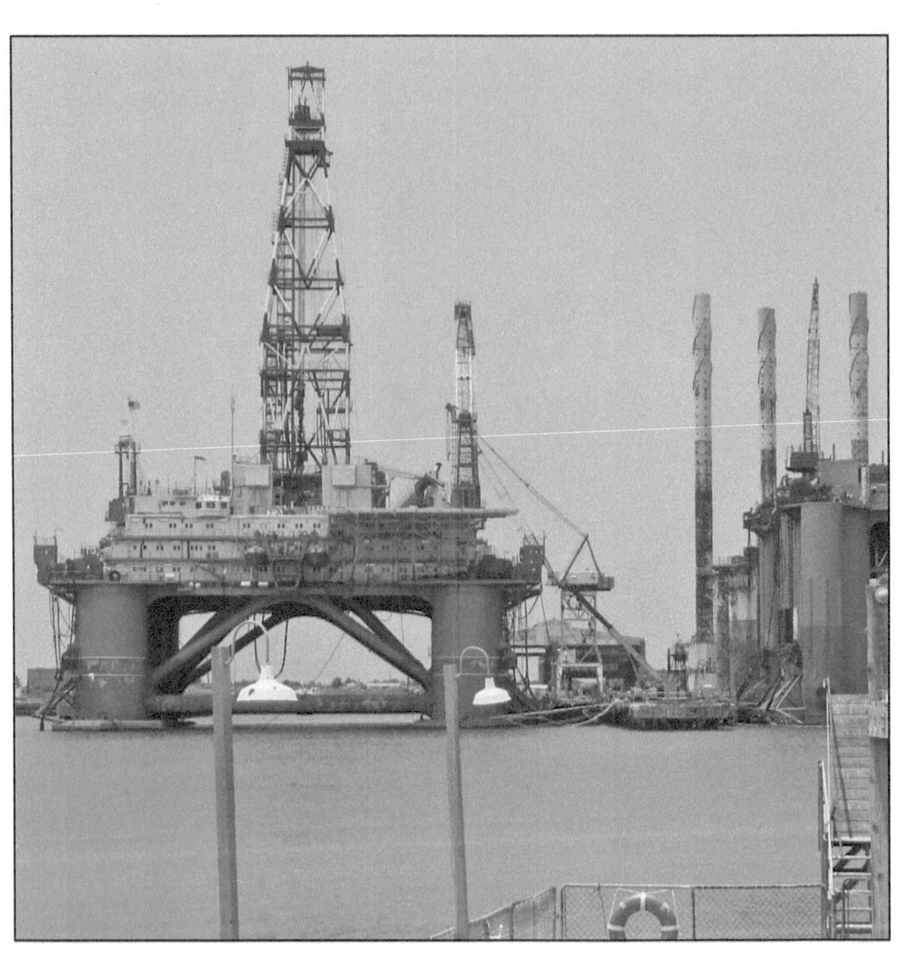

The look

Sudden death misses me
and my carload of teenagers
by three inches
on summer-stuffed Highway One
when a kid in a muscle car
carves around a curve
aimed right at me
using my lane
to pass the traffic in his lane
I stare into his velocity-inflamed eyes
as we sardine three cars wide
on the two lane
guillotine blade
between ocean and continent
I see his ecstasy of power
without care for who's around the bend
I've seen that look before
in parking lots
history books and committee rooms
campaign ads and evening news
and just up the street
while walking my daughter to school
I wonder if that look was around
the time my dad happened upon
a half dozen burning teenagers
after their own drink-fueled head-on
using the wrong ramp to go nowhere
he couldn't get them out of their car
or his mind or apparently mine
what happens to others
happens to all

§

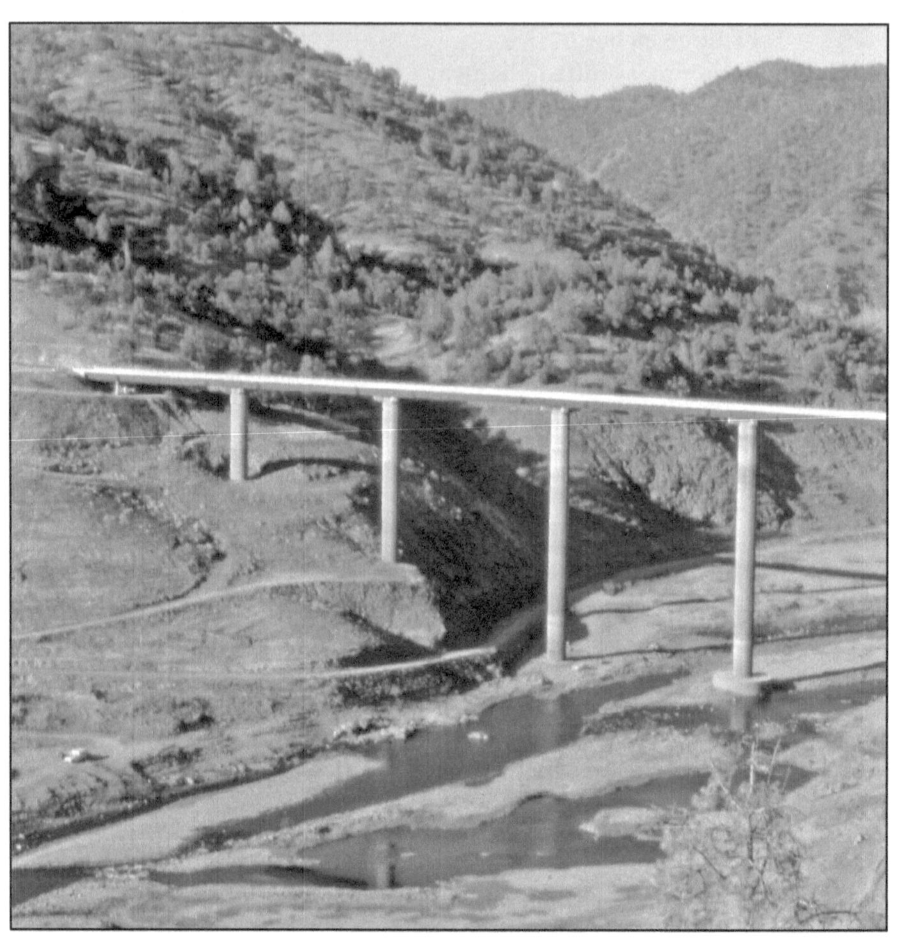

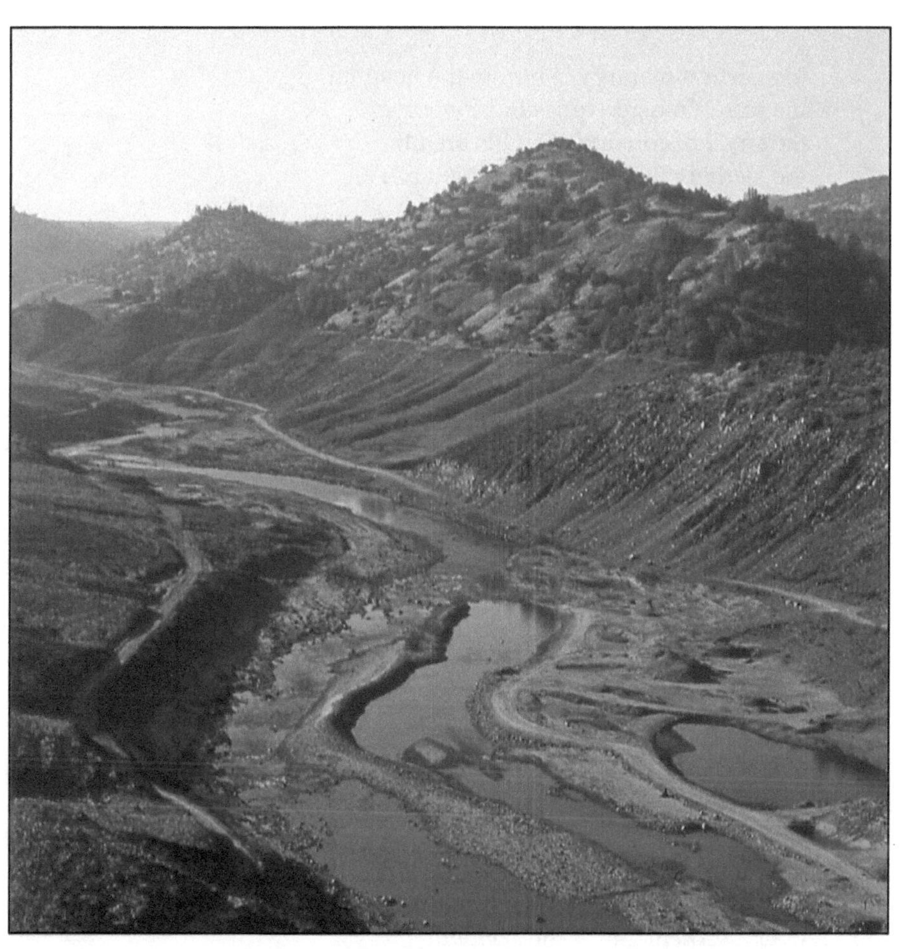

Home economics

My grandfather was killed by tobacco
when I was two and Ike was president

My earliest memory is him in the hospital
the hiss of oxygen tubes in his nose
the smell of corruption in his breath
the leathery face of a southpaw boxer
who built aerodromes in France
and then farmed Iowa
drilled for oil in Oklahoma
and traded farming magazines for produce
to carry through the Depression
a family of five kids

Meaning the ones who survived infancy
one living on insulin till age twenty
one who made it to the Solomons and back
and later two to Korea and back
plus his wife burned and scarred
when her flammable nightgown
touched an open-flame space heater
in an uninsulated house
one arctic-blasted plains winter

While the market was still crashing
a drilling rig accident cracked his skull
and he had to return to lower-paying work
with a metal plate in his head
when his cheap attorney got out-maneuvered
over a settlement for the accident
and his son who delivered papers for dimes
never got them back from a failed bank

They never considered themselves poor
just hard working and stubbornly independent
but he still has the plate in his head in the ground
and the smoke in his unbreathing lungs
somebody made a profit off of him

§

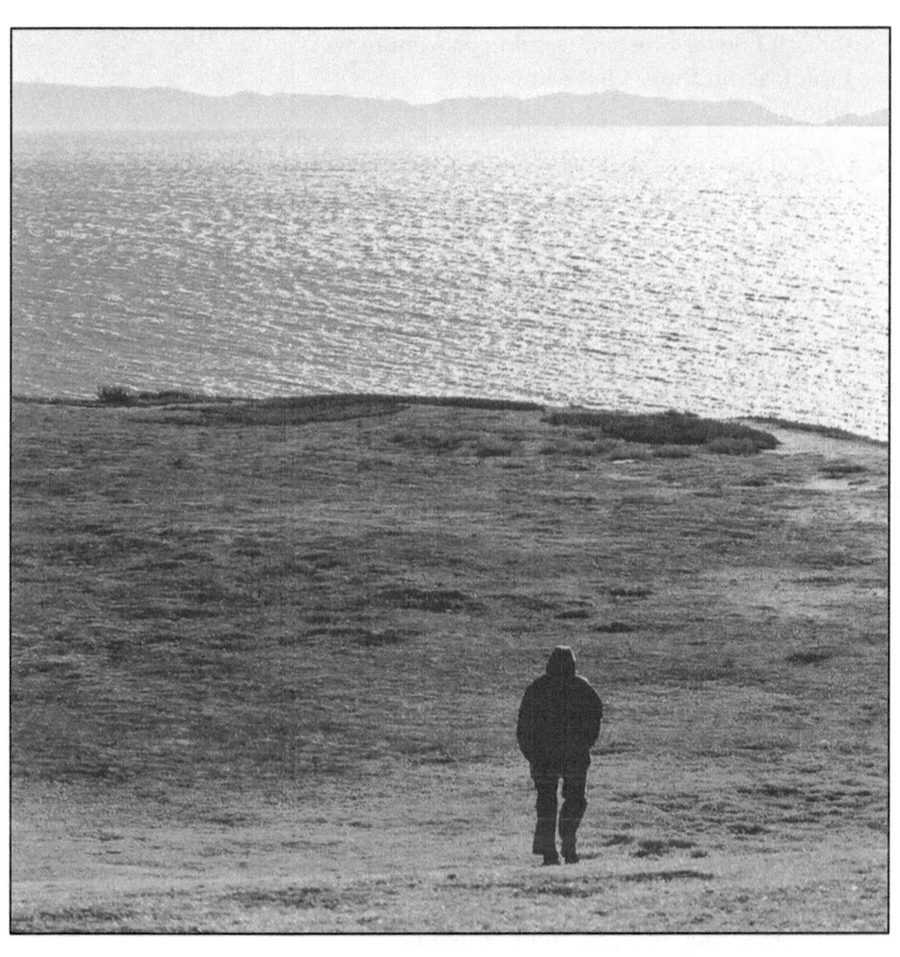

Wounds

I put on a uniform
and came home in a wheelchair
though I never finished training or went to war
I think about those I have known
who did

What good is *thank you*
without cost or commitment
to those who come home missing limbs
friends
parts and pieces of minds
sense of belonging
ability to walk on the sidewalk
without hitting the ground face down
chest thumping wildly
at the sound of a delivery driver
dropping a hand truck

Many in uniform wearing honor
some feeling naked carrying honor
they don't even realize is theirs
and some unsure where they left it
some with welcomes
and some wondering who to call
some with axes to bury or hatchets to grind
some with sharp strange metal still inside them
many with newfound purpose
and a newly tested steel spine

All with something you and I cannot know
but can listen for in their stories
if we save the space for them to tell when ready

Except that too many put on uniforms
and come home in airplanes
lined with flag-hidden boxes
I think about someone I knew
who did

§

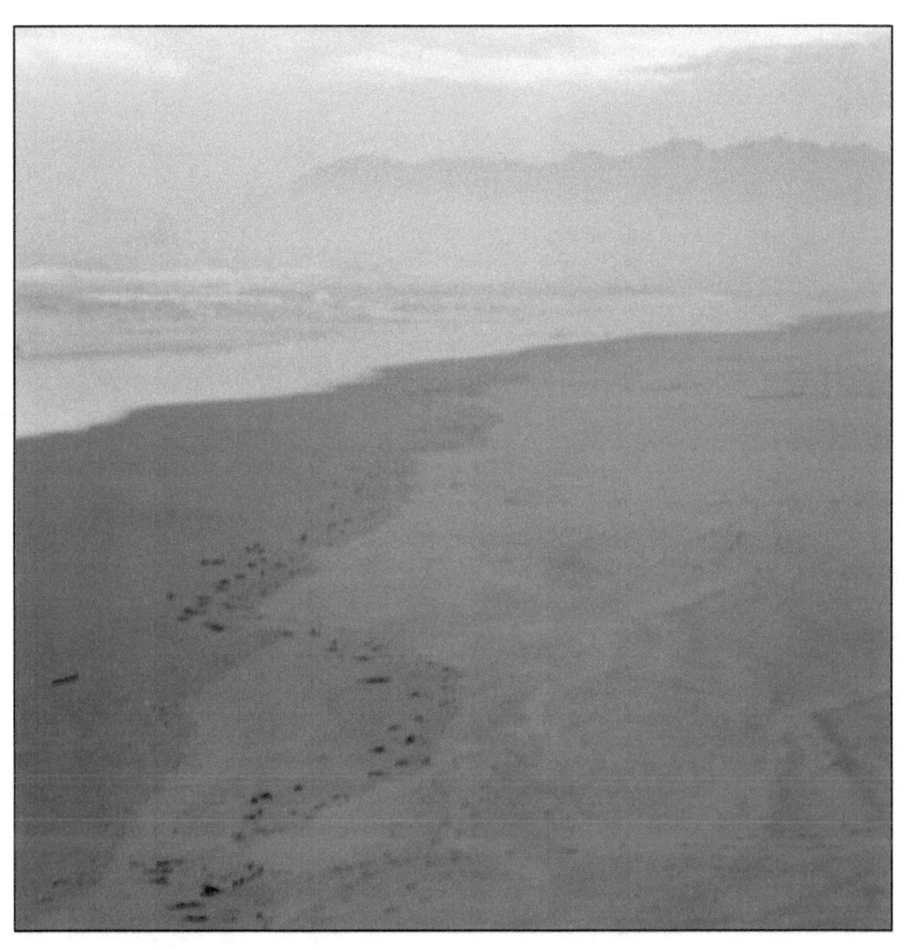

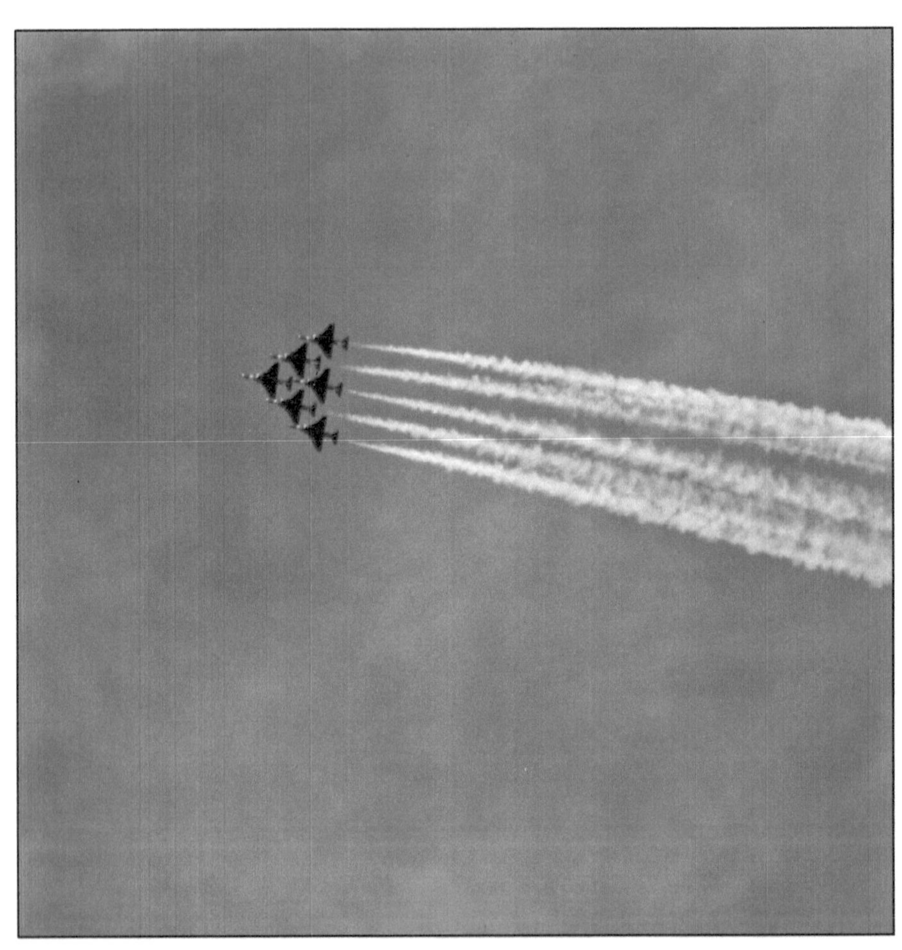

III.

Physics lessons

1. General relativity

As the light of truth
fills a world of self-deception
it bends in the presence of massive bodies
and I am surrounded by them

2. Gravity

The drooping curvature
of my responsible shoulders
is all that keeps me
from flying into space

3. Centrifugal and centripetal force

I can never recall which is which
my mind is scattered
in so many directions
as I spin through life
trying to find my center

4. Entropy

Inevitable decay
the long collapse
into cool bland disorganization
of any closed system
the only law of physics
empirically verified
in human society

5. Solids liquids and gases

The reflection of sunset
on the still-wet beach at low tide
freezes my gaze until it fades
and my lungs expand again

Turning to my right to leave
I am struck in the face
by the full white moon
risen behind me
while I wasn't looking

Some time later
as my bath water swirls down the drain
a thought comes to me

6. Laws of motion

Watching my generation
rocket away to fame and fortune
on so little apparent thrust
while my own low orbit hardly budges
though pushed so hard my veins burst
I can only conclude
that something enormous and inert
rests in peace inside me

7. Orbital period

Evolved with ten fingers
on a planet spinning 365 and a quarter times
for each lap around its star
and then a scribe mistakes the year of a nativity
that anchors our calendars
tell me again what is so important
about the new millennium?

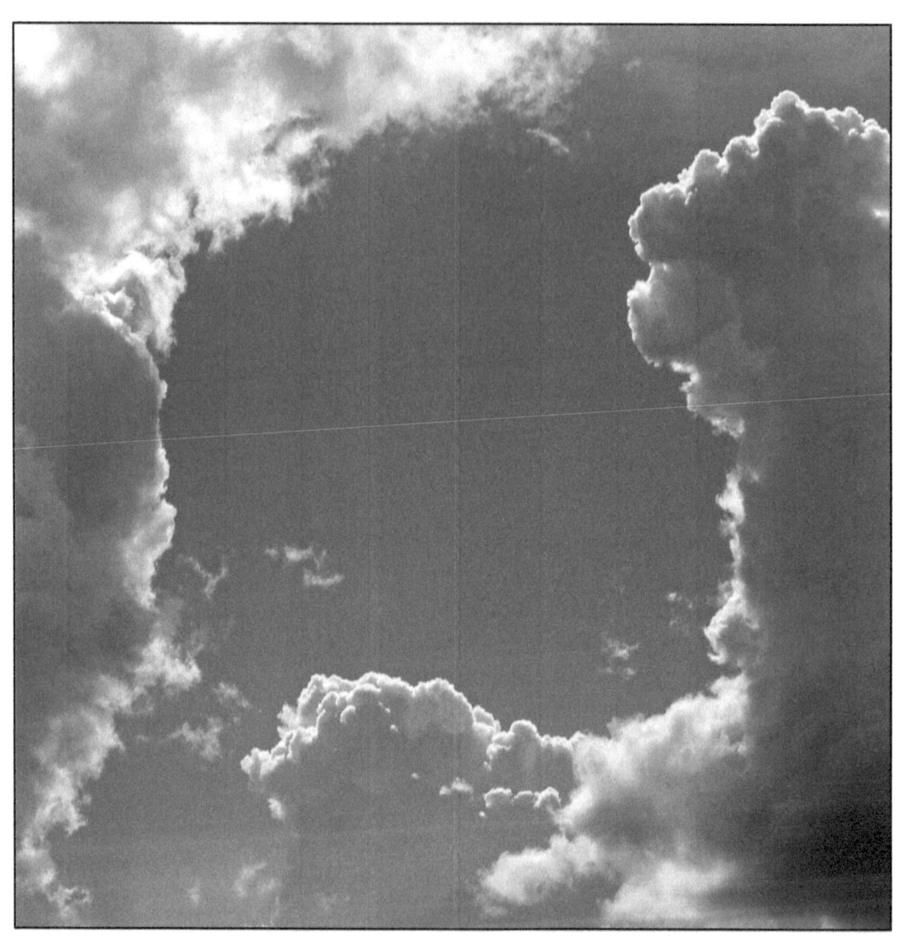

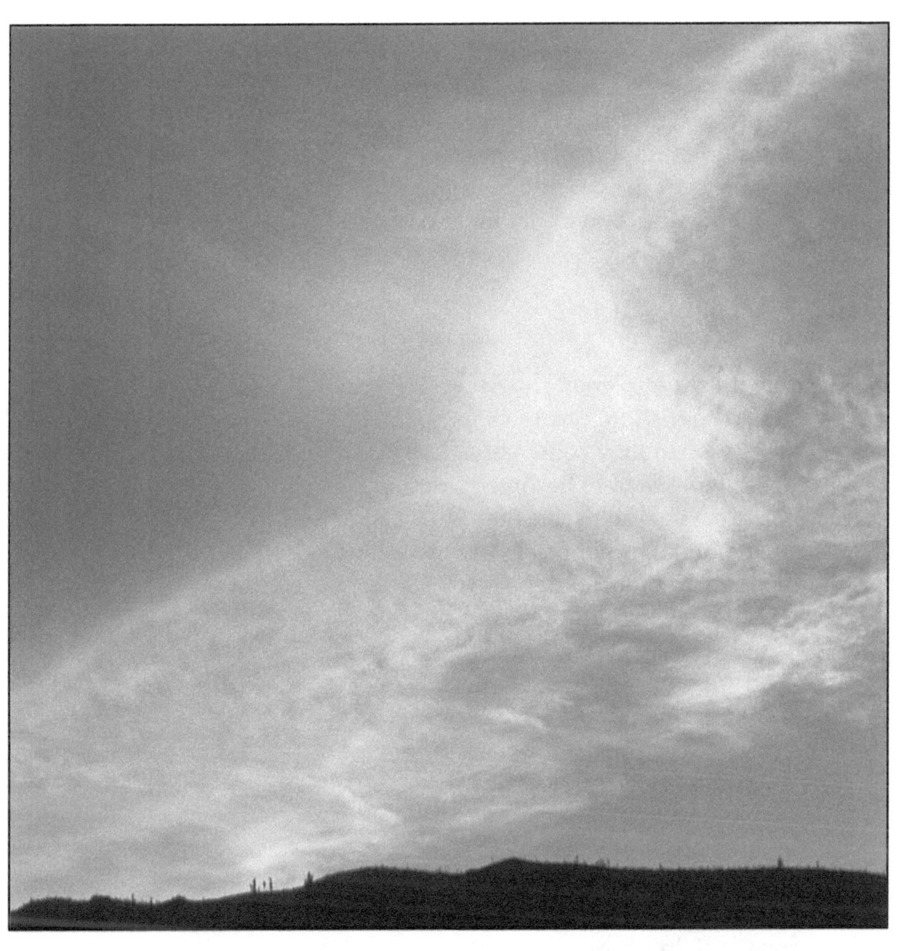

8. Magnetism

Whatever caused the Nietzsche
to leap from its niche
on the bookstore shelf
and into my pious young mind
might have been an affinity of opposite poles
but decades later what can explain
the continuing tug of *terra incognita*
drawing me ever deeper into heresy
as I follow the devotion of my inner compass?

9. Strong nuclear force

The only glue tough enough
to fuse two hearts into one nucleus
only works when they come very close
but causes them then to become something else
sacrificing part of themselves
as heat and lethal radiation
binding them to one another's orbit
in celebration of shared trauma

10. Weak nuclear force

Mathematics proves its necessity
long before it can be understood
the subtle decay
of what was once a core belief
announced by the release of tiny fast particles
everyone exclaims how negative
these messages are
yet the center becomes every moment
more positive

11. Anthropic principle

It is indefinably large
but made of inconceivably small things
it is far older than knowledge
but each moment is surprisingly new
it seems beyond comprehension
yet makes more complete sense
than could ever have been expected at random
one thing it does not do is explain itself
but it tries when I try
which makes me an agent
of my universe
examining itself

12. Cosmology

The stone at the bottom of this turtle pond
is the center of the universe

13. Earth

Riding a blue marble as it splashes
into the black lake of space
counting the ripples that spread out
and bounce off the wall of beginnings
a time ago so short
we could name the billion-year waves
for toes and one handful of fingers
that didn't exist then
which makes it hard to keep score
against other galaxies
but easy to hold hands with someone
in the same gravity well

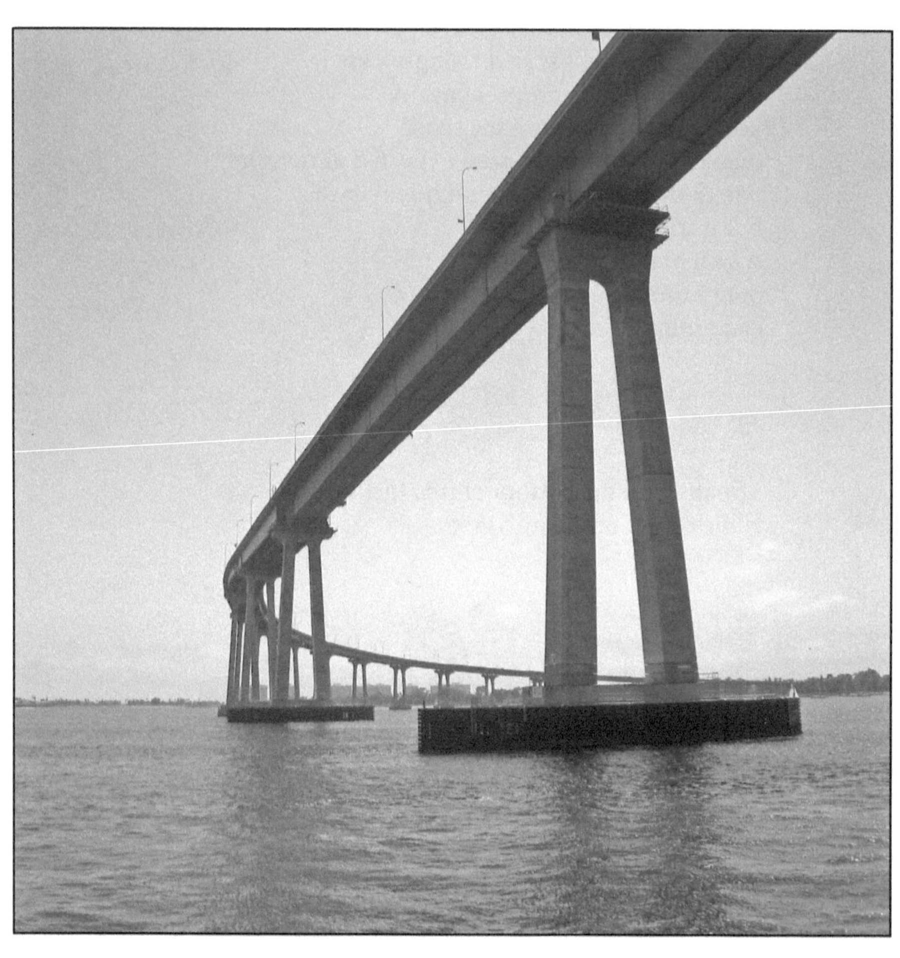

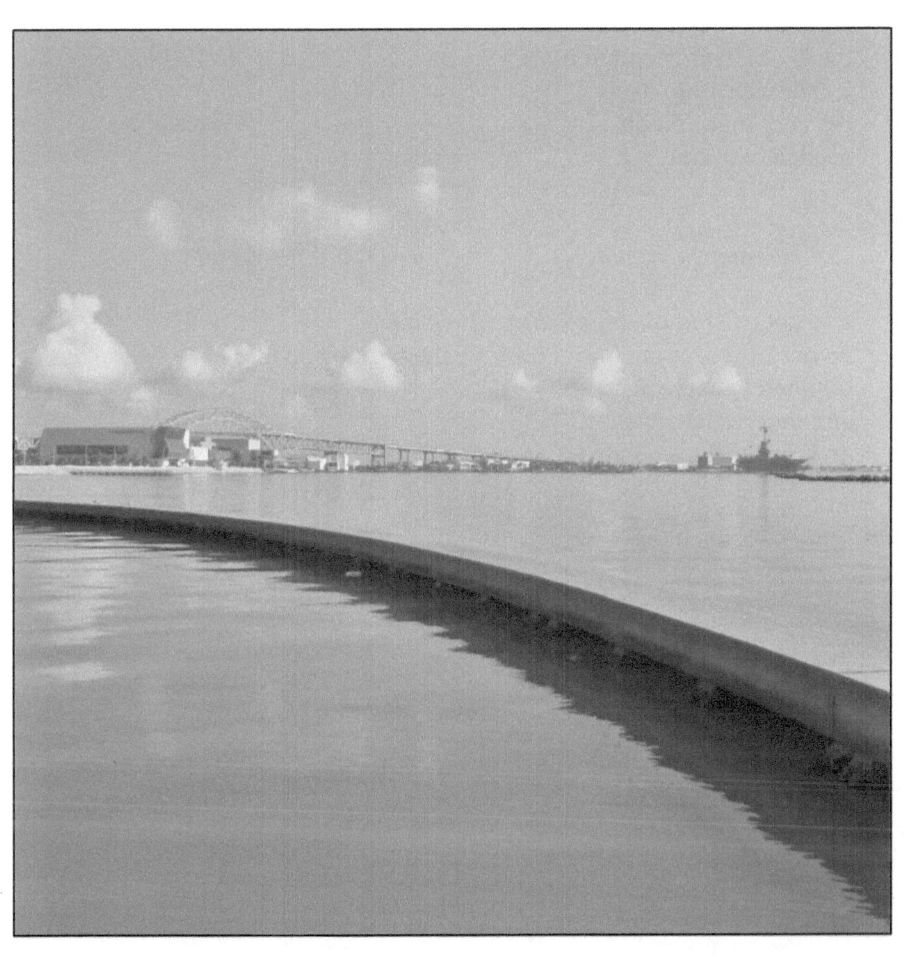

14. The speed of light

The worth of a life
cannot be measured
without living it
the given in any equation
it calibrates unto itself
the very instruments
needed to quantify it

15. Quantum mechanics

I do not exist until someone observes me
no one observes me until I observe them doing so
but then I am changed
and they are changed
and the world is created

16. Uncertainty principle

The cat and I meow
at the same harmonic frequency
along the curve of possibilities
we are both equally alive
we are both equally dead
the difference is I have books
to explain my sensation of half-death
it's all in the half-life of an isotope
and whether anyone cares to look in the box
the cat does not understand this fate
but is only lonely

17. String theory

An infinitesimal needle pulls my thread
through the fabric of the vacuum
which seems to be tied in knots at certain places
where I can't help circling back around myself
only to find infinite possibilities
vibrating in tiny pieces of emptiness

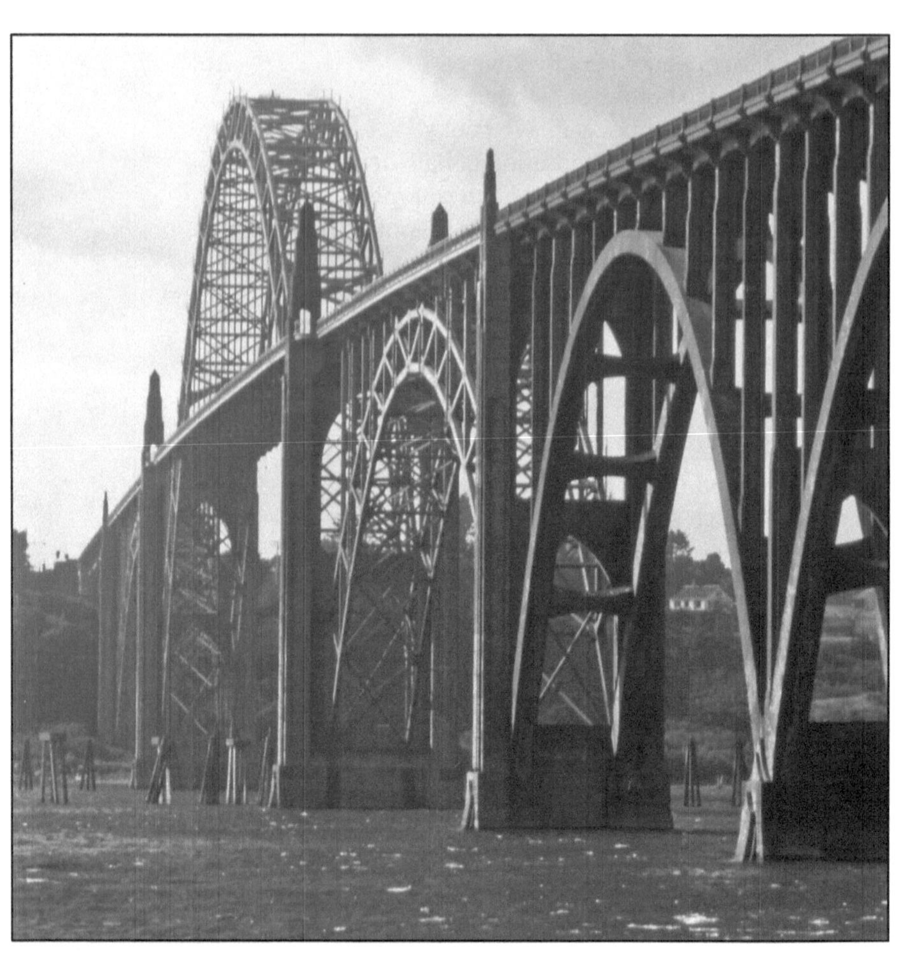

18. Time and information

Over three billion years after the solar system is born
the dinosaurs grazing and fighting for their rights
are struck down by a comet as old as the sun
leaving bones for us to discover
with an occasional worried glance at the sky
knowing Andromeda is already headed in our direction

During the month after peace is signed
indecisively by envoys in Europe
Andrew Jackson's ignorant lines east of New Orleans
conquer the assaulting British
in the most decisive battle of the forgotten war

About five hours
after Thomas Jefferson dies
John Adams dying without the news
asserts as though it relieves his mind
that Jefferson survives

A half-second after the winning ticket has already been sold
without my knowledge
if I buy a scratch-off lottery ticket
what are my odds of winning?
what should I have put in my calculator
ahead of time?

When you read these lines
whether floating in a capsule on the hot greenhouse ocean
buried on the ancient pages of a frozen civilization
or plucked in bits from the bowels of servers on the moon
I am not there to hear your critique
and you do not know what poison I am leaving in the words

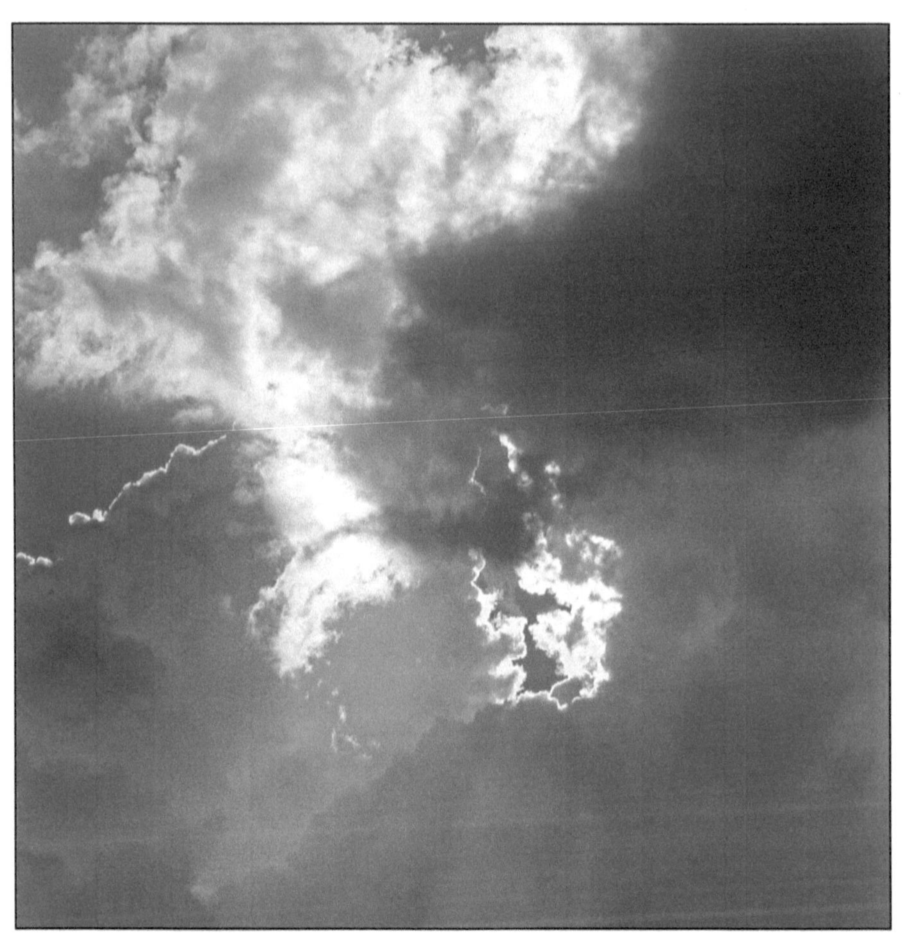

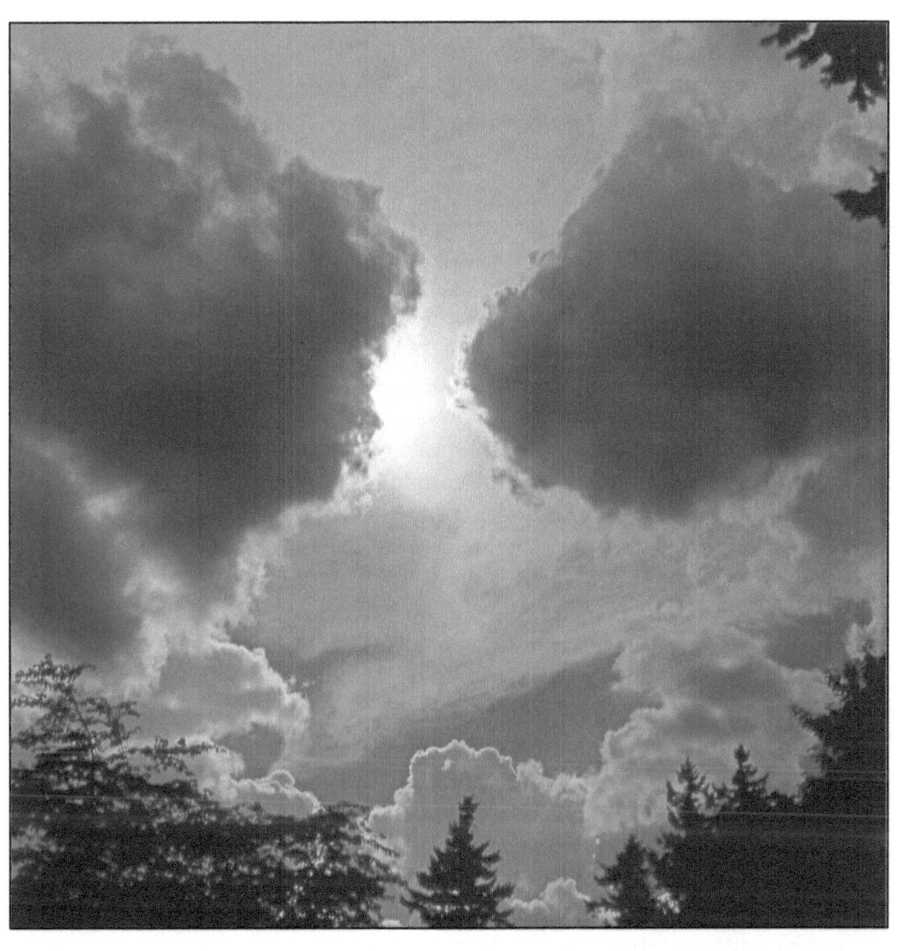

19. Electromagnetic radiation

This room is flooded with invisible waves
prove it with your tuning knob
violins on one wavelength evangelists on another
local rappers and their DJs
seekers becoming has-been celebrities
distant soccer goals in Spanish
voices from every streetcorner
pull one out of the air

Football skating tennis golf
seduction lies betrayal murder
entangled passions of daytime lovers
bloody beaches of invasion
French cooking for the masses
quiet canoe angling streams
amplified outrage about who isn't outraged enough
children of crossdressing parents compare
their public grief with parents of crossdressing teens
the worst fears of the school board
have come to pass — film at eleven
this weekend only special financing on used cars
psychics beg credit card calls
light beer makes young people sexy
laxatives make old people wise
hold out your open hand and channel what you dare

Shortwaves carry Thailand and Spain
and solo sailors in the Tasman Sea
while VHF waves cut through
to untangle jets stacked overhead
and ELF waves longer than a river
swing through with warcodes
for distant cold submarines
without a cold war to fight

Microwaves sizzle with corporate data
cellular arguments buzz all around
amid wirelessly webbed sarcasm
while dispatchers send emergency crews
and delivery trucks squawk by

And through it all
from every nameable direction
flows leftover energy
from the childhood of the universe
shifted so long it's no longer visible
but you can see it on a fuzzy old untuned television

All these photonic energies
vibrate every moment
through every space of this room
through my hand that I hold up—right there
through the thin-walled cells of my soft-tissued brain
I am an antenna to the world
all I lack is circuitry to pick one channel
and filter out the rest

20. Atomic number

Compounding the world
how many elements does it take
to make rain forest fern mushroom
beetle jaguar anteater parakeet
swelling sea and leaping whale
children playing soccer in the mud
noisy city with quiet library
stinking pile of rejection at the dump
gray-celled engine of human sapience
a sudden laugh
a broken life
is the periodic table big enough?

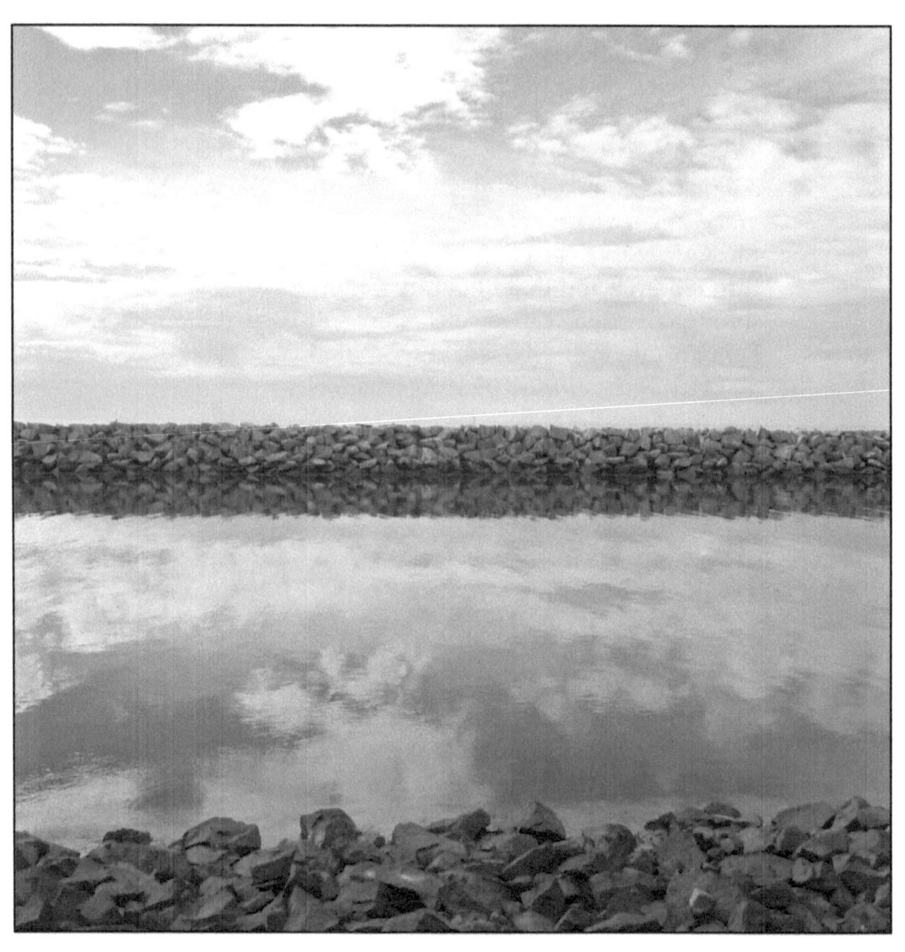

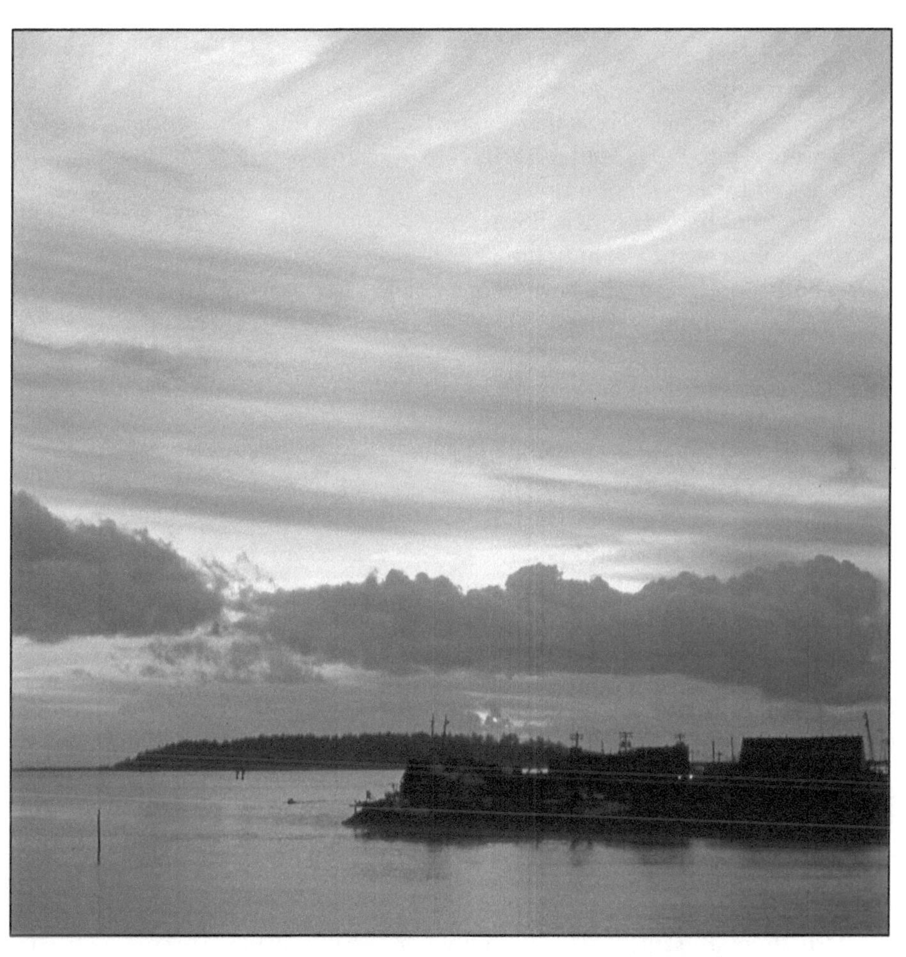

21. Space-time

Wind-filled canvas stretches taut
above a classic wineglass hull
of hardwood bent around fair molds
curling crests of lime-green seas
caress a sandy half-moon cove
while the sun arcs across the skybowl
to plunge into the globular horizon
followed by a crescent moon
young trees bend before a storm
along the brow of a rolling hill
smooth stones lie at the bottom of a creek
under an arching waterfall

Succulent outline of a woman's breast
streamlined warhead penis tip
lens-shaped window of the opened eye
whorls of identity on every digit
sausage shape of a nice firm shit
fragile edge of an orchid petal
shell of an egg—peel of an orange
abdomen of a widow spider
clever pitch hooking over the plate
line of a race car through a sweeping turn
flight of an arrow to a distant mark
or the long graceful fall of a burning plane
etching its signature on a lifetime of dreams

Good vibrations of guitar strings and vocal chords
sines and cosines waving back and forth
across the continuum
derivatives and integrals coupling wherever you turn
supply and demand dancing spiderwebs
to the music of convoluted schemes by self-seeking minds
wheels within wheels in the middle of the air

Radiant novae of unexplained joy
giant red stars of swollen anger
feeding on their own dead planets
galaxies spiraling into black holes of depression
roundabout logic of self-justification
concave awareness of solitude
fetal position of perfect peace
marvelous pebble of love

Curvature of the universe
curvature of all within

§

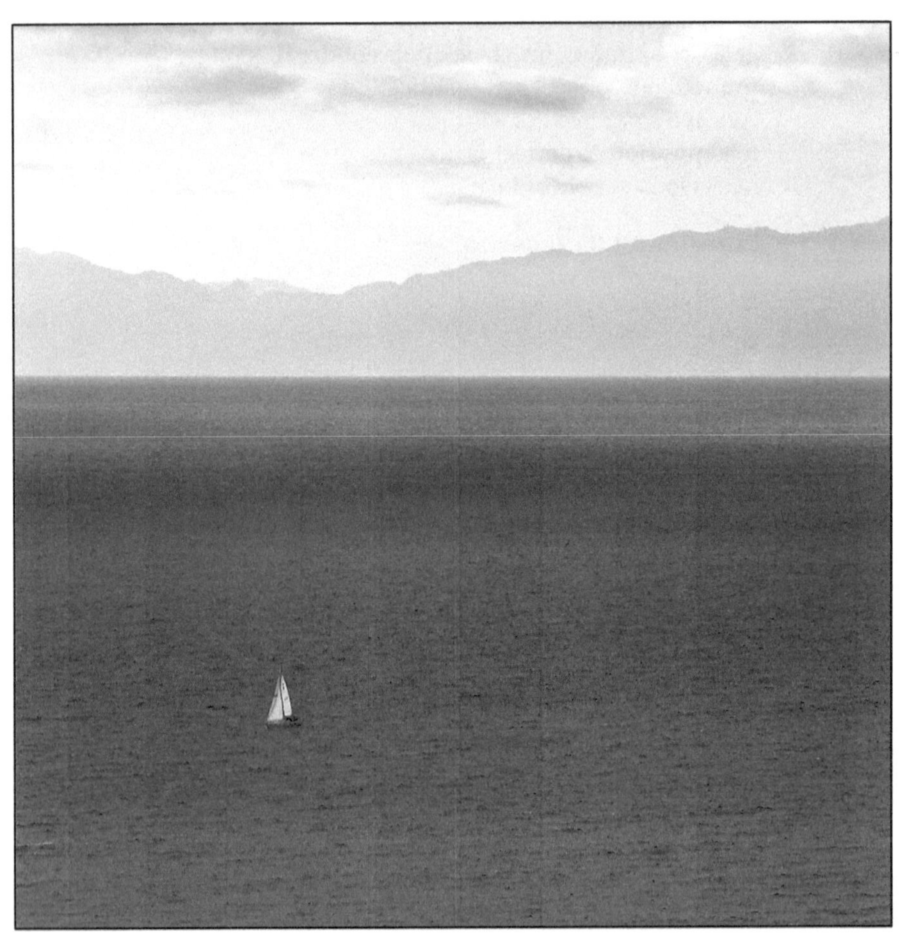

IV.

Variations on a Theme by Joshua Slocum

1. Muse

I propose to author a passage
alone around the world
and since I am an old Yankee
educated in liberal seafaring
excuse me for a hand
that has grasped the sextant
more than the pen

Critics labor over my shoulder
my craft's ends are too short
she needs stronger beams
thicker planks
fasten here calk there
and always asking will she pay
I'll not hew to their specifications
though my book be constructed
of rough timbers and not brightwork
she'll sail smartly enough in any weather
when well-handled
unlike the lilies of the sea

I knew a writer whose seas
were smooth enough to plant flowers in
fertilized with lovely words
but once he faced a real deepwater storm
he became a changed man
where after all would be the poetry of the sea
were there no wild waves?

The words of the sea
belong to uncounted hands
what could I write that would be
as ancient and as fresh
as the spray from a single wave
unless it be my self?

2. Precedents

Magellan gave his life for this dream
De Elcano completed it for him
afloat but barely alive
Drake made it look like sport
I think I'll take Magellan's strait

Bligh made a noble attempt
against the worst the sea could throw
but foundered on a reef of human pride
he never learned to master
my crew and I will see eye to eye or else

Clipper captains raced it for a bet
and a better price on tea
but drove their ships and men so hard
many never returned
I've served my share of bully mates
my new ship's owner forbids cruel usage

So many salty skippers seasoned like myself
blessed with graceful tall ships
and robust hands before the mast
have sailed around or failed in the try
what makes me want to do it alone in a little sloop
or think I can
or should?

Never mind
I will be myself
and say what comes to mind
and do what I happen to do

And what I will say is that
I am not for old ideas when new ones are better
and what I will do is go to sea
and keep on going to sea
until there is no more sea
or no more me

3. Metamorphosis

The fellow I got you from intended a jest
and a fine one indeed
a rotted out oyster boat as old as the republic
retired in a pasture beside a cherry tree
far from salt spray
never to float again

I built you with my hands and adz from the keel up
new ribs and beams
new planks along the lines of the old
native pasture white oak
Georgia pine
New Hampshire spruce
with a foot more freeboard
for southern seas
and double breast-hooks
for plowing ice

Bought or built?
new or old?
you are my riddle to the world

It is a rule with Lloyd's that the *Mary Jane*
rebuilt from old one plank at a time
until she is entirely new
is still the *Mary Jane*
philosophers have argued the point
far longer than Lloyd's
building new ships out of old under cherry trees
since the time of Plato
how many have actually done it?

By the end of my voyage
I shall be ten years younger
than at the beginning

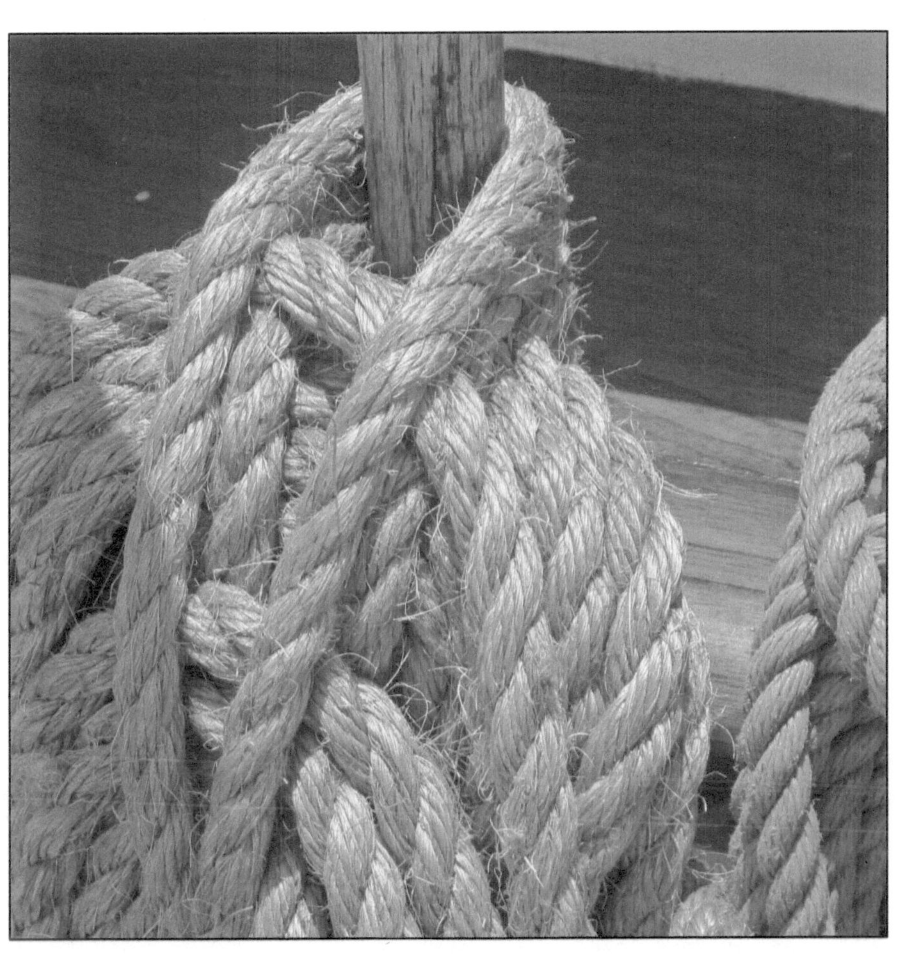

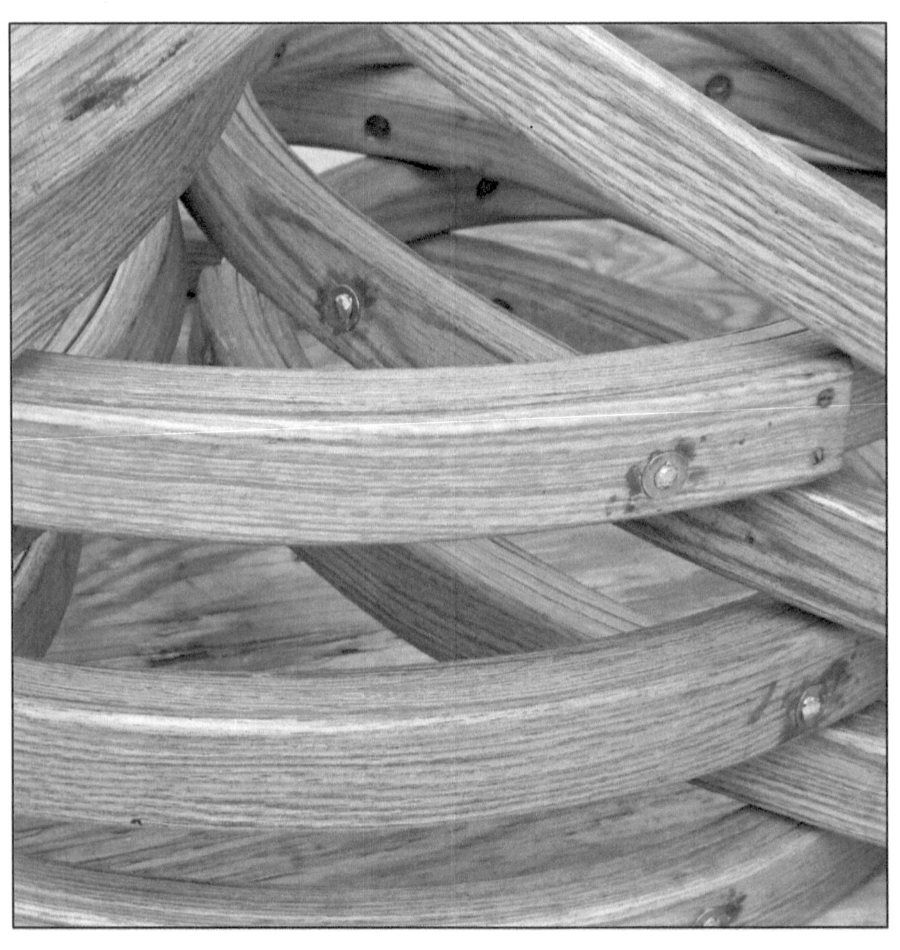

4. Departure

As I round the last point
a hundred pairs of arms reach out from shore
to beckon me back home

But the shore is dangerous!

It's a place to spend a lifetime
walking through leafy woods
chatting with earthy folks at rock-fenced farms
sitting by a fire of native oak
with someone warm and welcoming
while snow falls quietly outside

No—give me green water for my leaf
white spray for my flake
Sargasso for my rock-fenced farm
and flying fish for neighbors

My little ship skips along smoothly
away—away from those well-meaning
solid-rock citizens who beckon to us
stretching our sea-legs southeast
toward the wide horizon
and our destiny
and the round wet world

I tell you this
the sea will take me someday
without a trace
no land will ever own me

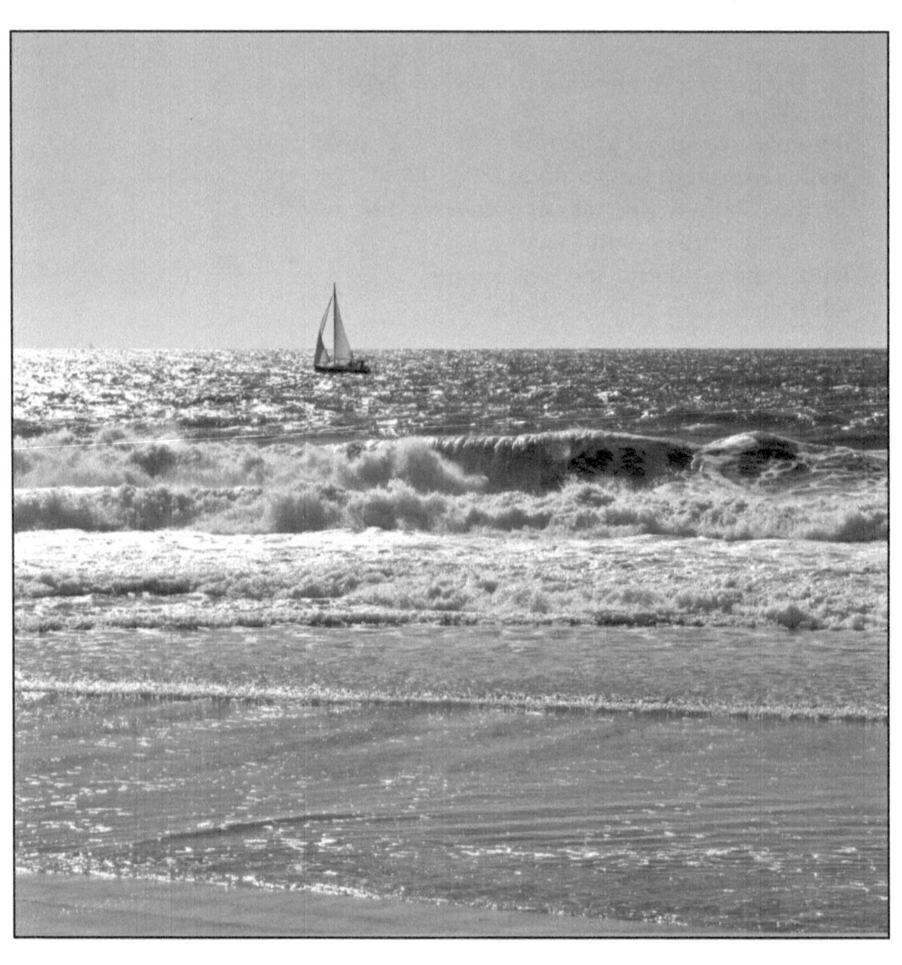

5. Sailing

Joyously buoyant in your dance
nimble lady
carry me bounding through tumbles of green water
hot sun on my shoulders

Be silent!
hear the water rushing by

Jewels of spray splash about your heaving breast
sparkling necklaces you snatch from every surge
and as soon toss back
ah—cascade of diamonds

Lovely above me your smooth bellied sails of flight
glean the cool wind
in their white canvas curve
while I caress with my salt tasting hands
your bare pine deck
your wheel spokes
your mainsheet

Hold me!
hold me close
as I lay you lightly
across the lifting swells

6. The whale

As I doze and dream
my vessel hooks her anchor into a whale
and is towed a long way at great speed
by the beast

The ocean boils with the toil of his fins
explodes with jumps higher than my mast-top
cracks like cannon when he slaps his broadside tail
then he races and dives
and my poor craft leaps in chase
her ribs heaving
straining at the tow chain
crashing into wave crests
throwing aside great wastes of foam

I cannot fathom the sense of the whale
what powerful flanks
what profound soundings
what groans of effort and yearning

Great cetacean stranger
to what sunken city do we flee?

Oh pull me!
pull me down to your peaceful depths
I shall quit the unquiet surface and plunge with you
together swim the canyons of timelessness
what fame—what voyage 'round the waking world
can match your submarine sensation?
I renounce my feeble project
I will follow—I will follow
I surrender all

In my dream!
In my dream!

But here is my compass
there are the stars
the sails are drawing full and by
this is my true voyage—my sober dream
I know—I know—I do know where I am going
and I have far to sail for my pledge
to circle a watery planet by my own Yankee wits
and the virtue of a hand-crafted ship

I do not yield to any madness but my own

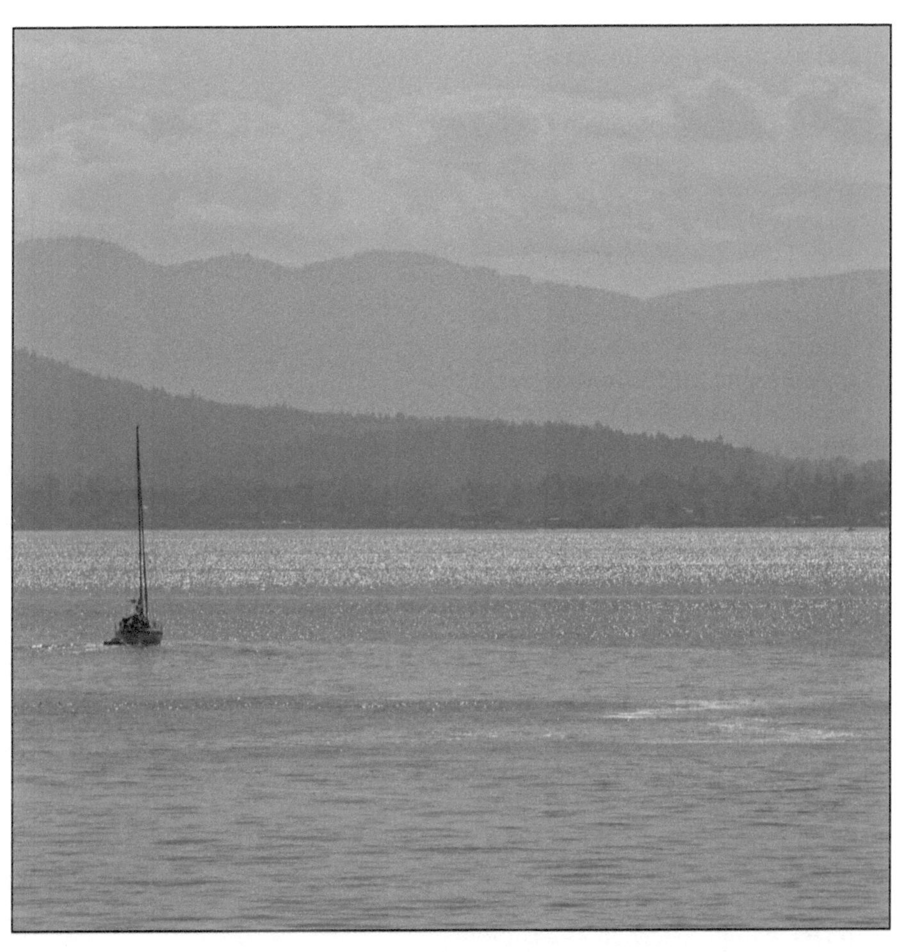

7. Equipment

My craft cost five hundred some dollars
and thirteen months effort
she boasts no labor-saving appliances
but a windlass for the anchor
blocks for hoisting sail by hand
and oars for pulling in and out of port in calms
yet she logs thousand-mile passages
with no hand at the helm
so sweetly balanced are her lines
once I give her the mizzen she deserves

My tin clock with a smashed face
purchased for a Yankee dollar
according to time's fashion
serves me as well as the brassiest Bristol chronometer
my longitudes may not be as strict as a man-of-war's
but we sight by the same noon sun
and I go wherever I will

My hand-stroked bilge pump
disposes easily of what little sea leaks in at first
while planks swell to their seams
but it becomes unneeded thereafter
and stays in its box the rest of the voyage

My defenses consist of sprinkled tacks
business end up on deck at night
to deter barefooted cannibals
and a modern repeating rifle
for fending off musket-armed pirates
a lesson I once learned as a captain
repelling mutiny with a carbine
unpleasant work compelled by unpleasant people
best be prepared

My shortened Cape Ann dory riding bottom up on deck
is an unneeded lifeboat and a ferry to shore
once I swamped her rowing out an anchor
to kedge off a beach I ran *Spray* aground on
three times I went under
and was ready to say 'now I lay me'
but—determined not to let doomsayers win
saved myself dory ship and voyage

The sea I sail on and the stars I steer by
I cannot take credit for

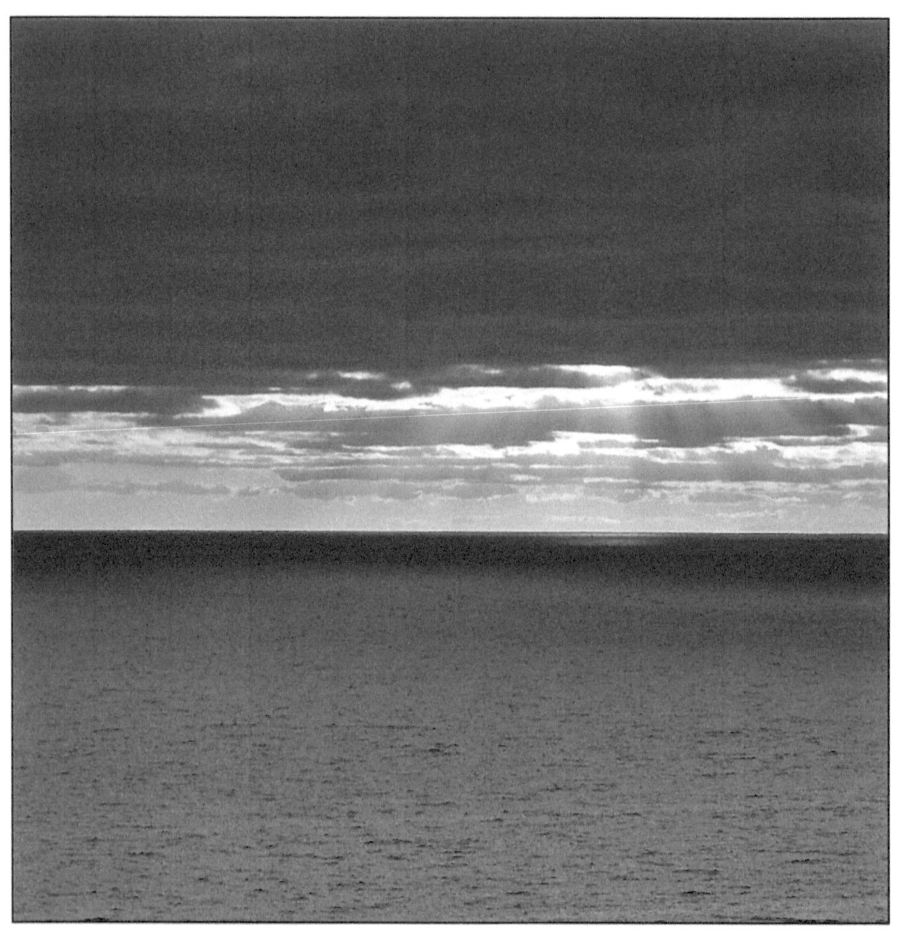

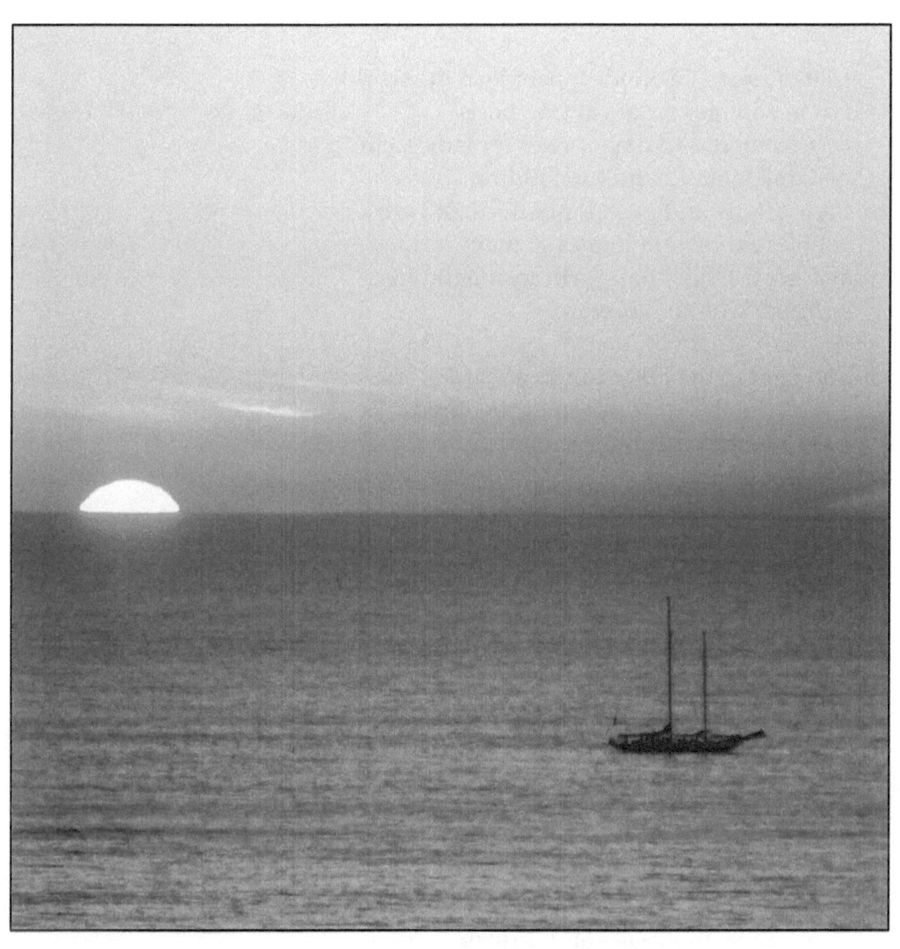

8. Society

I sing to porpoises who splash in delight
and I greet the man in the moon as a friend
even coral reefs keep me company

Islanders are the kindest people in the world
I dine with governors at tiny ports
give lectures and day-cruises for ladies' clubs
make sleight of hand for children
trade tallow and nails for native handwork
get blessed by religionists of many stripes
and good-willed flat-Earth cosmographers
worried over my itinerary

The pilot of the *Pinta* comes aboard
and steers the *Spray* when I grow tired
I am honored that the Admiral of the Ocean Sea
has lent him to me
a dependable helmsman
he has good advice about my diet
though I can never get him to change a jib

Steam freighters bound by schedules
are welcome encounters
but do not take the time to speak
let alone back sails to gam like the old days
it is a prosy life when we have no time
to bid one another good morning

The battleship *Oregon*
hurrying to fight the Spaniards
flying enormous Stars and Stripes
gun turrets and towers like a citadel
bellowing black coal smoke
returns my flag-dipping Yankee salute
but declines my offer to sail in company
for mutual protection

I have done hard voyages
lost ships cargoes crew and my own good credit
I have stood trial for my life
in the aftermath of violence in foreign waters

This time around
I meet a good many
very good people
but my greatest companion
is the crew of my own ship

§

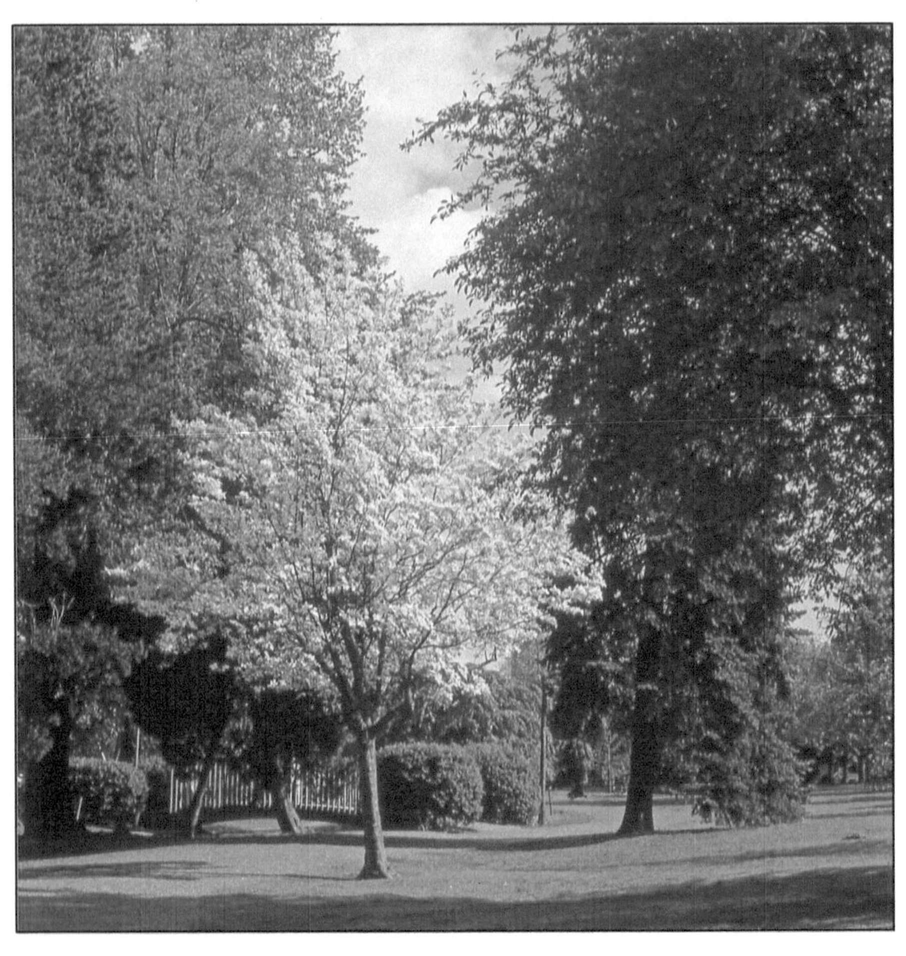

V.

The Secret of Ladd's Addition 1992-1997

Morning walk in Ladd's Addition

Yesterday's mown grass confronts my toes and my nose
lilac blossoms and roses on fire my nose and eyes
beat up old sedan and city bus my nose and ears
that is bacon and coffee
wood smoke from a stove
that is perfume
a whiff of natural gas
where the street is dug up and flagged off
horse manure in someone's garden
and that is definitely fresh dog shit—I check my shoes

A big dog and a little dog bark in the distance
a whoof whoof and a yap yap yap
sparrows starlings robins jays and crows
singing chirping calling screeching
I watch them flying between the trees
and pacing the lawns of the houses
cottages too small for a grandmother
mansions too big for a commune
but most of the houses just right to covet

A black cat sits on the porch fence at that house
a white cat in the window at that one
piano practice comes from this house
repeating Chopin until perfection
a newspaper slaps against a front porch
another and another right down the street
a few house doors and car doors slam
there's a train over on the Southern Pacific
the whistle announces it
the rumble on the track I have to listen hard for
then I also hear a ship on the Willamette
and a drawbridge horn

Steam rises where a man in ragged clothes
pees at the front of the hardware store
UNICEF graffiti at the elementary school
gang graffiti on the 7-11
house sold and house for sale signs
lost dog picture stapled to a power pole
children's yellow and pink chalk games on the sidewalk
grownups' orange spray-paint marks on the street
yellow plastic recycling bins and rusty garbage cans
on dark gray sidewalk slabs lifted by tree roots
weeds rise through the cracks
and white cement squares show off recent repairs
where trees blew down in the winter storm
rhododendrons and dogwoods in full color
cherry trees already past bloom
fallen petals everywhere I step today
remembering last fall's maple tree spinners

Brand new sunlight works its way through the trees
and down the criss-crossed streets
my own sweat drips down my face
mixed with salt forced from my eyes by the breeze
alert and open
I spend an hour searching
for the secret of Ladd's Addition
among the elegant homes
and return to my cluttered apartment
full of joy
the secret still unfound

§

Herons

A *pas de deux*
of great blue herons
on the airport service road
I watch them from the Columbia levee
where my Sunday morning walks

Slowly circling on spindly legs
politely bowing their long curved necks
flapping dark barn-door wings
they look so awkward
but move with stately grace

In the way of a yellow airport service truck
that blasts a klaxon horn to scatter them
again and again in the cool silence
giving the birds a raspberry
I flip the truck a bird

§

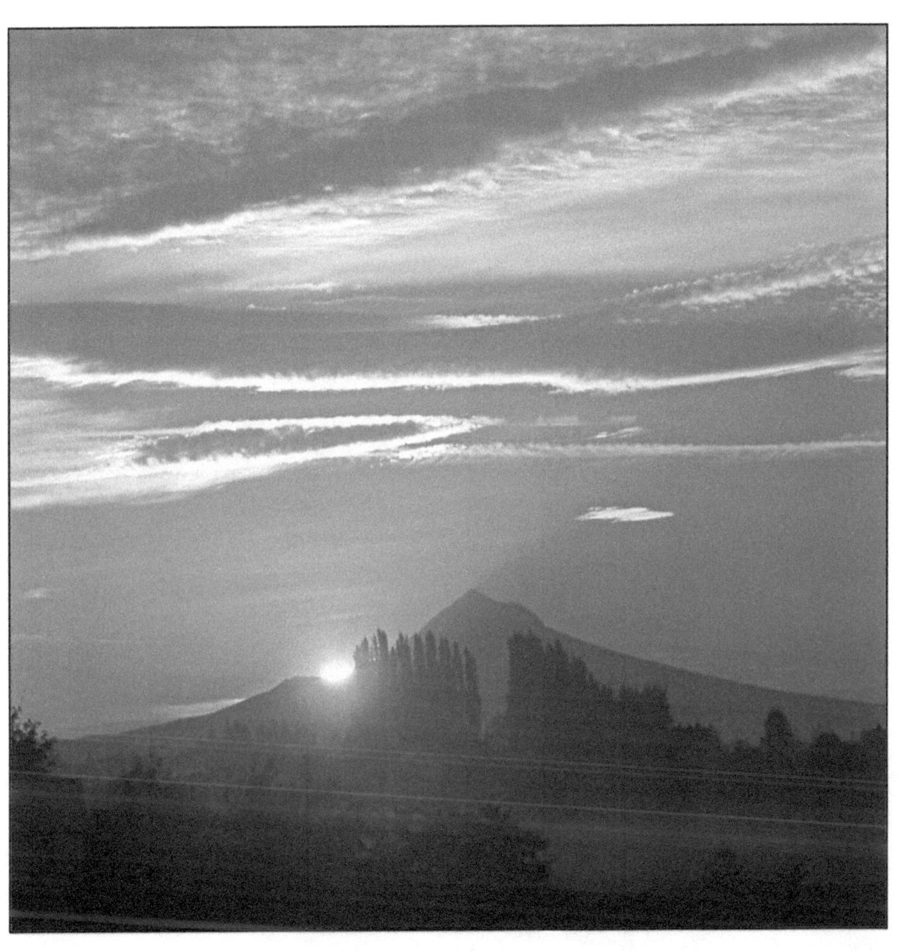

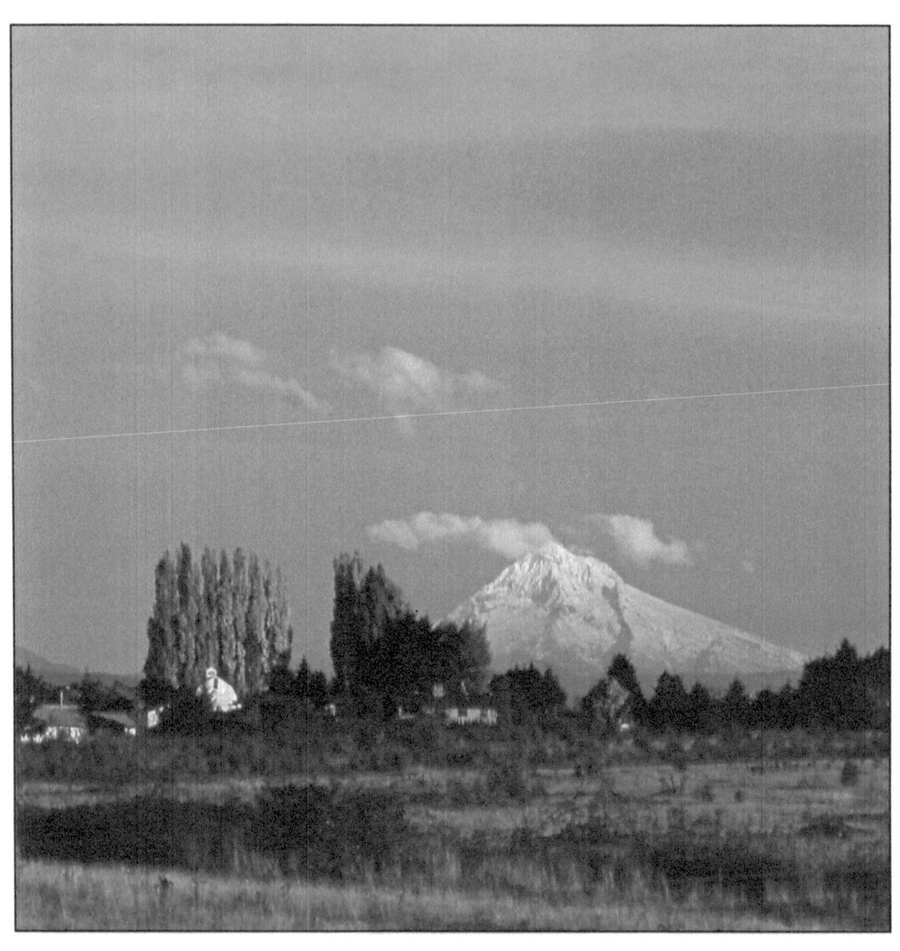

Where we live

There is nothing solid between us and Jupiter
we feel the chill of its methane storms
as we gaze on dry summer nights
Japan is closer and sends storms by sea
I remember green glass fishing floats
and still have one from my childhood
but haven't found any lately
we were the only state out of forty-eight
bombarded by Japan
but now we have sister cities there
and a Japanese college
within sight of our capitol
that slab-sided ship you see by the river
is rolling off Toyotas for sale
our car is a Honda

Today we have a submarine of our own
commanded by an astronaut
but only the mast and smokestacks
of our famous old battleship that fought the Spanish fleet
and was moored for years right across the river
from where the submarine is now
until used as a barge in the war against Japan
and then sold to Japan for scrap
the smokestacks are stuck in the parking lot
of an import emporium—goods from every land

Spanish is what you hear in the mall these days
or when the kids come home from school
unless they're taking Japanese instead
one of our fastest local industries
sells sportswear made in China
marked with a Greek name
and advertised by descendants of Africa
our nuclear power plant is shut down
but its tall tower still commands the river
there's a little college right here in town
with its own private reactor
just up the road from the rhododendron gardens

We were the first with initiative referendum recall
the first to require pop and beer bottle deposits
many western states allow an armed citizen
to stand and fight like *Gunsmoke*
but we make it a duty to flee if possible
with shooting a last resort
like most states our universities
have savage predators for football mascots
ducks and beavers
and you don't say O-rah-gone
say Or-eh-gun instead and say it real fast

Here we protest so much one president
called us Little Beirut
another bully president took his friends fishing
on the Clackamas
where we take our Sunday drives
we rank number one watching public television
have the largest bookstore
the most colleges parks and hospitals per person
the world's largest strawberry shortcake
once a year a city block long
in a town named Lebanon for its cedars
and we have our own sick whale as well

Stern-wheeled riverboats are coming back
but not cloth-covered wagons
except the giant ones over there
you can see from the freeway
the highways too crowded for wagons now
and we're in too much of a hurry
long-time residents are certain
they can drive fast in any rain
by virtue of statehood
watch them spin and crash
when autumn's first showers
loosen the oil slicks of summer

Jefferson's captains explored this place
but British sailors discovered it first
well—it was already settled by then
sometimes we complain about the bad air
in modern cities placed in places
previous occupants avoided
because of what they called bad air
and we are still amazed at the heights of the floods
we get after stripping forests bare
to develop concrete riverbanks

We live downstream from three dozen dams
and a dozen volcanos
The city parks where we play soccer
and chase our unleashed dogs
occupy flood-plains or slopes of extinct lava cones
earthquakes are few right now
but they say a big one is overdue

Our native forests are coniferous
not from so much rain in winter
but from so little in summer
contrary to reputation we have a drought every year
forest fires strike in their season
put out those embers cold
the green is what I miss the most
when I have to go away
the solid darkness between the trees
when small towns go to sleep
I remember and miss already

Oregon is twice the size of England
but has fewer ghosts
the ones we have are less civilized
they beat their drums on clear nights
while we name the nearby stars
and they chant to us of a wildness and wisdom
that once possessed this land
under the very same stars

§

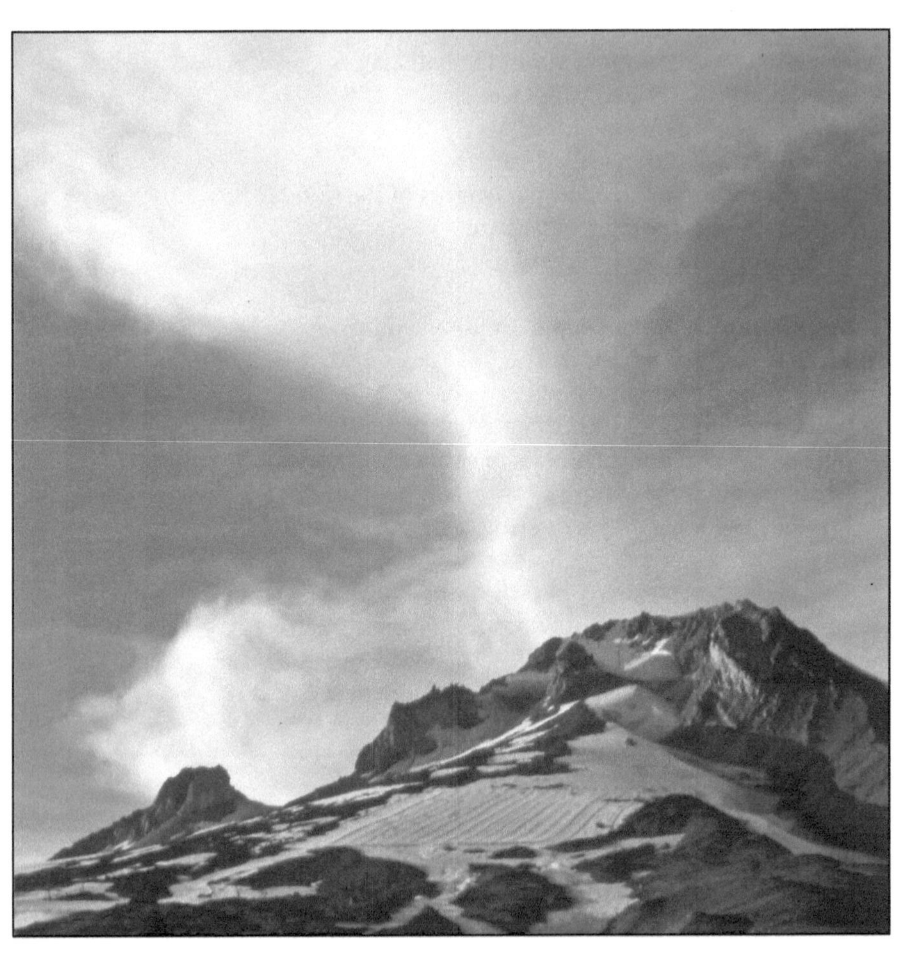

For Erin

I have never seen you frightened by the future
or slow to speak political ideas
that would shock my parents' generation
or unable to turn conventional arguments surprisingly upside down
but your optimistic energy frightens me sometimes
as when you ran into the parking lot at the rose garden
and a car was coming and I yelled *ERIN STOP!*
because I couldn't have reached you in time
but you did stop and you turned toward me
more from curiosity at my unaccustomed firmness
than from obedience

Once when something awful happened
I don't remember what
I told you to say *life is tough*
and you sobbed *life is tough*
and I told you to say *but I'm tougher*
and with trembling lips you echoed *but I'm tougher*
I'm not sure you knew what it meant

You have designed original things all your life
I kept for future use many drawings
and folded paper prototypes you made outside of school
you solved problems that had me stumped
and asked questions I still have to ponder
but the moment that I cherish most
was your birthday when we went to dinner
at the Italian restaurant on Burnside
and I gave you the sketchbook and pencil set
then we went to a comedy double feature
and when we walked to the car in the back alley
you danced and swung around the lightposts
and you yelled out to the quiet night
I AM SO HAPPY
but my eyes were the ones that suddenly got wet

Now I want to yell at you again
as you swing around a tough world
of rushing cars and critics
whenever that world gets in your way
listen to your father yelling *GO ERIN GO!*
and this time don't turn around

§

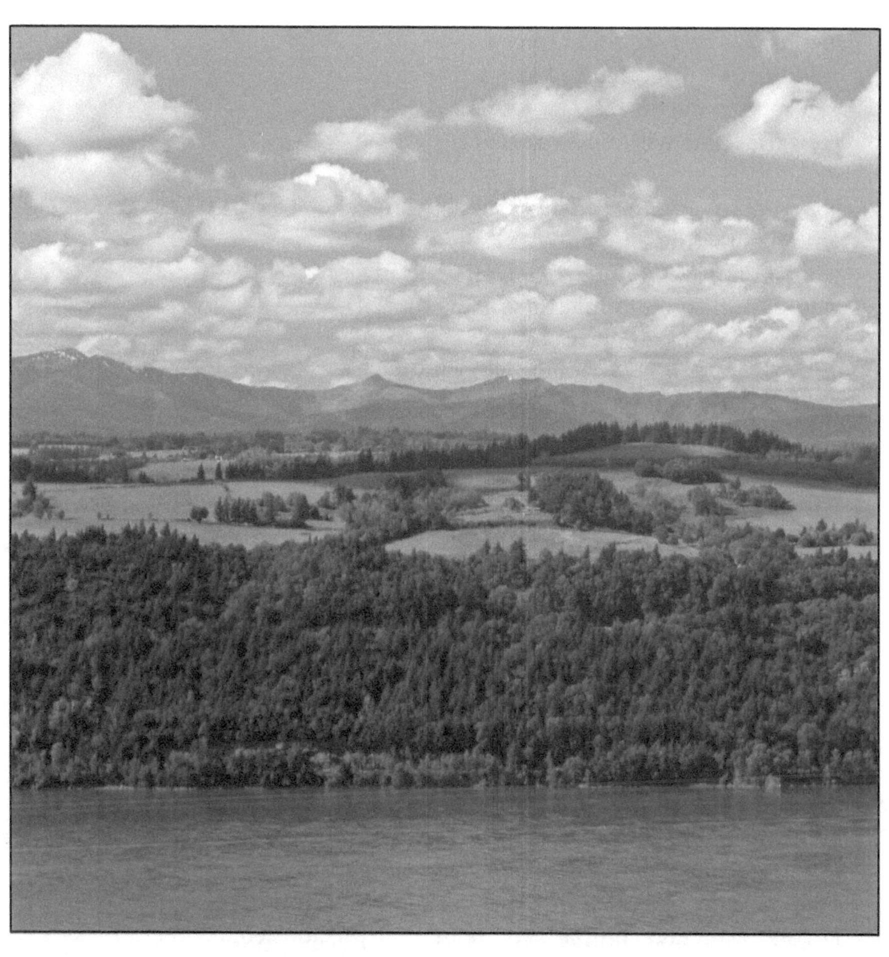

For Robin

You screamed and I swooped you up
and plunged your tiny hand
in a handy bowl of cold tapioca
yelling at your mother to bring ice
you rode to the hospital on her lap
your first time without a car seat

For weeks we changed your crusty bandages
with fresh white ones and cool salve
when you preferred to leave well enough alone
—for months you toddled in a wide margin
around the offending stove
and played more gently with your toys
—for years you hesitated to stir the spaghetti
favoring one hand behind your back

Forgetting the stove you continued to be burned
by teachers who labeled your slower brilliance as an attitude
I remember the fractions homework you did at the dinner table
with me on the sofa concentrating to check your work in my head
and when you were done I walked over to discover
you didn't write down any answers or work
and never got credit on paper for problems you solved
in your own head

You were burned by classmates who teased and threatened
and later by employers who took advantage of your gentleness
ministers who could talk endlessly about pain without feeling any
and I'm sorry to say by my own various inabilities
I even teased and complained about your precious collection of rocks
until you became a geologist and started teaching me their names

If I could go back and give you any gift
it might be a world where you could
reach out your hand and not get burned
but if I did you would not have that other gift
—the one you gave yourself when no one else could
the boldness to be different and still to touch the world
even though it might hurt you

§

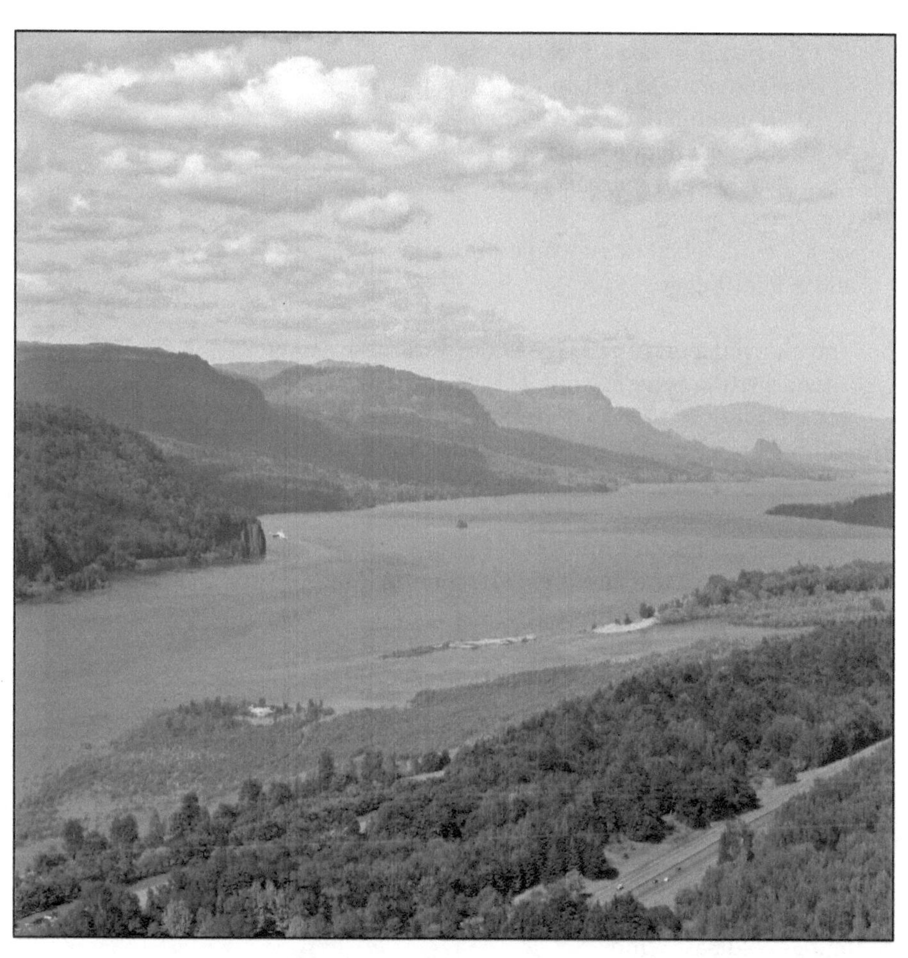

The honker

This is for the driver of the black Mercedes
who honked at my back
and startled the crap out of me
as I walked across Sunnyside with a green light
at 7:20 p.m. on Sunday the 30th of January 1994
in Clackamas Oregon
having just seen *Tombstone*
you know the one
with the deathbed catechism on life and love
and not letting go

You showed a lot of courage in our little showdown
it took a real *hombre* to honk at a pedestrian with a cane
in a well-lit intersection of deserted streets
when there were three lanes available to you
and I took up one at most
what did you prove?
was your girlfriend impressed?
will you sing of this conquest along with others equally brave
to your children's children?

But more to the point
did you happen to notice
Sirius shining brightly
in the southern sky
the faithful dog
at the heels of Orion the hunter?
did you smell the nearby mountains
and the distant Arctic ice
in that cold east wind
or did you even know it was blowing?
did the thought blow across your mind
as it did mine
both before and after our brief encounter
how very good it is
to be alive?

§

Terrified at Powell's

In the poetry section
the walls of books cave on me
has so much been written?
the very cream of the iceberg I'm sure
but more than I could digest
in a thousand incarnations
where is room for more?
these shelves are stuffed from my toes
to beyond my reach
which already exceeds my grasp
the flame shrinks within me
how many variations on a theme are possible
when the number of poems already born
nears infinity?

Dizzy
I grab a book from the shelf
open it slowly
focus on pages that don't spin like the room
and the miracle occurs again
the host is transformed
the elemental forces erupt
I take out my pocket notebook
and conceive a new poem
right here in the public aisle
and only after the act is done
does the terror begin to subside

§

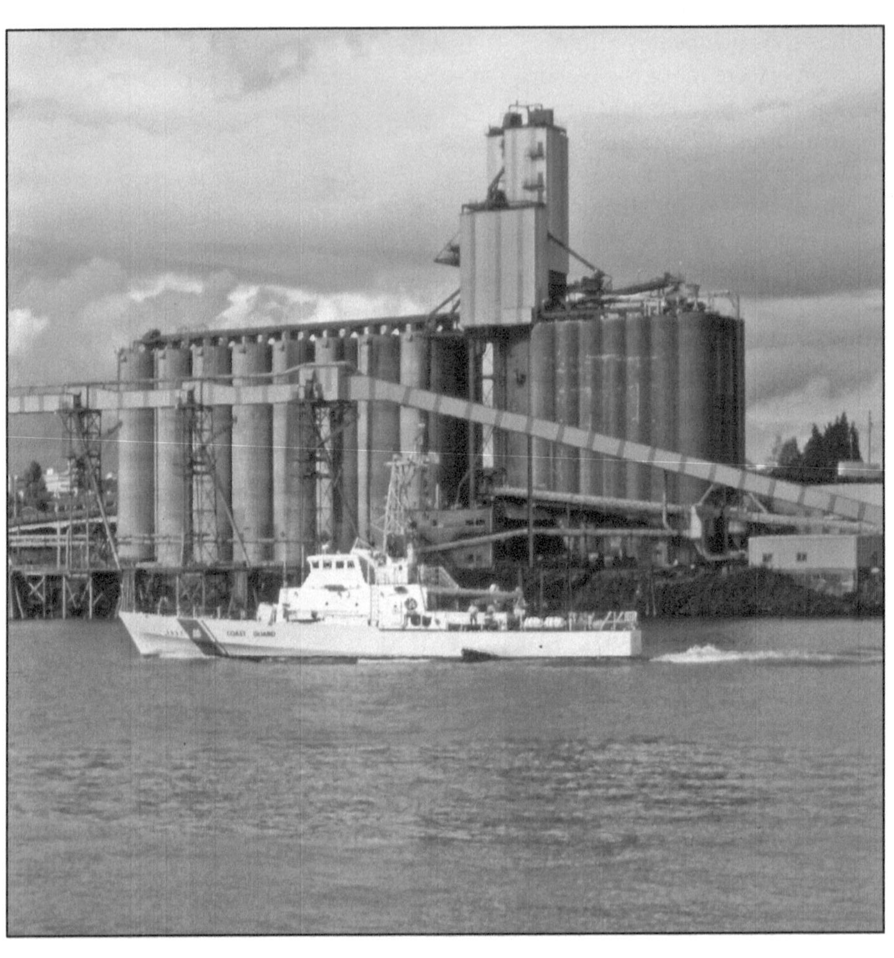

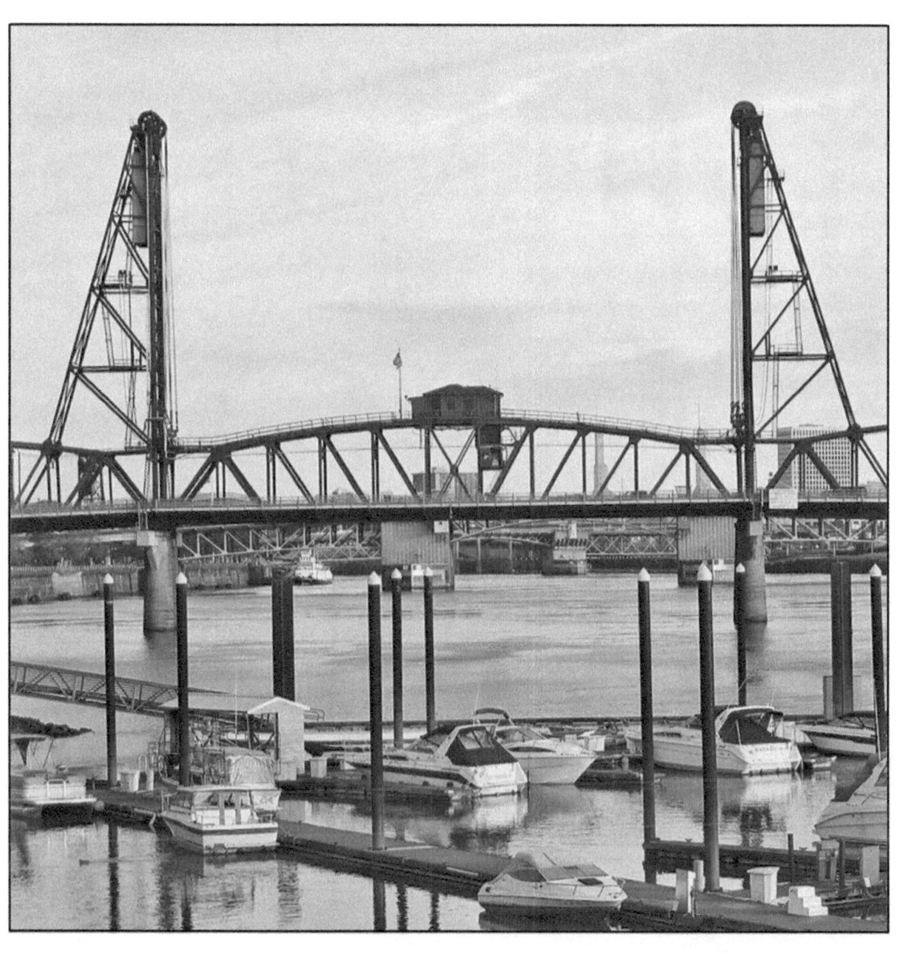

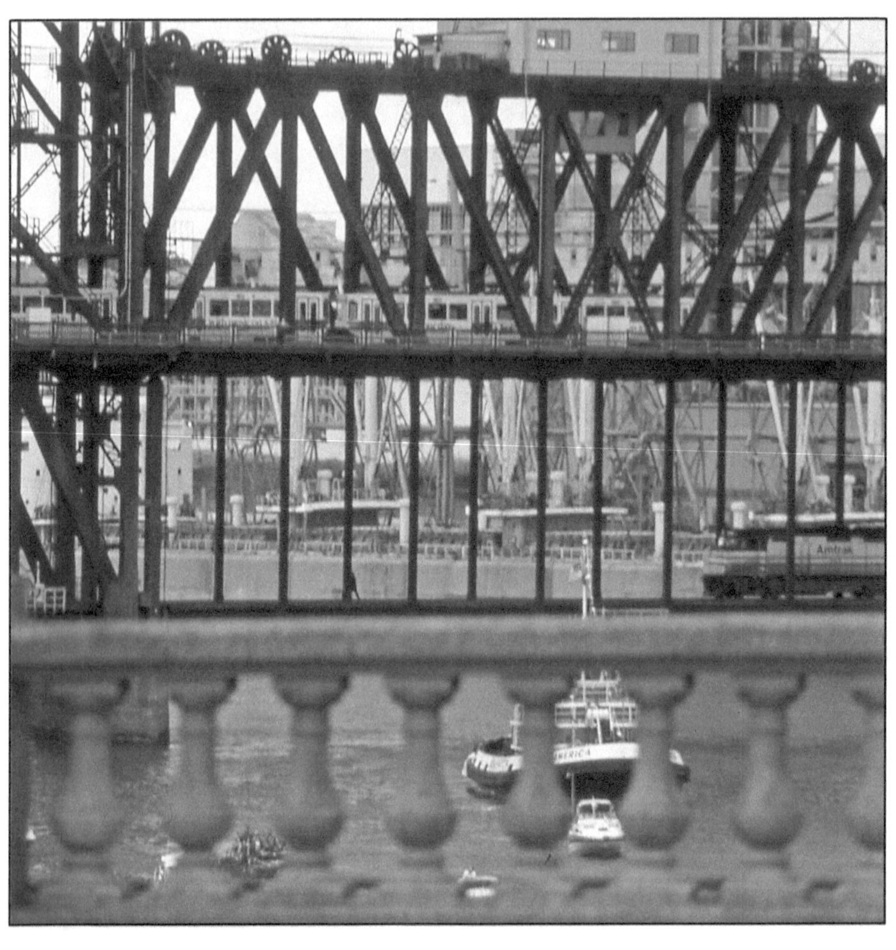
Amtrak

Journey

Starting from these stone-walled rooms
over the middle terrace of the palace
stride across the courtyard past guards in armor
between the monstrous gates
then through throngs of merchants and beggars
in narrow city streets
and finally out the tree-lined river road

In the gorge where the river runs
through the perilous mountains
I watch my step on the winding trail
and listen under the thunder of the falls
for soft bandit footsteps behind
at night my fire casts shadow ghosts
against the circling cliffs
while I eat my modest rice
and unroll my mat on the stony ground

Then across the high plains in cool morning mists
burning off slowly in the sunlight
I stride along through drift-piles of dry leaves
yellow and red and crackling under my feet
I watch wood smoke curl as it rises from yonder house
smell it in the air

Through the worsening afternoon
my legs become weary
the rain falls cold on my back
a village awaits at dusk
there will I take my rest
among groves of fragrant sandalwood
wine and baskets of fish await
and young faces like peach blossoms

What will it matter then that the road has been long
that the path was rocky to my feet
what will it matter then
that my journey was made
without you?

§

Personal ad

Grouchy manic depressive
with attention and other deficits
walks with a limp and runs with the hyenas
never insults anyone who doesn't deserve to be hit
doesn't smoke except through his ears
been divorced more times than married
wits and money abandon him when needed most
apartment decorated as a late Victorian city dump
bad luck follows him like tin cans tied to a getaway car
to know him is to wonder what love is
some assembly required—tools not included

§

Poet seeks partner

Your unheard music stalks my daydreams
and pine needle tears sprinkle softly
into the caverns of solitude
shaped by your prolonged absence

This poor apostle of the refractive mind
seeks you in all the windswept bookish places
but fears finding and turns and hides quivering
in the cockroach cracks between prosperous walls

So come to me bravely – passionately
as a child nurses a strange lamed cougar
and sail on my laughing shoulders
beyond the islands of stars

§

Silkworm

Adventurous little one
your smiling eyes touched me lightly
and woke me from a restless dream
trapped in tangled vines
how did you know?
why have you come so far?
tell me your name again
and all the places you have flown
describe the moonlight on snowy peaks
in a land I can only imagine
spin silk for me
and I will show you a valley I know
peaceful with mist and wild blossoms

§

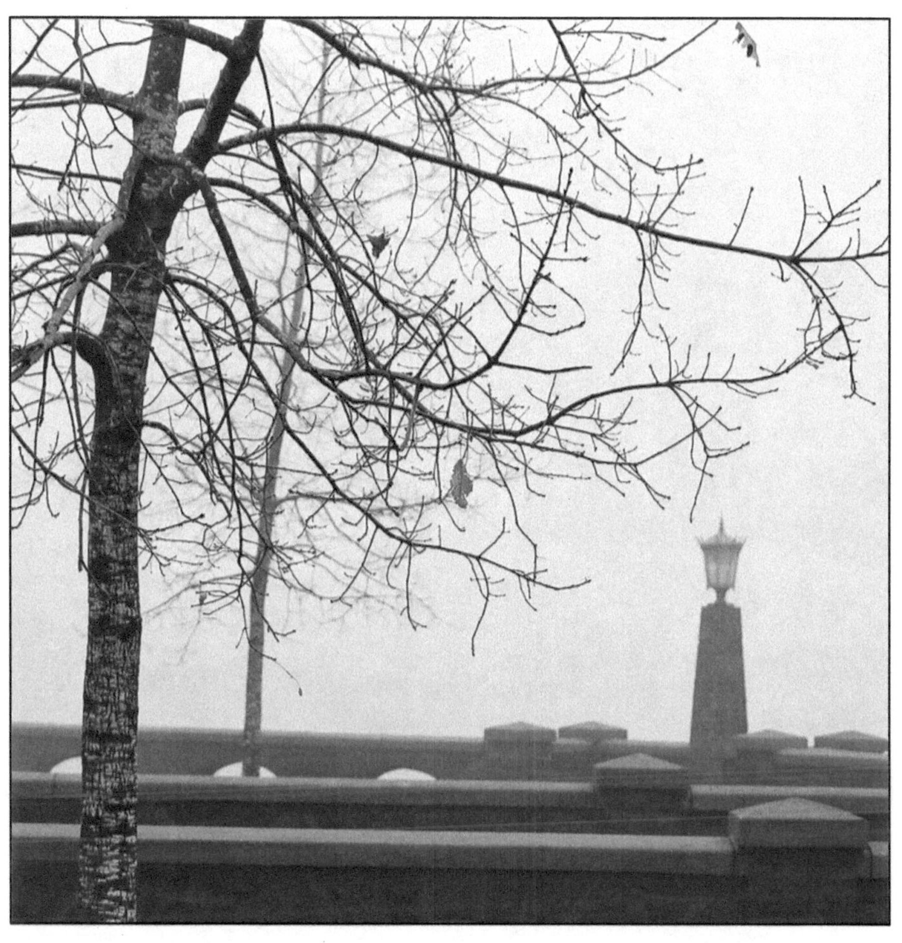

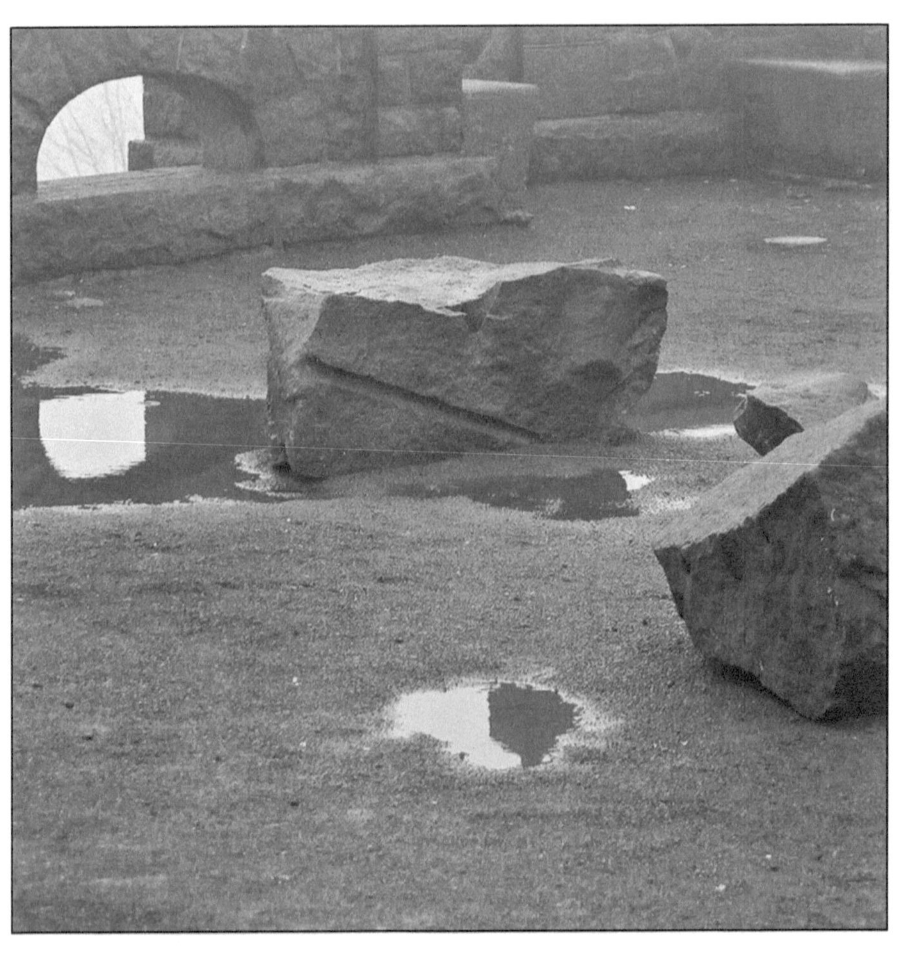

My love

The ocean
I sit for hours and stare at waves rolling in
and listen to gentle thunder of surf
and never tire—each wave a fresh surprise
a gift from far away

A rosebud
sweetly shaped and saturated with color
pressing toward your fragrant destiny
you are so lovely this way—I don't mind
if you take your time opening

A country road
challenging to drive but worth the effort
twisting through fertile valleys and over green hills
humming a tantalizing tune—an invitation
to explore in new directions

A squirrel
waiting for me to chase you around the campus
up and down trees and across busy roads
and fleeing just fast enough to keep me close
I haven't stopped chasing yet

A city lane
lined with exotic shops and sidewalk cafes
with sunshine filtering down through green leaves
and whenever I stroll along looking and tasting
I discover something new

A song
I enjoy more each time I hear
and carry where I go
strangers see me smile
but don't hear the song

A rare book edition
hidden in the shelves where I browsed
unsuspecting I opened the pages of a treasure
it doesn't matter who else has held you and put you down
you're in my hands now

The new crescent moon
so delicate at dusk
so low in the dimming sky
but setting so soon—I blow a kiss and wonder
whether you'll return and swell to fullness for me in time
or leave me only this slender image

§

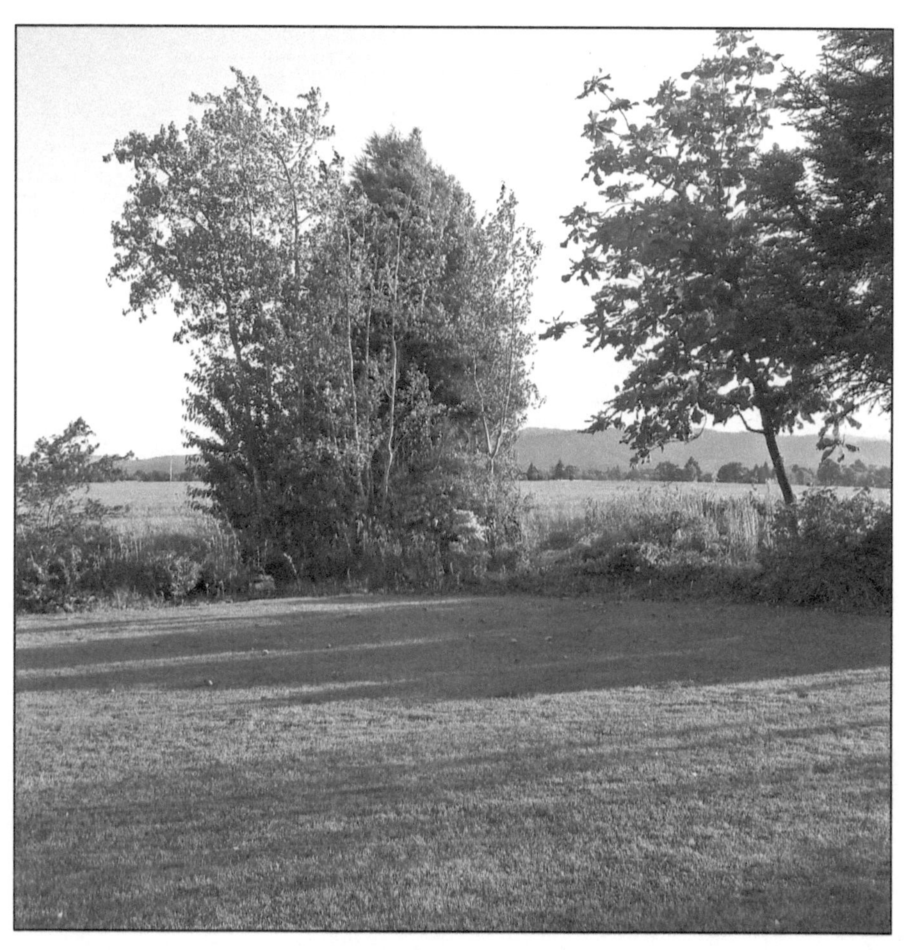

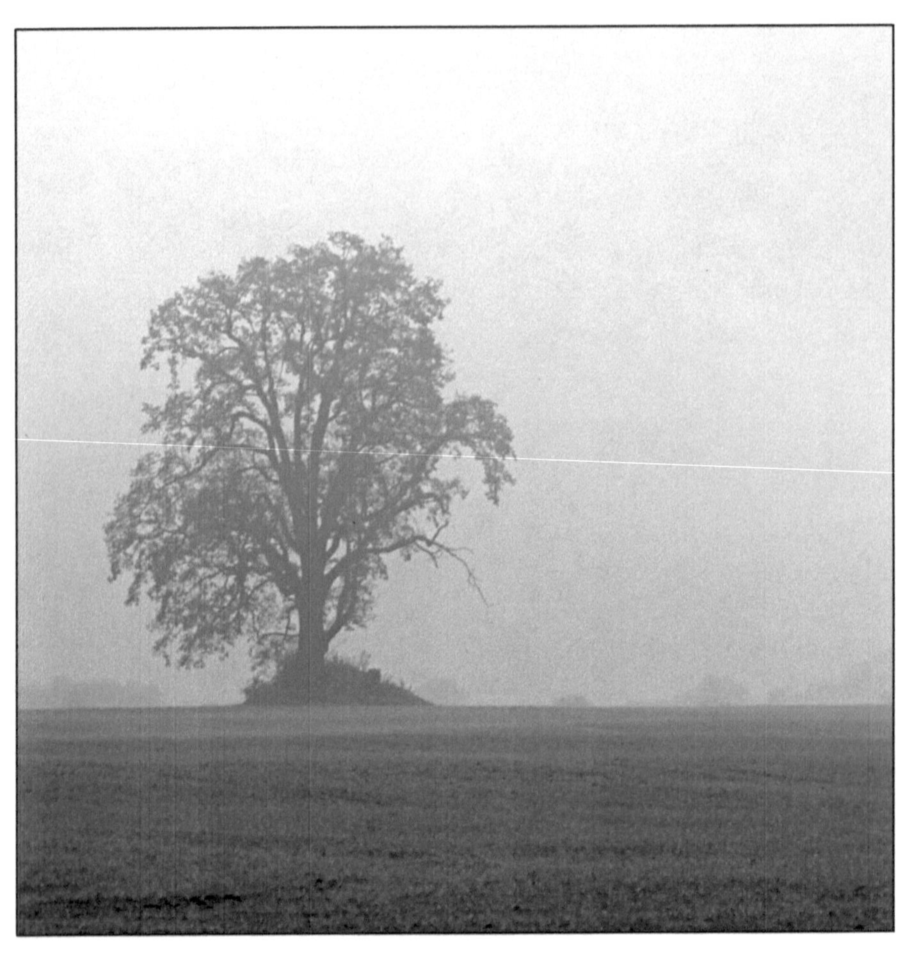

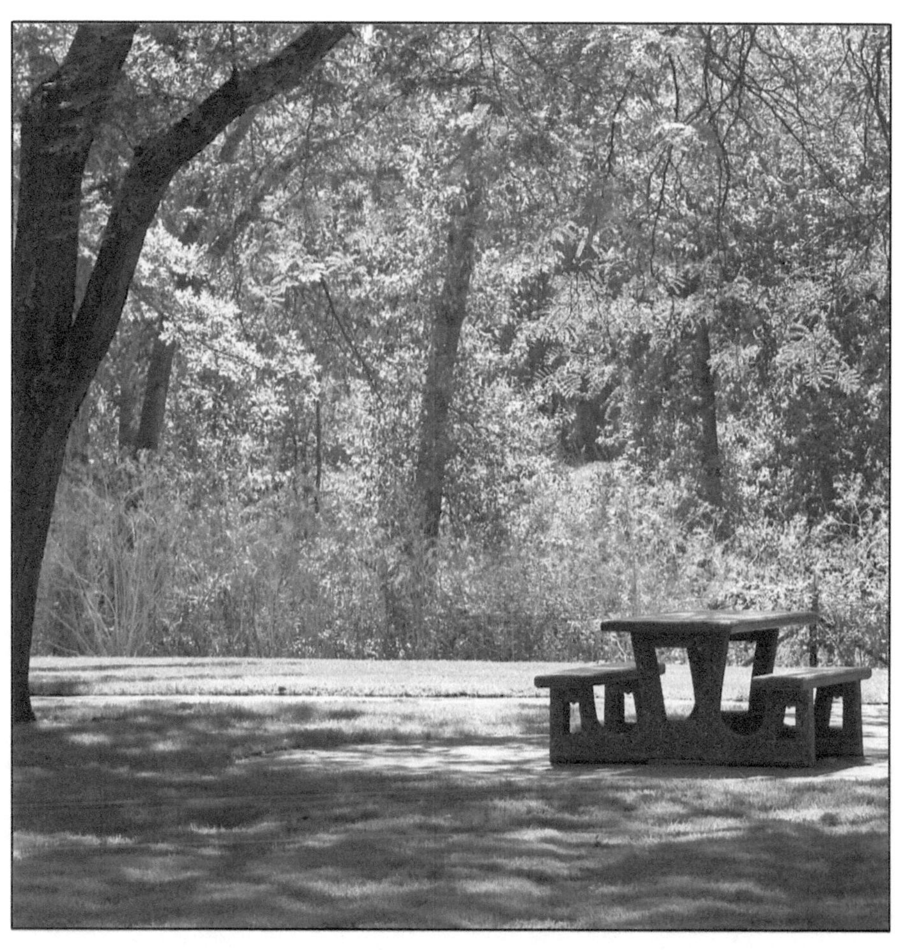

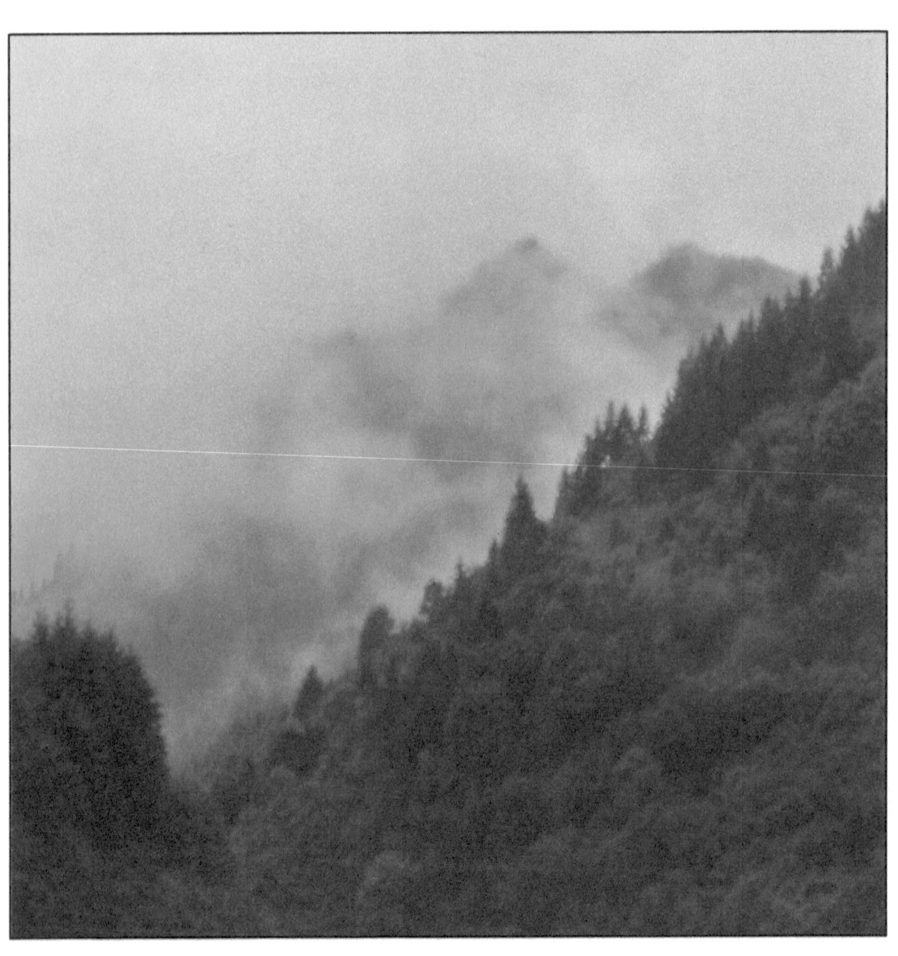

VI.

Ancient Forest Talking Blues 1992-1994

1. Encounter on the Clackamas

Out here in two cars to cut Christmas trees for three families
canyon viewpoints evacuated for winter
empty boat docks behind the rain-filled dam
we turn through a cut in the highway's beauty strip
of wild trees thick enough to hide clearcut behind
slowly cross the rusty single-span bridge
up a narrow dirt switchback logging road
past thick straight stands of identical skinny firs
replanted where the old growth used to breathe
park in a gray gravel truck loading spot
copper cartridge cases under our feet
from someone's target practice
among abandoned stumps in an open scar of land
I climb over a ridge
near a tall and naked spar tree
unemployed since portable metal towers
took over the work of pulling logs
out of ravines like this one
a big rain puddle in the bottom reflects
the blueness of the cloud-gray Sunday sky
better than the sky does

There on a higher ridge stand two dozen giants
Douglas firs maybe two hundred feet tall
a dozen feet thick with deeply grooved reddish-brown bark
heavy green branches hang outward from the bole
a hundred feet and more above the root
so far for sap to climb to reach the sky
so much tree so little greenery
it's a wonder they've lived so long
maybe living slower helps
in a mixed stand of woods
a few red cedars on guard in green fur coats
middle-aged hemlocks with tilting-lance leaders
and dainty fingertips
overlooking precocious young firs
earning their space as skirmishers
outside the grove
not straight-row cadets
like the renewable tree plantation down the hill

The black clumps in those high lofts might be eagles' nests
no birds are flying on this cold day
the northern spotted owl doesn't migrate like the clever duck
but sensitive owls wouldn't stay in this small grove
with the logging road and debris so close
the spaces around the old trees have been hacked out
it's not an old growth forest after all
just some ancient trees left behind to watch over the wasteland
where a real forest used to be
in the thin battle zone between humanity and wildness

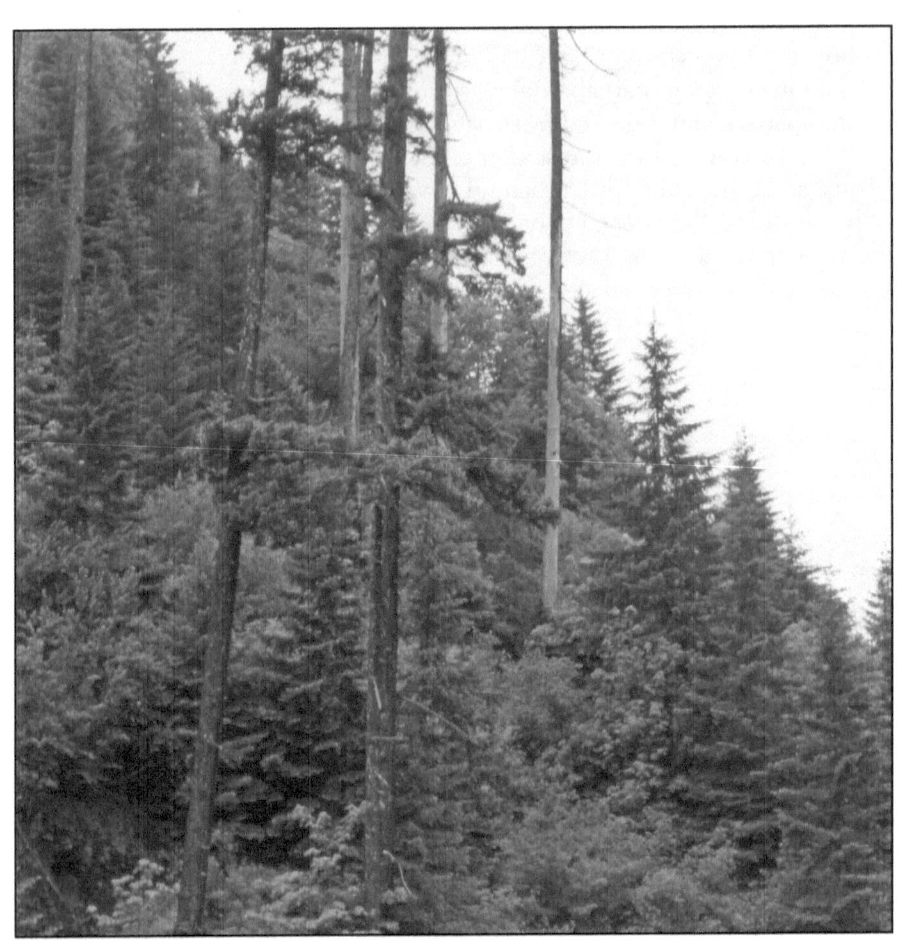

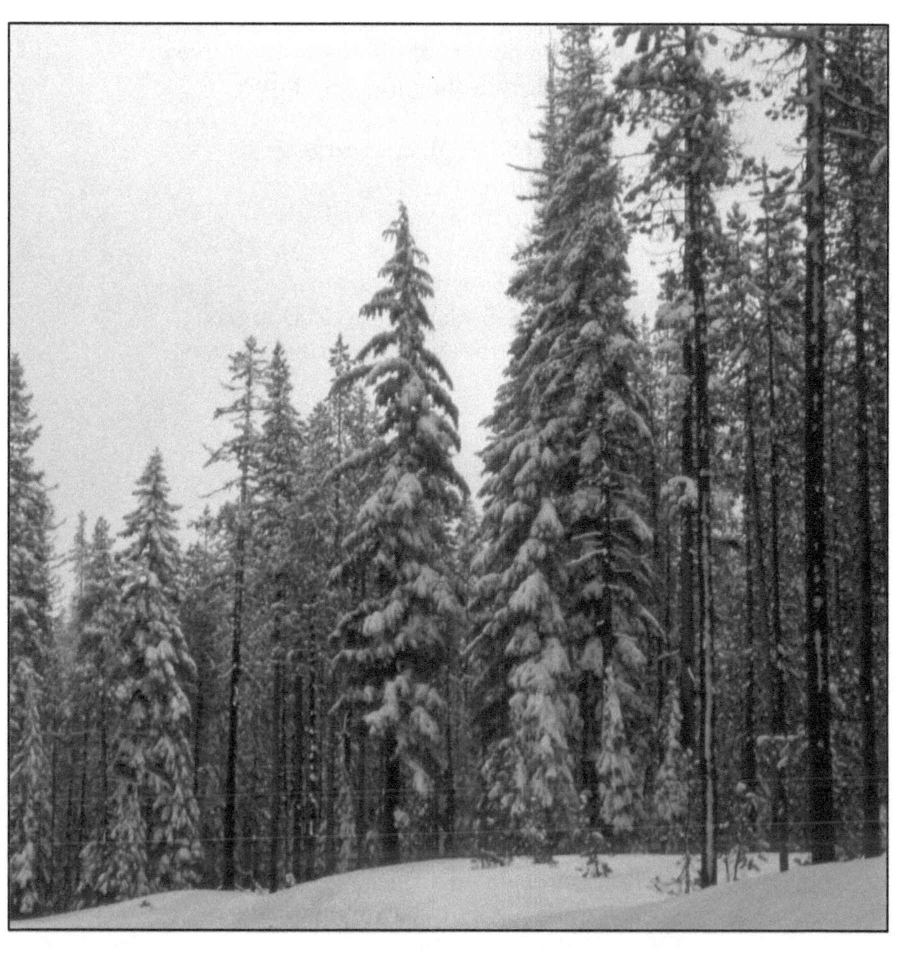

2. Older than names

Not holiday shopping mall trees
not statistically modeled economic political trees
not messy kindergarten fingerpainted trees on butcher paper
not four-color printed travel posters of photographs of trees
not fractal mathematical self-reflecting images of trees
actually not even trees
if they were here before the Old English word *treow*
evolved into the Middle English *tree*
yes Douglas firs grow that old unless attacked
by fire or insects or chain saws
the most important timber in the world
not really firs but named so by Scotsman David Douglas
two centuries ago when these trees were already dignified
and didn't care about names

These giants were growing tall
when Gutenberg printed his Bible
Pacioli invented the bottom line
and the peoples called Maya Inca Aztec and Pueblo
and the fishing tribes around this spot
inhabited the old continents we later called the new world
and named after an Italian

Growing here growing tall
when the Mayflower folks ate Thanksgiving
before the nation was even a gleam
in George Washington's paternal eye
and Paul Revere shouted at the night
when young Tom Jefferson penned a Declaration
and later sent an expedition led by two captains
who passed not thirty miles from these woods
guided by a woman named Sacajawea
not long before Douglas himself arrived to name the trees
growing here growing tall
for millennia before anyone white arrived
to call the locals *Indians*

I haven't been to holy Jerusalem
or touched the ruins of ancient Rome
but I have stood behind the firing line
where General Jackson stood
and I have stomped the wooden weather decks
of great steel ships
where Admiral Halsey paced across the Pacific
yet what I see here is older than anything
in my white American History books

I've been to redwood and sequoia groves
to see and touch trees bigger than these and older
as tall as a touchdown is long plus the extra point
trees a thousand years old or two or three
growing in days of prophets and sages
Isaiah Jeremiah Lamentations Ezekiel
Gautama Siddhartha known as Buddha
Socrates Sophocles Aristophanes
wise old Lao Tzu
honorable Kung-Fu Tzu
and of course silly Chuang Tzu
who dreamed he was a butterfly
and wondered the rest of his wandering life
if he was really a butterfly dreaming he was a man
or the other way around

Growing when Rabbi Hillel
taught one version of the golden rule
and Jesus of Nazareth taught another
when Bodhidharma crossed into China
and Mohammed fled to the desert
when monks drained the swamps of Europe
and barons cleared the forests

You know some olive trees in Gethsemane
that heard Jesus pray
listen there still
and some bristlecone pines
high on a California mountain
have stayed there five thousand years
growing there during the forty years
Jacob's children wandered Sinai
a different sort of wilderness experience

For the record I testify
these bit-fingernail arthritic hands
a handful of decades old
have touched a still-living being
older than Jerusalem

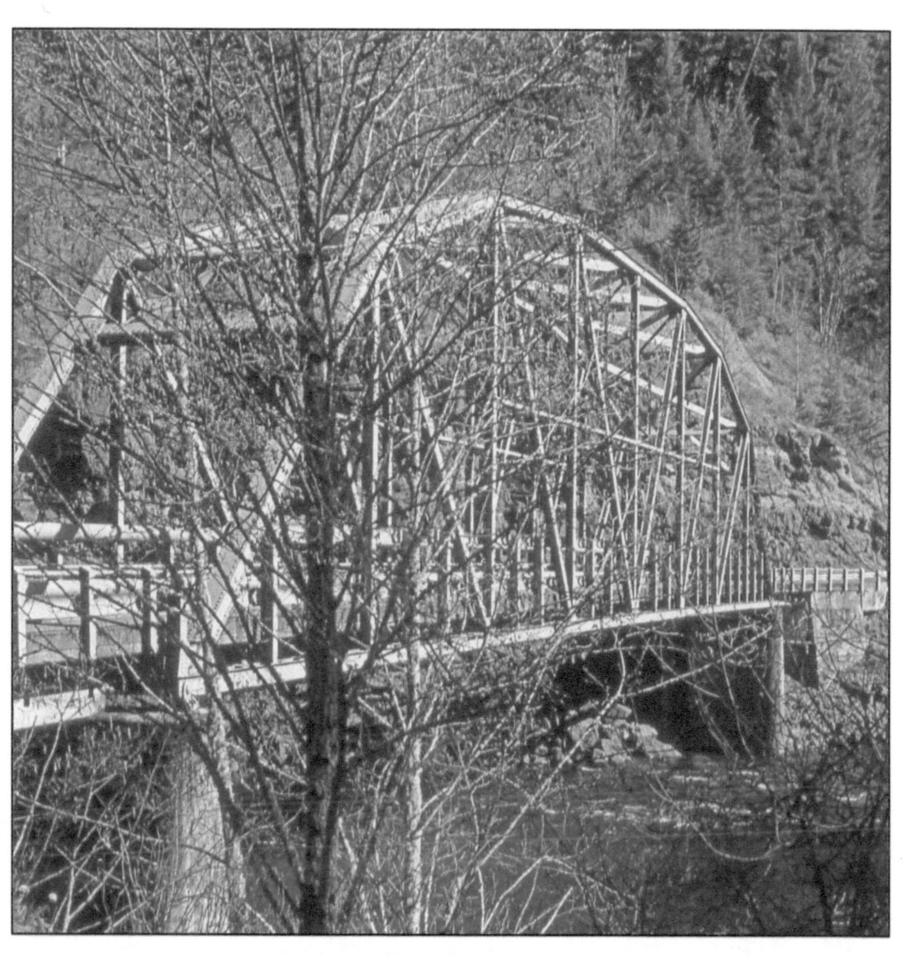

3. Mount Baker

When I was younger I worked two summers
near Mount Baker
for an old-time logger turned preacher
turned campground superintendent
we boys cleared brush and mowed grass
for Brother Wilson
washed dishes and towels
chopped firewood and shingled cabins
drove pickup loads of garbage
to an open trench dump in the woods
where I picked up some great used book bargains
we got up early and walked half a brisk mile
to build a big fire in the cold chapel
and once in a while trimmed limbs and set choker
when the logging bug took over
and we hauled big firs out of the back forty
or converted a half-acre of alders into firewood
in one sweaty day's preaching

We took turns driving the old green Chevy pickup
with its stump-pulling low gear
and we rode the step-side running boards
hanging on with one hand and waving with the other
as we hollered around the campground
teenage motorized rebel cavalry
though I once got thrown off and skinned through my jeans
when the driver of the day downshifted into reverse
instead of second
on a gravel hill

Brother Wilson told of his own brother slashed open
by the whipping end of a broken choker
close friends crushed by widow-makers
and the truckload of logs he himself turned over deliberately
at the bottom of a hill after losing his brakes
so as not to slam into a split-level house or a station wagon
he boasted of the three-log loads and one-log loads
he had put onto trucks or driven
can't see many eight-foot-thick logs on the road any more

He had more strength in his wrist than in both my arms
could drive a six-penny nail in two strokes
with hardly room to swing a hammer
once we had to fell a tree frightfully close to a cabin
Brother Wilson pointed to a spot on the ground
Babe Ruth pointing to the stands
and dropped the tree whack where he'd pointed

Another day we took that truck
and Brother Wilson's tractor
across the road to skid trees up from a muddy slope
by the bank of the plunging Nooksack River
we set a choker on a mighty log
and started digging mud with those big tractor tires
until the tractor buried itself up to the axle
so we hitched a cable to the truck
and started spinning its wheels as well
by now the log wouldn't let go of us
so we threw into the Procrustean pickup as ballast
all the chopped firewood that fit
and chocked a couple pieces in front of the tractor tires
and then with one of us in the truck cab tickling the clutch
and Brother Wilson on the tractor flinging mud
and the rest of us pushing and whooping like war
and the cable vibrating tighter than a violin string
and the big log dragging its feet through the mud
then scraping itself off against the brush as it finally came loose
we slowly slowly slowly crawled
that monster up out of the bog
I took that log home with me
and carry it around to this day
but one of the boys on that pickup truck
later took his own life
he never told me why

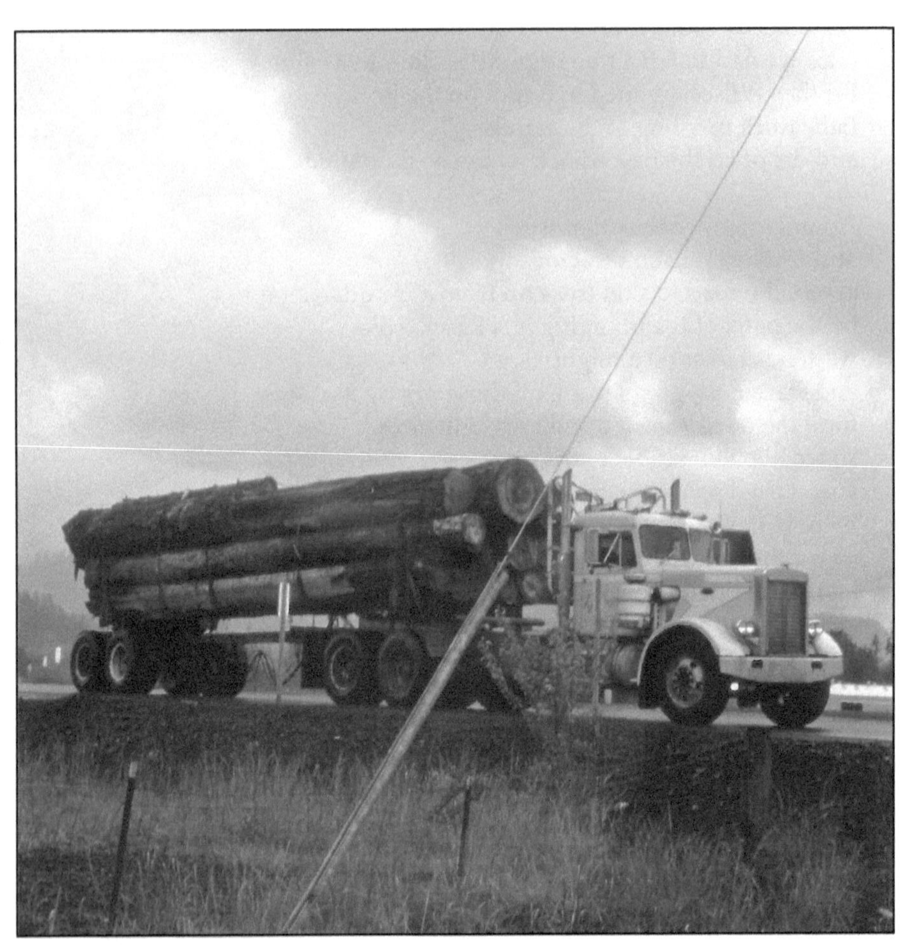

4. The woodcutting way of life and death

I love things made out of wood
and building them myself
I love to hold books made of dried wood pulp
and I love cutting wood
especially Doug firs and cedars
the scent of the wood filling the air
along with the slow thunk of the axe
I always loved log trucks
and had my own names for them as they passed
the fenced yard by the road into town
going to the mill
where my dad worked
before he went to help build the oil refinery

Woodcutters of all kinds are my friends and relatives
but many are losing their livelihood
like so many others in a shrinking world
the forest problem isn't their fault
any more than war is the fault of the foot soldier
but the anger and fear of losses are real

So is the work and so is the pride
setting choker among fallen trees
so they can be hauled up and out
grueling and dangerous work reserved for the young and fresh
if you prove yourself and survive with limbs intact
you can move up
riding the crummy down the mountain
body vibrating from all day with a chain saw
ears ringing in spite of protectors
although younger replanted trees can now be cut
trimmed and loaded by one person operating a machine
but the truck is still required
that one with the driver's signature
painted in white on the red cab-side
and those two chrome stacks mirroring the sun
kept cleaner than an ambulance
and skill and caution still matter
working graveyard in the computerized mill
as much as on the mountain

Summer mornings when I lived in Roseburg
I awoke to the sound of a silent log truck
the fellow up the street
always idle-coasted in the predawn dark
to the bottom of the hill
as a courtesy to the neighborhood
but I always heard gravel crunch under his tires
and the gentle babble of his diesel as he passed
and listened till I heard that deep-throated exhaust
when he opened it up and gunned the beast
always admired his early-to-rise work ethic
even though I was a lazy college kid
reading books about other people's lives and machines

Once I watched a man cut off his thumb
with a little carpenter's table saw
rode to the hospital with him and my dad
we didn't get there in time for microsurgery to be invented
today's miracles can't go back and give him what he lost

Statistics say the most frequent food
for a rabid chain saw
is a right-handed logger's left leg
and the most important part of felling a tree
after deciding how to cut it so it falls right
is planning where to run if it doesn't
or if it splits instead of falling cleanly

And I've drawn my own blood
with a whittling knife
building an airplane of soft balsa
we cut wood at our peril start to finish

To fell a tree in the good old days
you cut notches in the trunk
and stuck in springboards to stand on
chopped out the undercut with axes
then pushed and pulled a two-man crosscut felling saw
to finish the backcut and let the tree fall
then you limbed and bucked the great fallen bole
into manageable lengths
still working a two-man misery whip
sometimes from underneath cutting up

You hauled the logs down a skid road
or dragged them out with oxen knee-deep in mud
or a steam donkey engine pulling a high-lead
or floated them down a flume
but to make timber easier to haul out of the woods
you often sawed it into lumber on the spot
with a little steam-powered sawmill
where you had to worry about too much steam
as well as too much saw

Today a dozen workers can cut in one day
and drive to the mill and still go home for dinner
what would have taken weeks
for a camp of a hundred loggers living on tent grub
to fell and limb and buck and haul
so fewer loggers are now required
you're not alone in this world
big city factories
just like forest and sawmill
where it's hard to keep work if you have it
hard to find if you don't
and hard to keep up with the changes

It's happened many times
in history and prehistory
improvements in hunting
shift the balance
between hunter and hunted
decimating the hunted
and hunters have to change
it's happening now
for the hunters of wild trees
just different cuts from the same fibers
scouting for a new way of life

5. Counting birds

Jesus said every sparrow
is known and numbered
so what does God think
of spotted owls
which are easier to count
shouldn't we do divinity a favor
knock off the remainder
simplify bookkeeping
make some cash for ourselves
and give back a tithe
if we feel charitable that Sunday
as if the Creator would rather
have our money
than the beautiful owls
which were kind of silly to make
in the first place
if that were the case

6. The cathedral grove

The owl is the bishop of the cathedral grove
space and silence between the enormous old trees
for owls and their prey to thrive in
and that huge fallen bole in the middle of the grove
home to a million small creatures
its gradual decay returns an offering to the Earth

One sunny day at Mount Baker
we hike up a trail headed south
to a ridge on the shoulder of the mountain
and look out at rocky Mount Shuksan
across the wild-flowered valley between
where a black bear and her cub forage
a few hundred yards below us

The trail passes through unlogged forest
through dark shadow-spaces under the canopy
and over immense fallen trees
rotting and roofed over with moss
dark shelters for mushrooms and ferns
homes to millions of insects for feeding birds
and foundations for ambitious young trees
starting the cycle over again

On the hike down I stay alone
to sit a while in the cathedral grove
toward the darkening evening
quiet enough to hear a distant stream
and the hoot of an owl
beginning its nocturnal hunt
by sitting and watching like me
I try to be very still
my eyes adjusting to the dim light
rewarded with the white flash
of the owl grabbing breakfast
I better hurry on down the mountain
before it gets too dark
and my dinner back at the campground gets cold

Another day at Mount Baker
we follow a creek uphill to the north
with no trail but the stream itself
beyond the trampings of campers and kids
beyond the cosmetic strip of forest left standing
and up to a clearcut canyon
both sides of the stream channel
strewn with stumps
littered with limbs
trashed with worn or broken tools
that have rusted away for years
and the v-shaped canyon visibly eroding
as its unreplanted sides
let rain or snowmelt run raw into the creek
without impedance
no giant trees remain here
no wide spaces shaded by canopy
no owls hunting
no cathedral grove to meditate in
no music of the spheres

If you want to see the glory of God
in everything that exists
can you see it in this?

7. The lost ship

The months I was in the naval hospital
I made a big model of the *Cutty Sark*
surgeons gave me hemostats for tweezers
and told me my knots were nice work
but the masts broke off and the rigging got tangled
when I tried to truck it from California to Oregon
so I threw it away
and all the grandsons of the clipper sailors
and all the granddaughters of all the whalers
and all the tall ship sailing schools
and all the wooden ship preservation museums
can't put a past glory together again

Trees are renewable resources
but forests are systems
not as renewable as their parts
we couldn't restore the vast forests
of Oregon and Washington
to their pristine complexity
and quiet cathedral grove spaces
in fewer than hundreds of years or thousands
if the species we'd need were not already extinct
and if we were willing to try
which we're not because there's no money in it
so we grow our trees in plantations
and remember the old growth
reading our paper books in wood framed houses

When you talk to me
you're talking to that lost ship
the canyon of stumps
the whipping end of the choker
the quiet clean log truck
the boys on the muddy pickup
and their enormous prize
the cathedral grove with its owl
and the giants on the ridge
they're all inside me now

8. Teeter totter

The kid in you knows
how helpless you feel
playing stuck see-saw
with too much kid on one end
a game with all winners
or all losers

This game will end
if the CO_2 makers
continue as now
eliminating CO_2 users
faster than all records
while sitting out there
on the wrong end
of the breaking limb
with a boast of leading the score

9. A little meditation

Start with breathing
the trees breathe too
let the spirit of the trees
breathe through you
simply stop moving
till you can move like the trees
bending to a breeze
then back anew

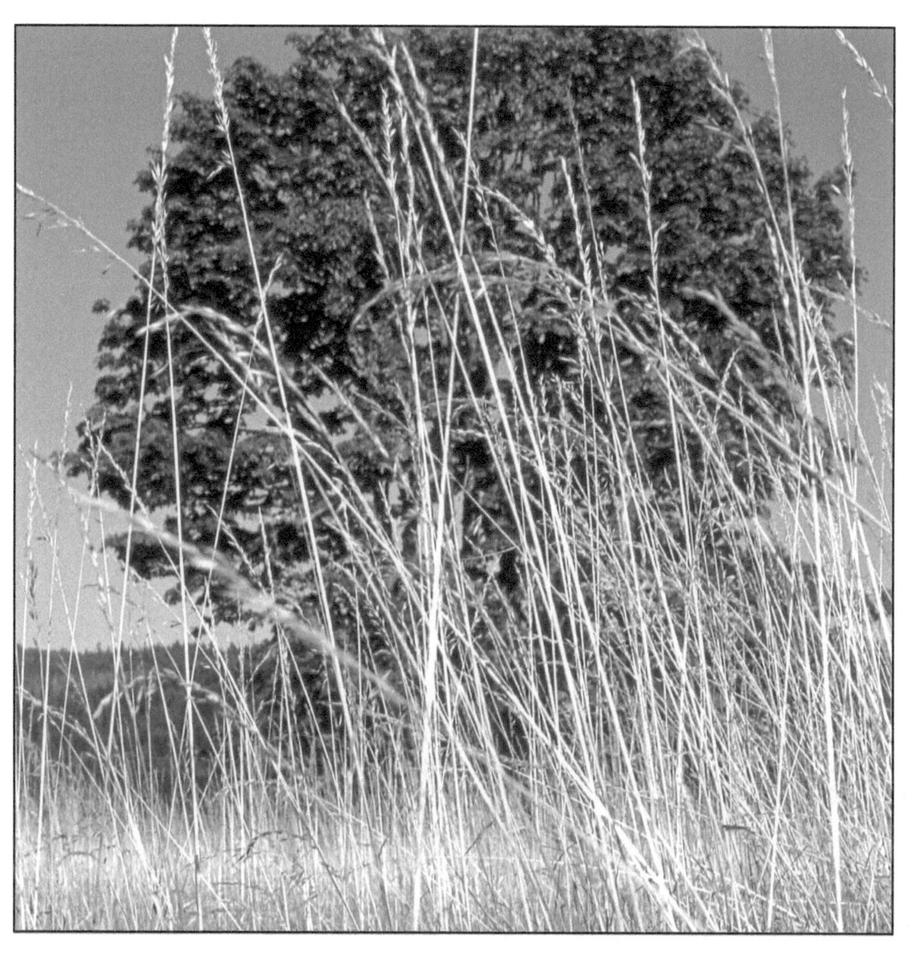

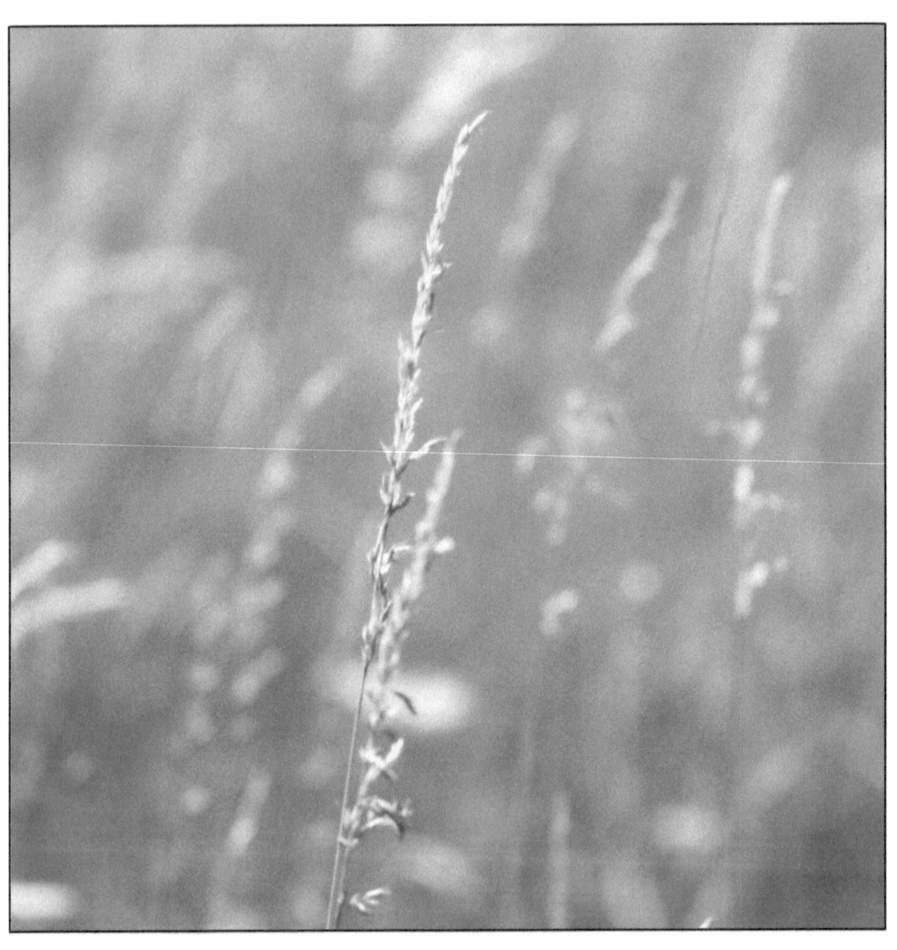

10. My meadow

High school biology in Lebanon Oregon
named for its cedars
required a field project on the subject
of local ecology

Every Saturday from January to June
I got up and dressed early
grabbed notebook and pencil
crossed a board bridge over a tiny creek
walked through a field of wild grass
dead stubble in the cold of winter
but once spring had warmed it to life
grown green and unmowed
it reached to my chest
and later yet it turned into gold
with seeds that stuck to my clothes
walked all the way down to the south end
along the field's eastern side
with a thick row of alders
on each bank of the creek that I'd already crossed
doubled back east and jumped over the creek
ducked under wild thorny blackberry briars
arching as tall as my six plus feet

There concealed from the world
between the creek and alders on one side
and the briars and firs and oaks on three other sides
maybe twenty by thirty in size
was the quiet meadow I called mine

Sitting quietly on the dewy ground
eye to eye with biology
I meticulously recorded the arrival of spring
from the budding and blooming of wildflowers
to the busy traffic of insects
who laid tiny eggs on thistles
and the birds of loftier ambition
who built nests for their eggs in the trees

The suspense of waiting for those eggs to hatch
kept me hurrying out each week
to see what had changed
I made drawings of flowers in colored pencil
and tried to capture bird songs on paper
but there were too many sounds and colors
to fit in my little notebook
which later got lost
so I can't quote from it here
and I can't tell you which flowers they were
or which bugs and which birds
though I distinctly remember blue jays
and croaking frogs amphibiously liberated from creek water
and the dew in the dawn on thistle-stretched spider webs
the breakfast bug catch still squirming

Out my bedroom window at night
in the glow cast by the floodlight on its pole
I could watch the blackberry bush mountains
guarding the secret of the meadow
on rainstormy nights I watched the water
dripping from trees through the sphere of light
on warm nights when the air rustled the leaves
what I saw was a shimmering curtain of green
and I knew on the other side all was well with my meadow

I must tell you though how my notebook ends
for one morning in May I walked out
eager to greet my little friends
and one entire end of my meadow was uprooted
and great mounds of earth thrown up
by bulldozers and backhoes cutting a sewer line
I knew it must happen sooner or later
because people with bulldozers
and city permits and contracts
and children to house and RVs to park
always win out over frogs and birds
delicate flowers and ladybugs on leaves

In spite of my feelings I stayed on the job as junior scientist
to study what happened with one end chopped off my meadow
the ecology clear to the other end could not stay the same
the balance broken
isolation gone
predators came in like neighborhood dogs and cats
I heard no more frog croaks
and the little birds
who had managed a stable truce with the blue jay
were finally supplanted by the raucous and rude crows
from the power lines a few hundred yards away
you know those crows had never bothered before

By the end of my study the ditch was backfilled
the soil packed down and made to look
like any other vacant lot with some trees
but the meadow was never a meadow again
and within the next year the field beyond the fence
was subdivided and built up in houses

Now I know that meadow wasn't really mine
and only a tiny niche
but most of life lives in small places
that are worth saving
if not for ethics or aesthetics
then at least for not putting all nature's eggs
in one big homogenized omelet

I also must tell you
that those quiet Saturday mornings in my meadow
could not change the noisy Friday night news
of the war in jungles and rice paddies far away
where people were killing each other
and blowing up villages
and little niche habitats of little living things
where someone in my biology class
later was sent and died

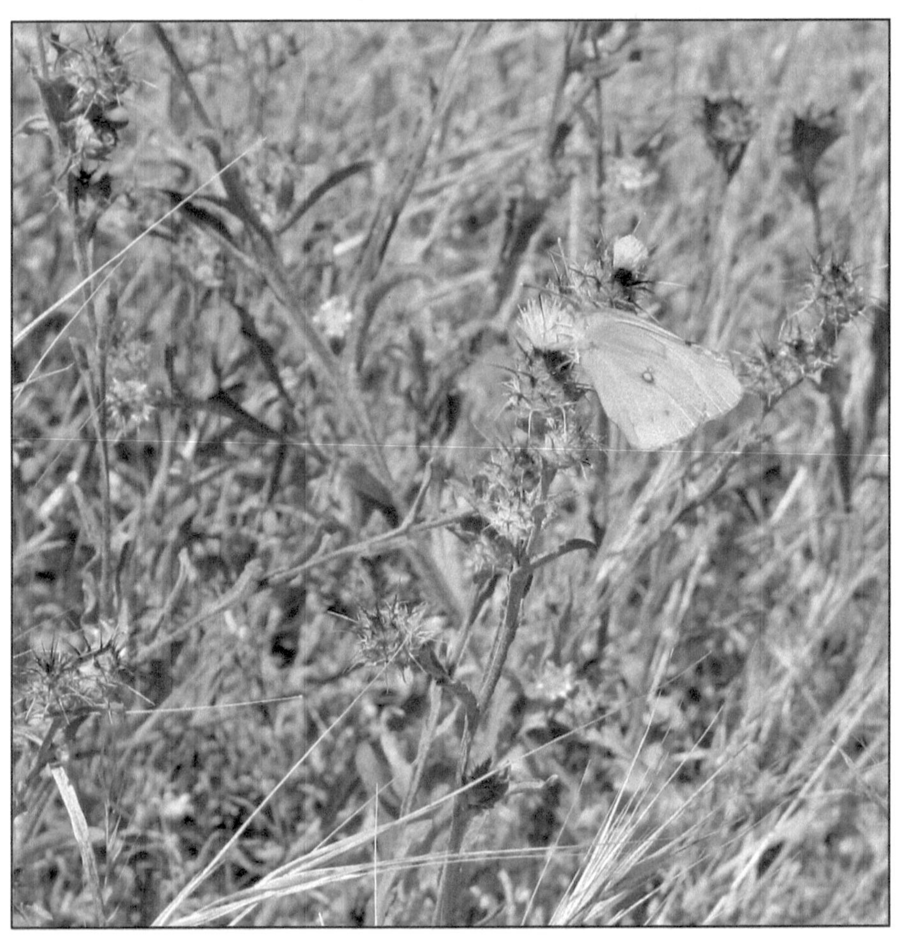

11. Emptiness

The Tao of nothing
the way of emptiness
the value of space in a too-full world
we need emptiness in our lives
and so does a forest
spaces between trees
matter as much as trees
one comes from seeds and time
the other from time and timelessness

§

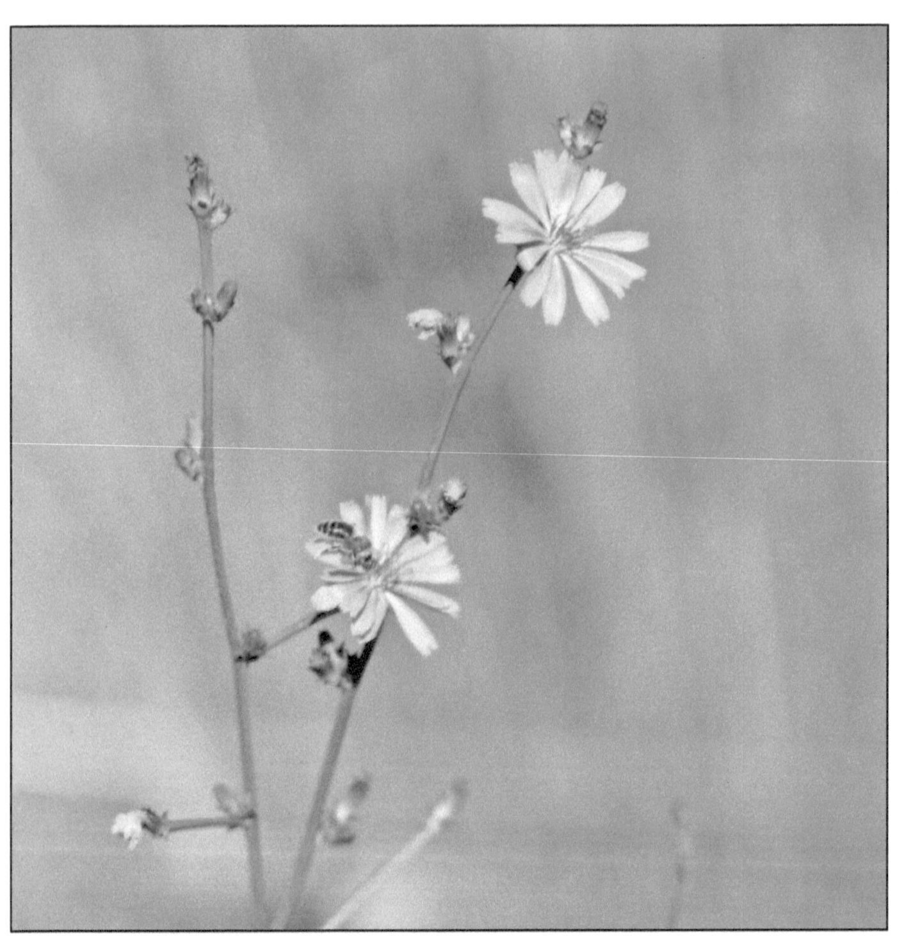

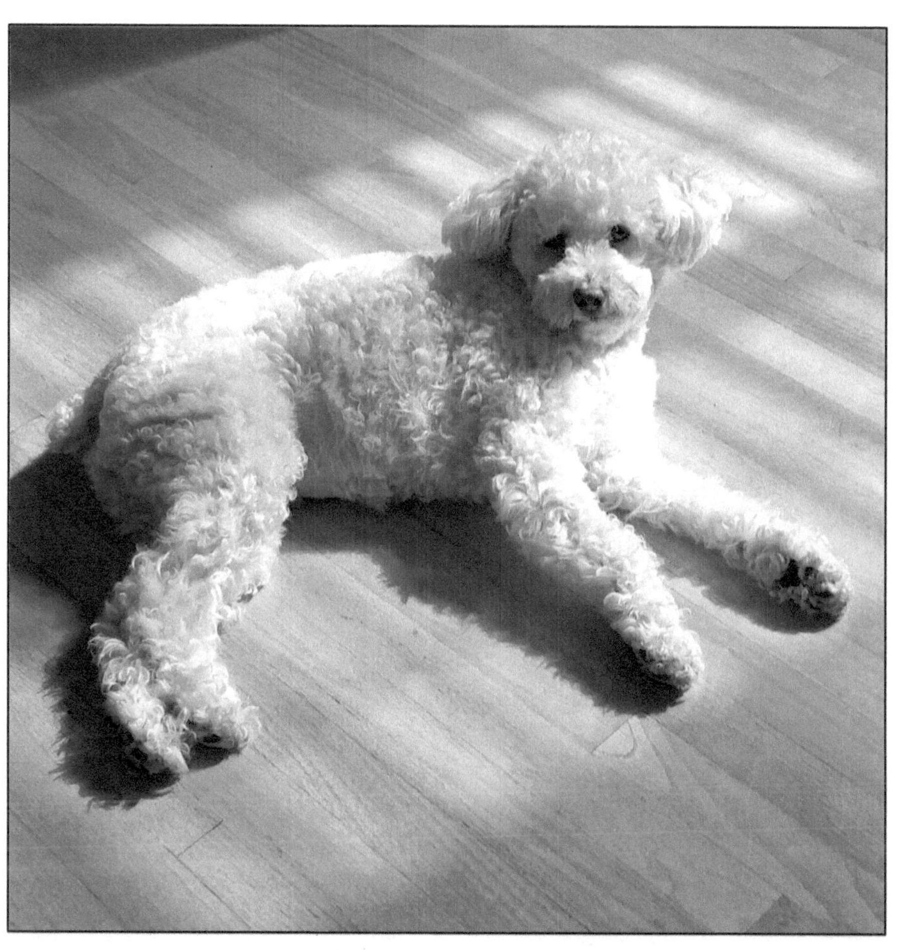

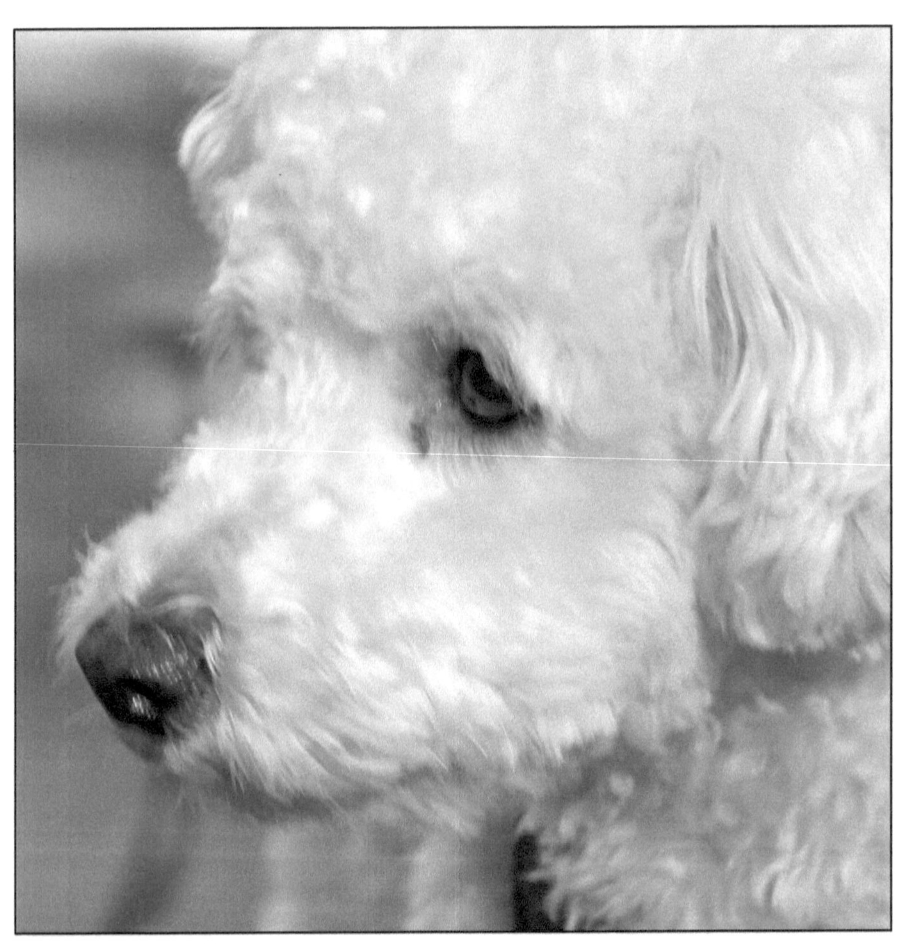

VII.

SIMPLE ODES

Oh kitten

Playfully you bite and scratch
at the white pagecorners as they turn
black markings are no symbols to you
curiosity arcs your eyes
you sniff the volume
and paw my face to ask
what the attraction is
then cry an injured meow
when I scold your ignorant intrusions
between me and my deep text
you scratch the back of your ears
against the sharp corners of the book cover
until finally I yield
and scratch you vigorously myself while you purr
I can feel the hard muscle in your shoulder
the running muscle
the jumping muscle
the hunting muscle
I can see the jungle in your eyes
burning with green fire
you dream of being a tiger
I dream of being a man
now I don't know what that means
any more than you understand tigers

§

Oh squirrel

Bewildered on that wire
stretched a hundred feet between poles
across the road
not a tree near
you stop
look for a green branch
balance yourself with your bushy tail
teeter above the pavement with its rushing cars
look at the distance to go
then gather yourself and resume your run
then stop again
look around again
run again
nothing in your evolution warned you
of telephone poles
high wires
concrete
and cars
I know your bewilderment
I try to practice your pluck

§

Oh gnat

Who just landed
on the open page
of my poetry book
you didn't fly away
when I brushed you
ever so gently
with my thumb
but instead
let yourself be crushed
and left a lifestain
that will always remain
on this page

§

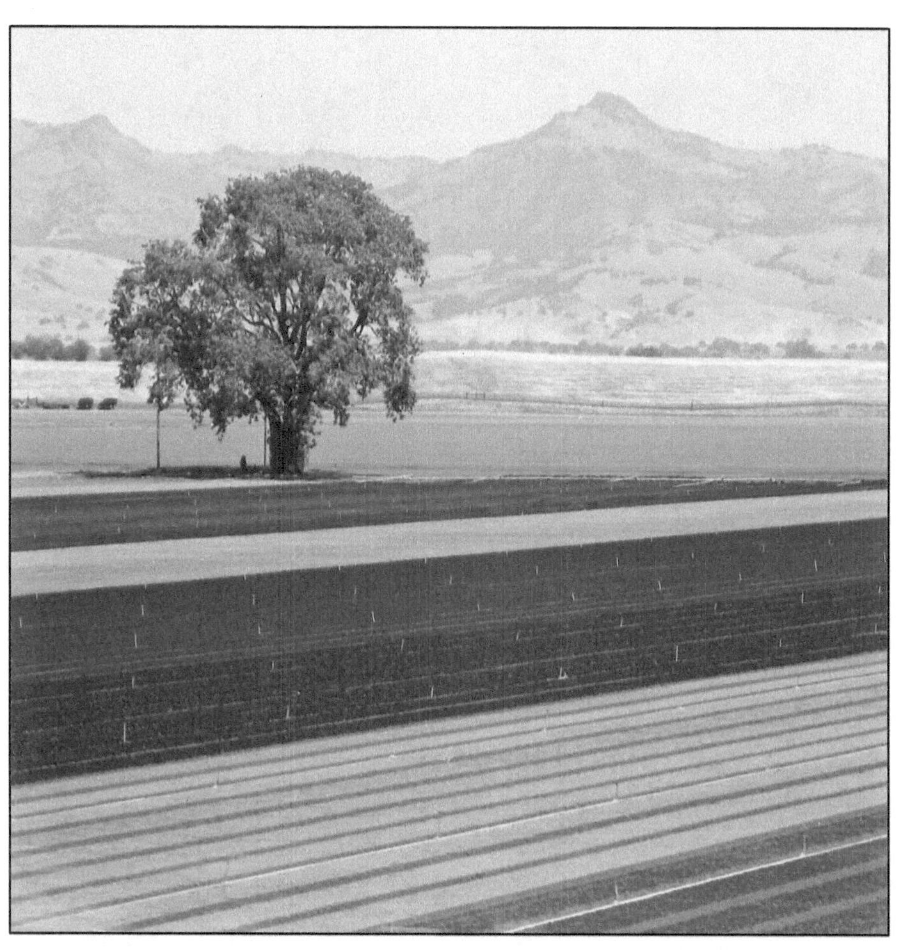

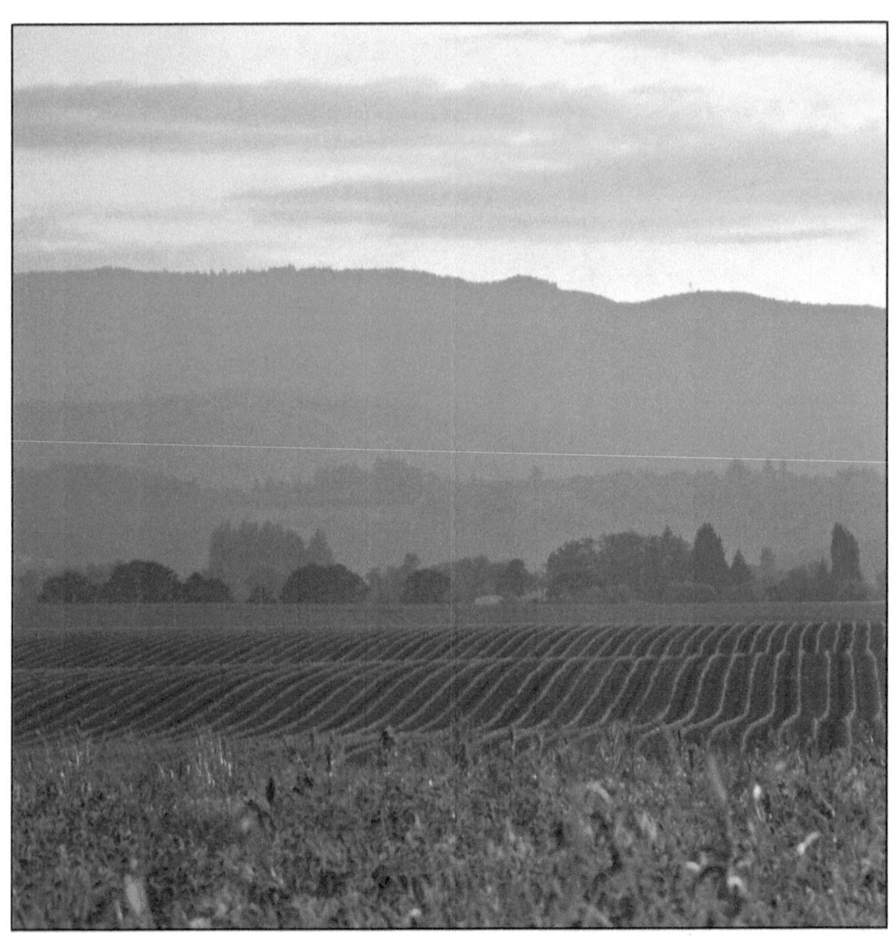

Oh dandelion

You are considered a weed
yet you gave me pleasure
when I was seven
plucking your petals one by one
rubbing yellow pigment between my fingers
making stick figures of your stems
mowing you down with green-stained sneakers
place-kicking you across the yard
and then when your yellow turned white
I would blow all your fluff in the air
and watch how far
and into whose well-groomed yard
you would drift away
by giving pleasure
you propagate your line
I have since learned
you're not the only one
to try that

§

Oh hemlock

Your little cones are so cute
compared to the well-wrapped cigar
of the Douglas fir
or the woody wide cone of the pine
your posture does not seem
so ambitious or arrogant
as their upward-striving reach
more like a thatched cottage
than a bank tower
you are the passive one
the civil one
your dainty dangling fingertips
appear to eschew violence
but you do poison your victims

§

Oh butterfly

Your crisp black lines
on orange-saturated wings
motionless on the sidewalk
fooled my daughter for a moment
that you were a painted toy
I am sorry
there is so much artifice
in her life
it's what she thought of
when she looked at your
still life

§

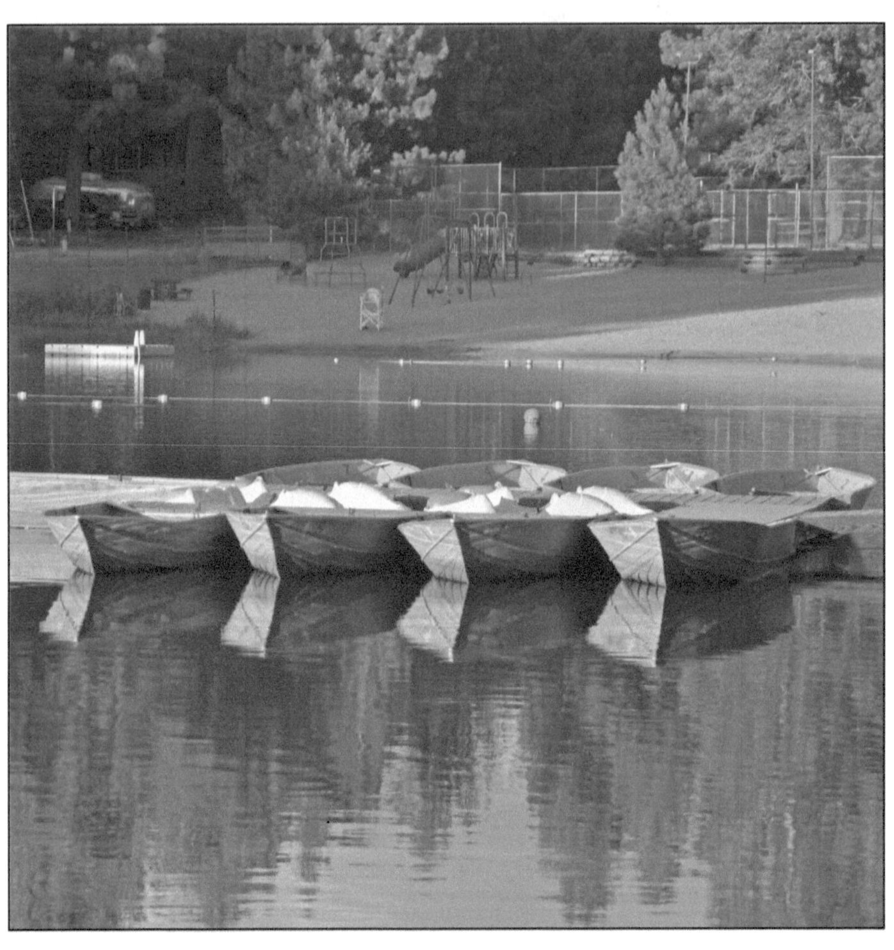

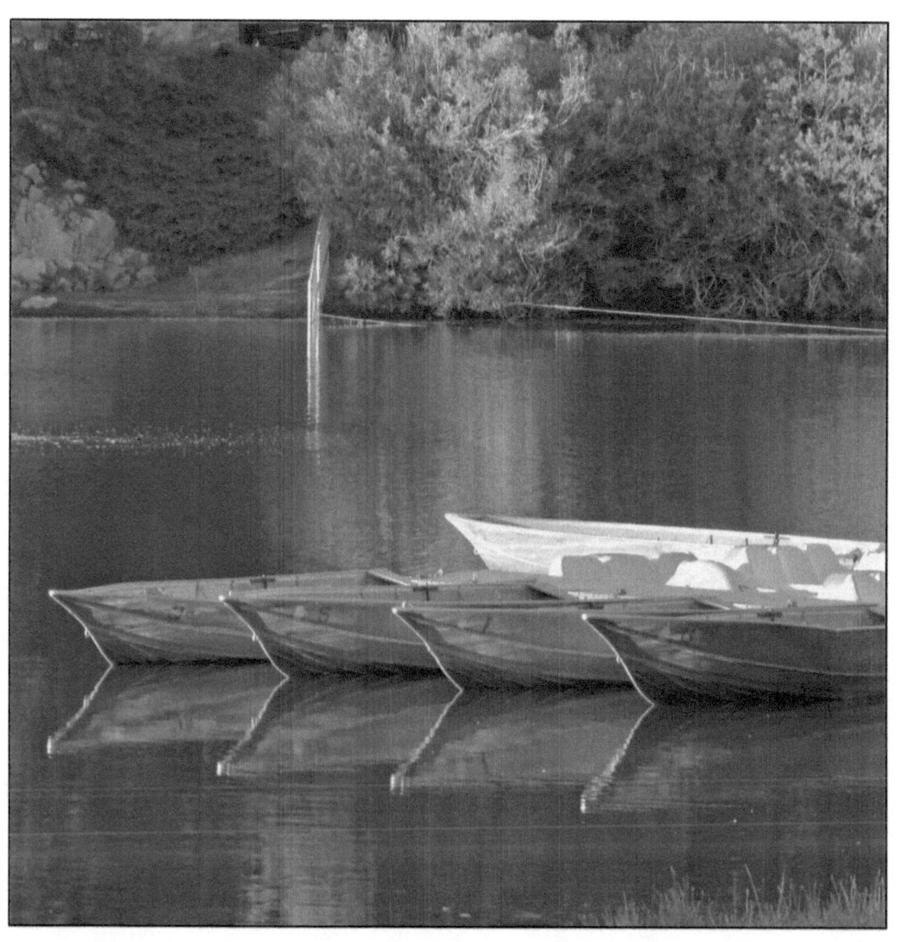

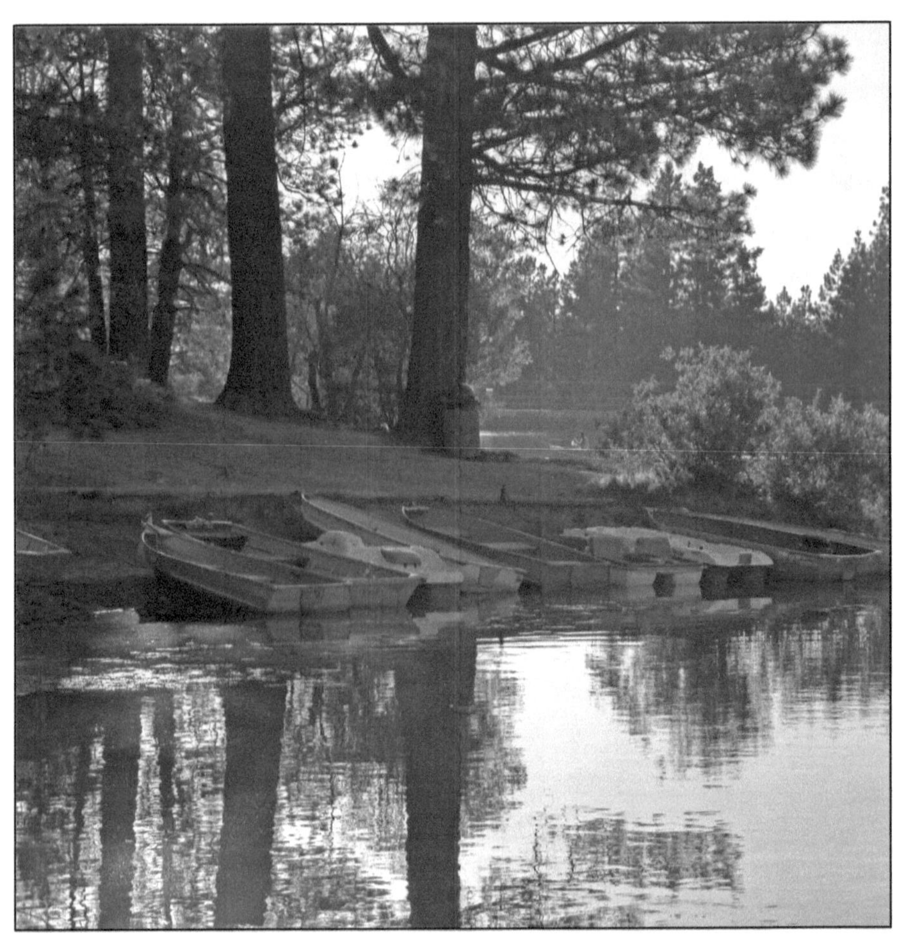

Oh dogwood

I miss your pink-flowered glory
your fall-colored leaves
even your winter bareness
there is your stump outside my window
where you grew so surprisingly large
gracing the street
where I walked in solitude for years
I never thought you would leave me
the ice that broke your back
broke many trees
but none as much a part of me
an empty hole gapes in my memory
when I look at the space where you stood
I think I have ignored other friends
who yet live

§

Oh sunflower

Buried too long and alone
in damp manure
with no light but a bright dream
that you refuse to forget
and when your time comes
tentatively at first you poke your way up
to the light and stretch your legs and drink
hot radiance from the yellow sun
then suddenly dizzy from your rapid climb to altitude
and your unaccustomed growing pains
you look around you
and find a community of bright faces
eagerly sharing in your giddy feast
of light and air

§

Oh hornet

You hit me so hard
on the back of my head
I thought you were a nail
sticking out of the board I backed into
while cleaning the campground shed
only later did I realize
you were minding your own business
when I invaded your space unwittingly
I wish I could defend my space so effectively
against those who
unwittingly or otherwise
act as if I'm not in their way
but after all you were not defending yourself
it was too late for that
in fact I recovered your carcass
you were only speaking up sharply
but selflessly
for all hornets
against future intruders
and died that others might live
we celebrate humans who do that
as the highest members
of what we consider the highest breed
but it's the commonest virtue
among all living things
and actually kind of rare
among humans

§

Oh hummingbird

Just a few feet away
sitting in your teacup nest on that branch
so well hidden among spring's green leaves
the other side of the window where I stand
I look for your dark tail feathers sticking out
to be sure you're there
in what I thought was my tree
in what I thought was my yard
and you fly away around the yard and back
stopping once in a brief hover
eye to eye
then away again
we've seen each other many times
and you've buzzed my ear a few
as I walked or worked outside
do you remember me like I remember you?
do you see me through the window
or only your own reflection?
do you enjoy your home as much as I enjoy mine
or is it the other way around?

§

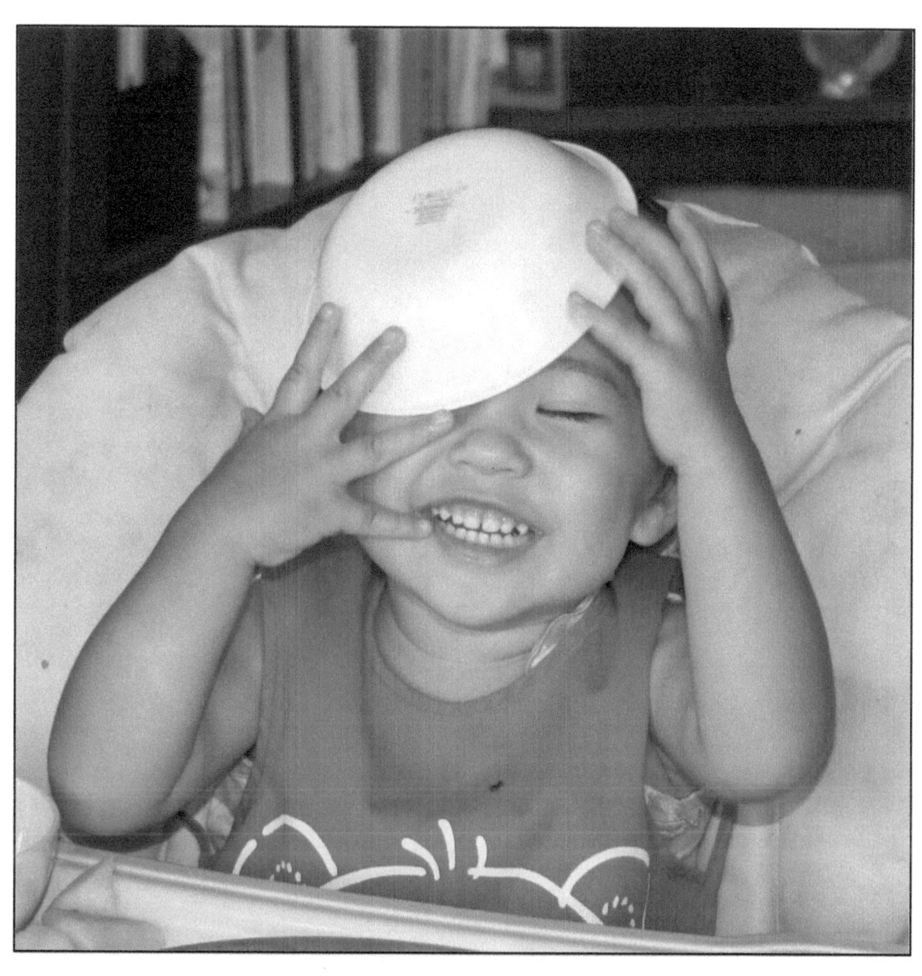

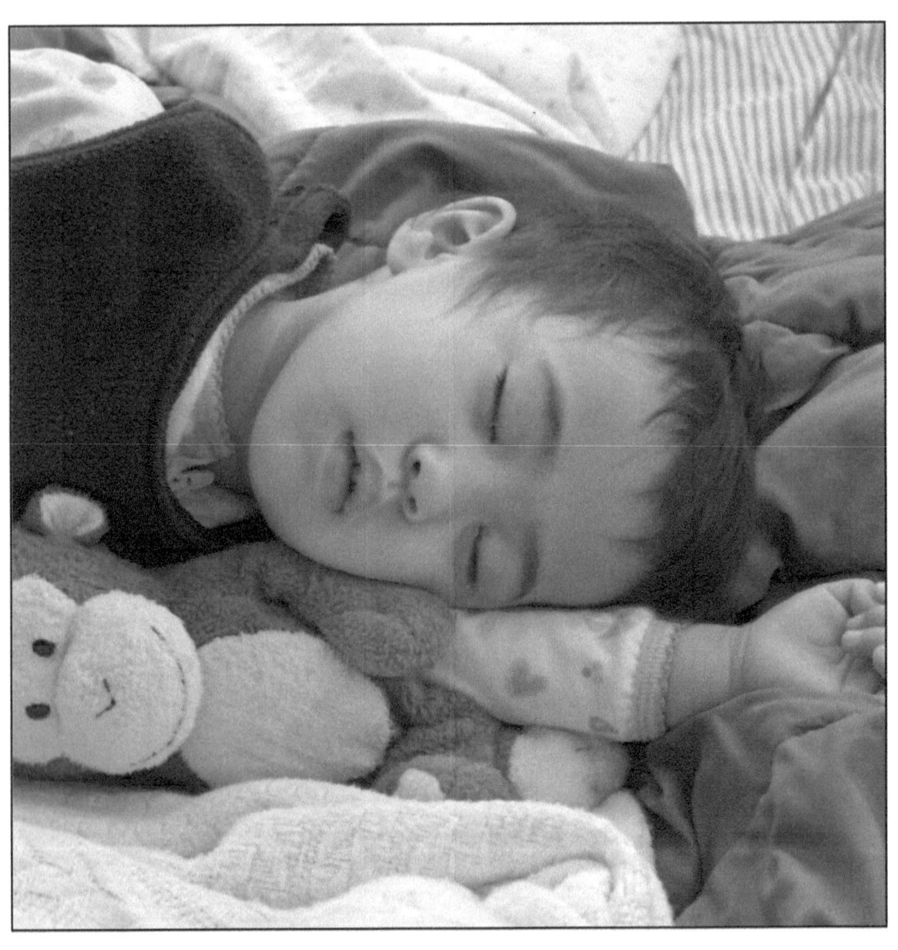

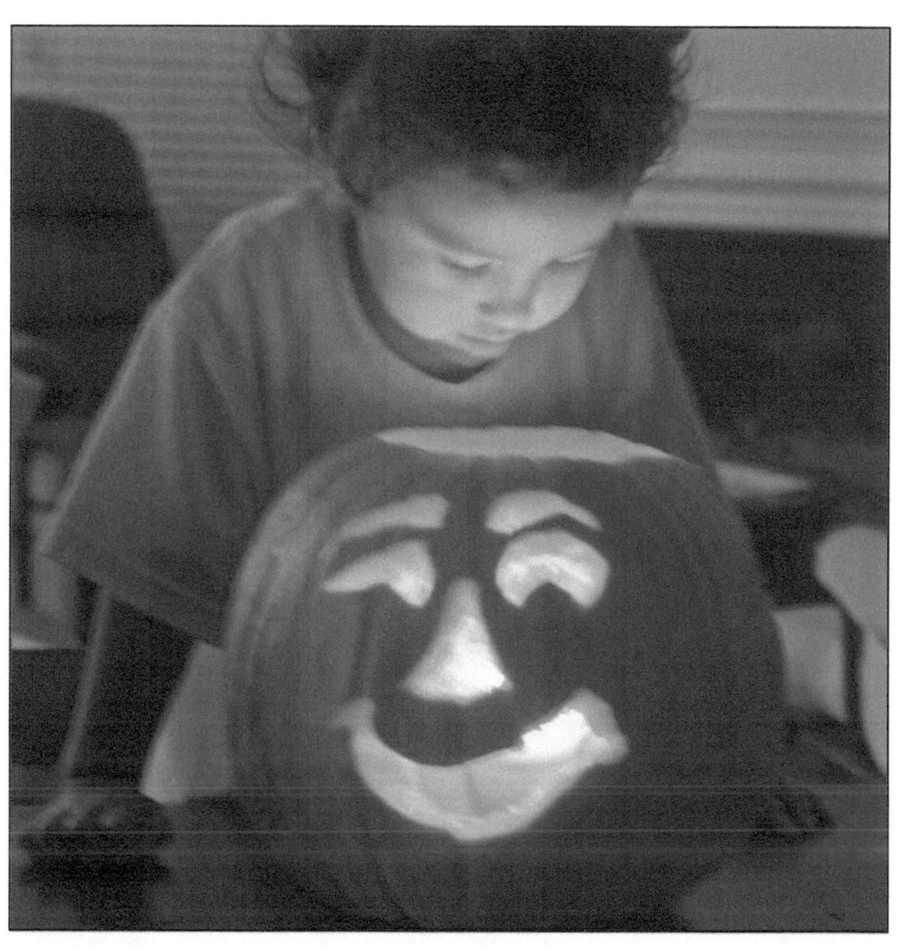

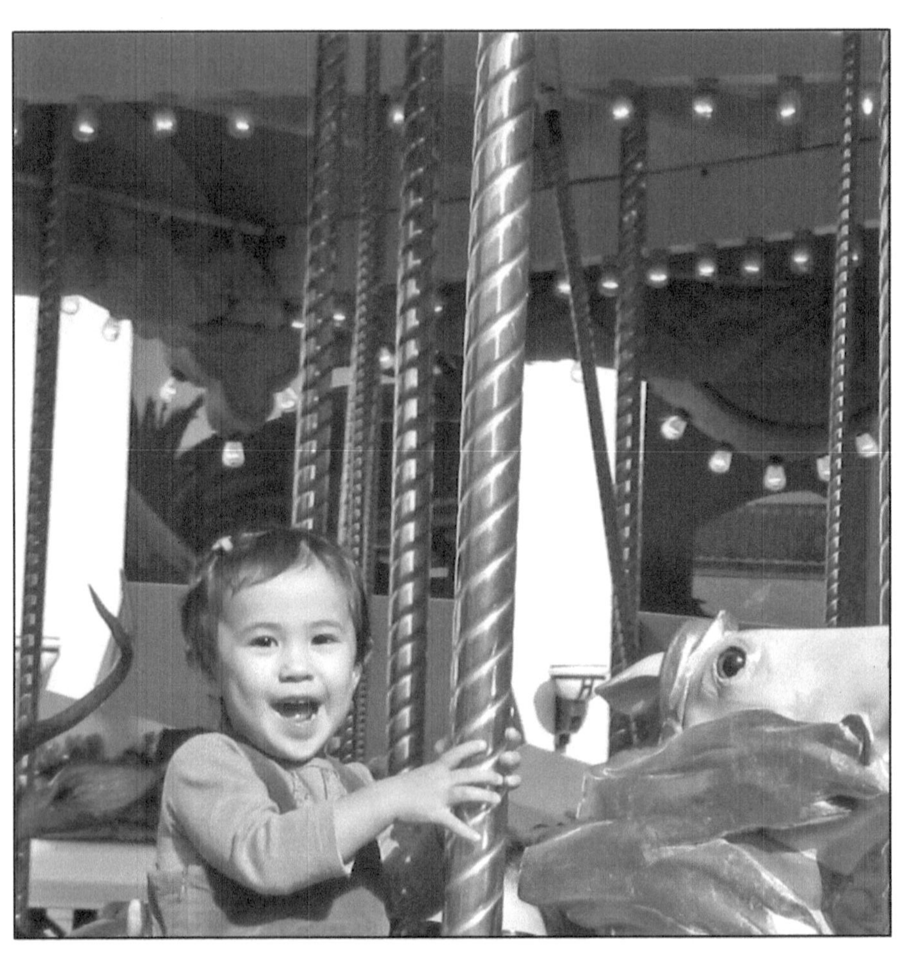

Oh rolypolybug

When I poke
you do what I have the urge to do
when people look at me
for faults to poke at
when you walk
your many legs and humpbacked body
move along like a gaggle
of children in the rain
under one oblong umbrella
when startled
you don't drop the umbrella
like the children would
you roll up in it
and put out a do not disturb sign
I could use an umbrella like that
sometimes

§

Oh silverfish

I open this old volume
and you scamper away
faster than my reflex
though I jump up
and brush my clothes
and turn over chair cushions
and check the book carefully
not to drop out pages
loosened by your appetite
but you're gone
and I wonder
how much of the book
you took with you
and how much
you left for me to eat

§

Oh puppy

Your little heart beats faster than mine
I feel it under your warm fur
holding you to my cheek
feeling the interplay of two pulses
at different rhythms
syncopating into a longer measure
that surges and recedes
one of many differences
between you and a stuffed pet
the heat of your body
your scratching claws
your stinking poop
your eyes that look directly into mine
like you're trying to tell me something profound
but can't quite find the words
rescued from that sweet bizarre dog shelter person
loved through weeks of parasite purging
all over our living room
and inside one designer purse
are those big eyes saying thank you
or time to feed me again
or please put me down and open the back door
to save the living room and both of us
from further embarrassment?
I do those things
but hear the thank you in that look
and I tell you
I should be thanking you instead
for sharing your tiny heartbeat
and the elemental knowledge
that the wonder of life
goes in one end
and out another

§

Oh flying fish

You whip your tail into speed
that leaps free of the water
and off in a new direction
in the harbor where I watch
waiting for my ferry
extending your winglike fins
you glide as far and fast
as a well-passed football
to escape from that clumsy sea lion
chasing you under the water
what an advantage you have evolved
for reduced resistance
using an atmosphere you can't breathe
and have no other use for
except to pop out of your viscous world
in one place
and re-enter another
moving faster when you fly
knowing the big wingless mammal
behind you
could never match
such quickness
and the strange clothed mammal
on the dock laughing
could never match
your acrobatic agility

§

Oh sea lion

Your little appetizer just jumped
in a different direction
out of the water again
into the free air
that you understand so much better
as a thing to breathe
than a source of lift
but your mammal brain
triangulates a vector
and you swim with your strong flippers
and smoothed wet hair
toward where you think the fish will land
and not where you last saw it
outsmarting it to be sure
though you can't jump through the air
as far or as fast
you almost catch it this time
surprising it into another flight
in another direction
so you recompute and swim
hoping to get there first
for the interception
or try again
knowing it will grow tired
before you do
what an advantage you have evolved
with that mental circuitry
and muscular streamlining
but what advantage is there
in your enjoyment of the game?
teasing the poor frightened fish
while you solve geometry and motion problems
in your head for fun
someday you may even figure out
how to fly like a fish

§

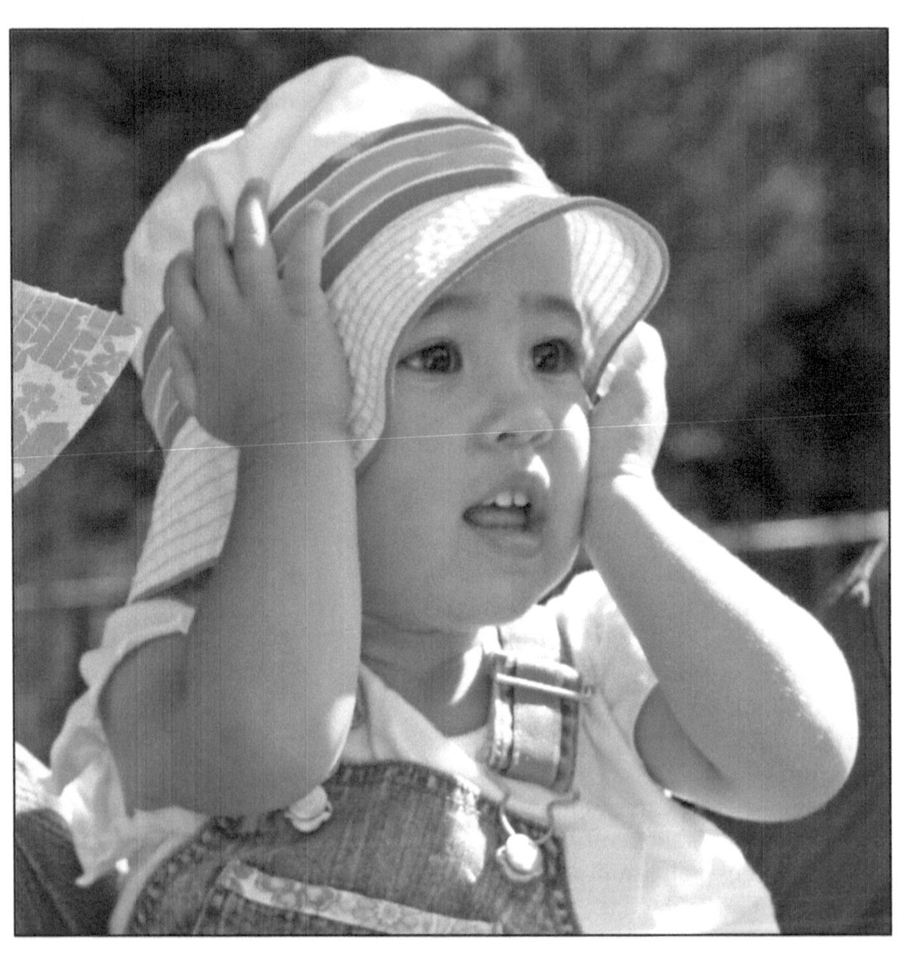

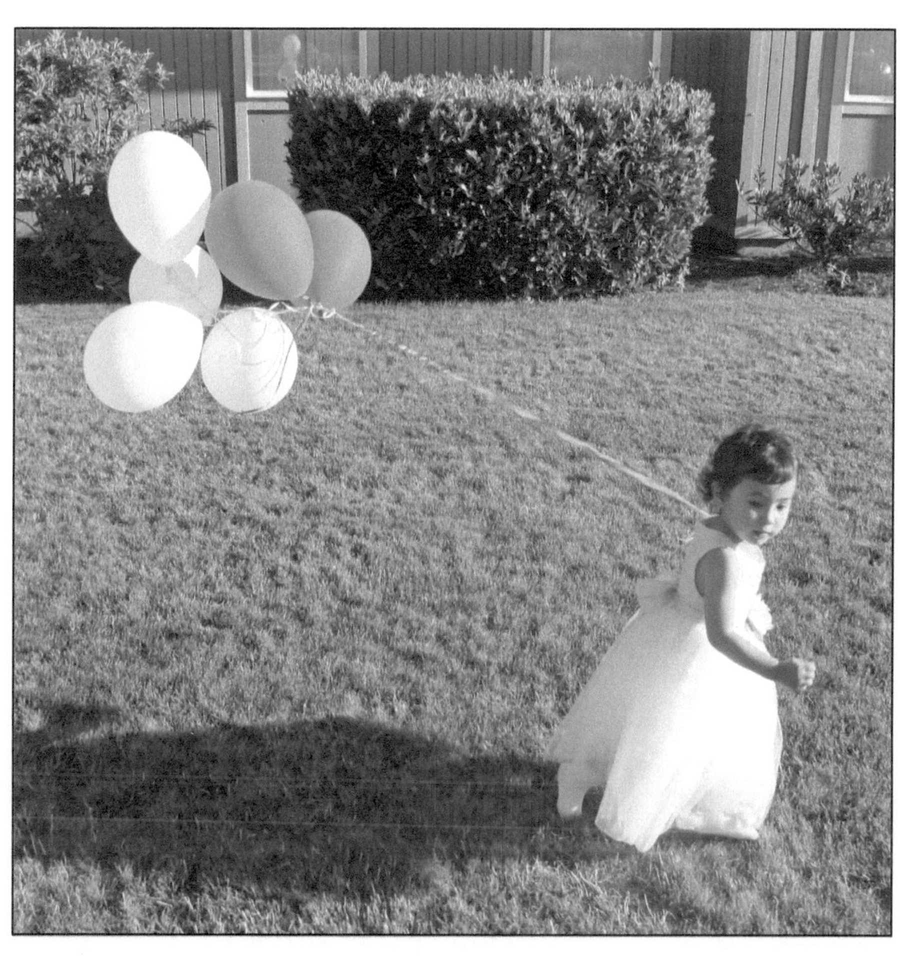

Oh tortoise

You are such a surprise
in this suburban neighborhood
not quite as big as a lawnmower
hobbling across your yard
faster than that rock you resemble
except when you stop to look me over
head cocked at an angle
your friend tells me you are over sixty
as am I
does that shell burden you?
such a weary metaphor
carrying your house on your back
like Thoreau's villager
is there so much difference
between protection
and social obligation?
never mind
keep your familiar shell
I'm carrying enough
old tropes of my own
to keep me feeling weary
to keep me feeling safe

§

Oh dog

You have me on a leash
taking me for a walk at your pace
I brought my office with me
but you don't give me a chance to log in
you stop to smell the tree trunks
and fire hydrants and stone wall corners
with the names of all the boy dogs
and then you tell me to get moving again
to catch up with you
so you can play your little game
of sniff and squat fake-out
over and over
until frustrated with your game
I stop waiting and forge ahead
and you can't hold it any longer
and pee a line across someone's driveway
dragging on the leash
you give me a dirty look
that asks what are we out here for anyway?
and haven't you ever wet yourself
when you were having so much fun
you couldn't decide where to stop the car?
and I say *yes dog*
but you're not satisfied
until I say *good girl*
and then you resume
leading me along by my leash
I feel a need to hurry home
for some reason

§

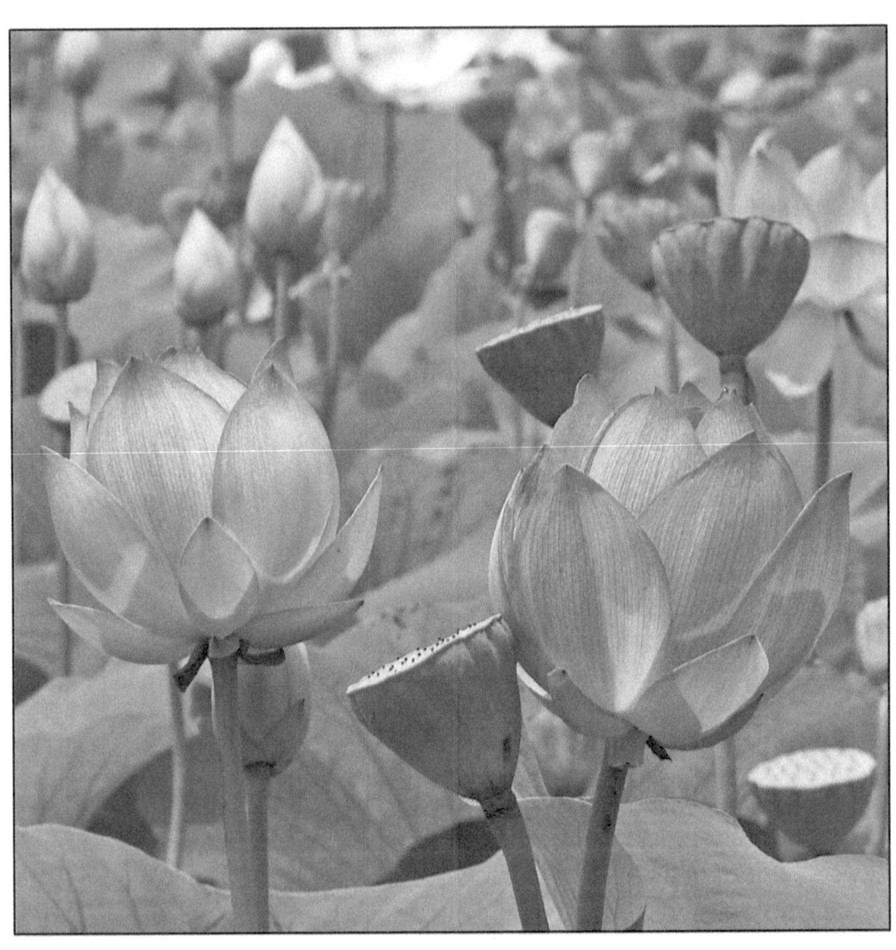

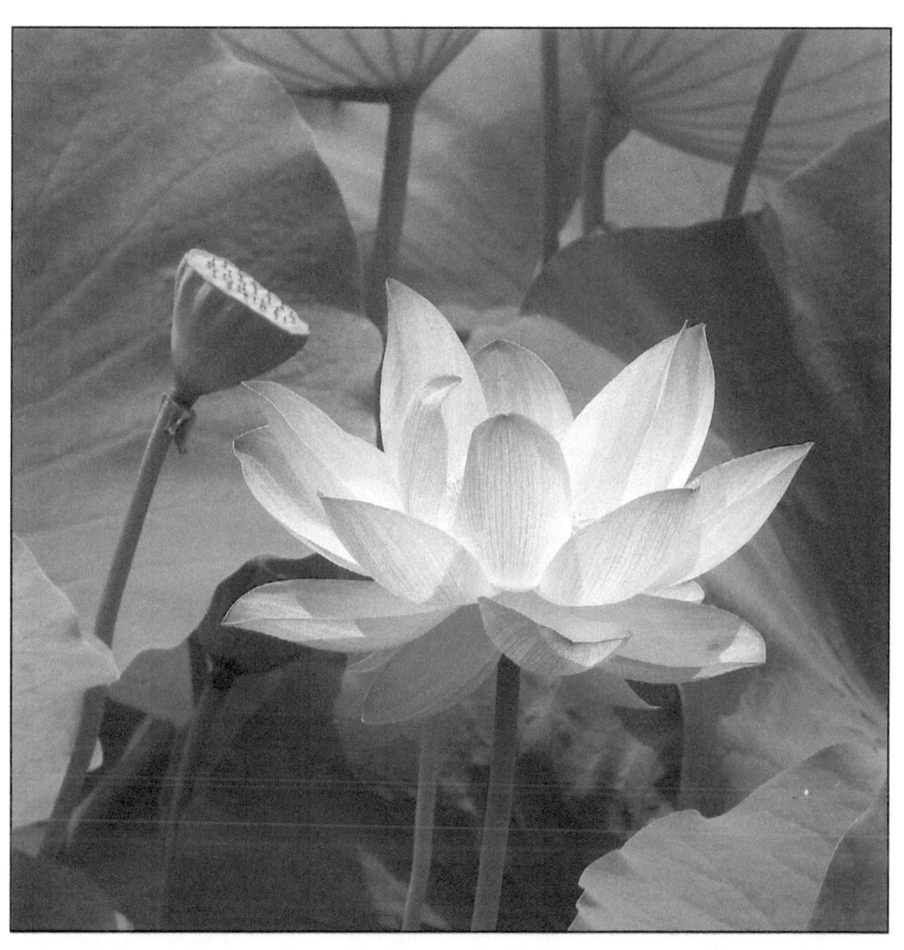

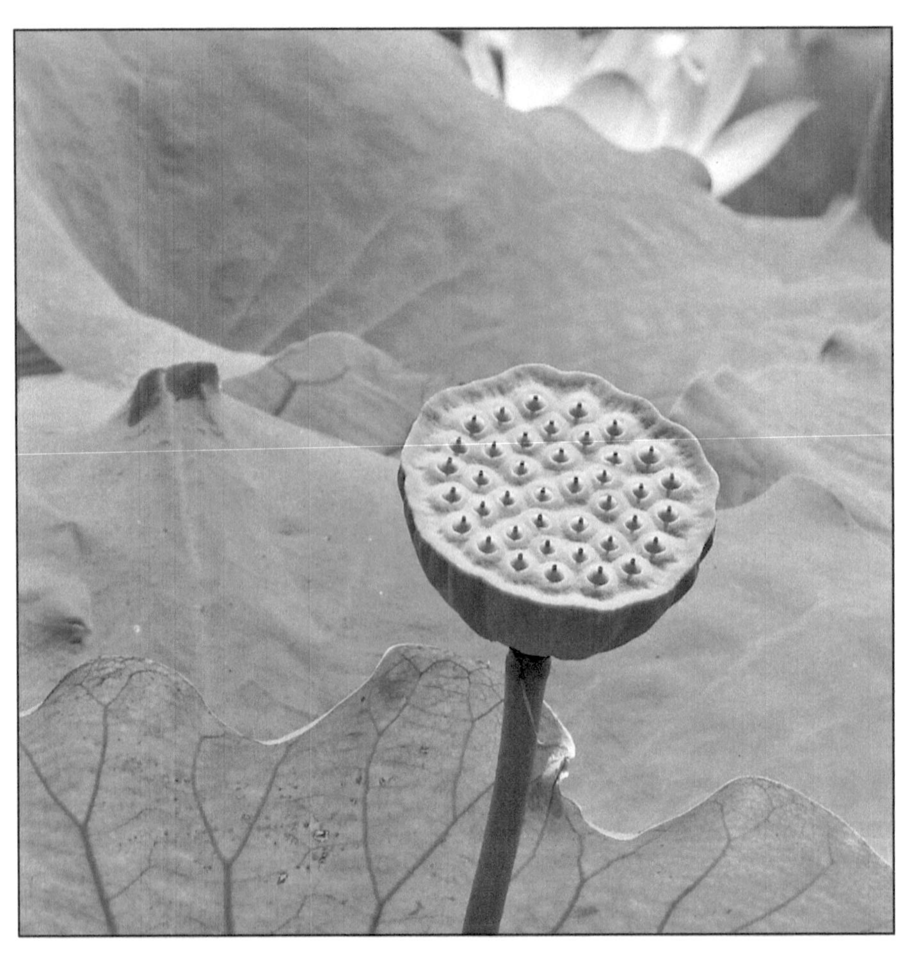

VIII.

TEACHINGS AND UNTEACHINGS

§

Successes that teach us nothing
are chains about our feet
failures we learn from
are gifts of wings

§

What philosophy is all about
you might not know what you will not doubt

§

My Gospel is simply this
that all meals are Eucharist
all Sundays are Easter
and all Fridays are good

§

The beauty of a flower
and the size of a life
cannot be measured
in dollars
or miles
or years

§

Limping away from philosophy class
I hurt therefore I am

§

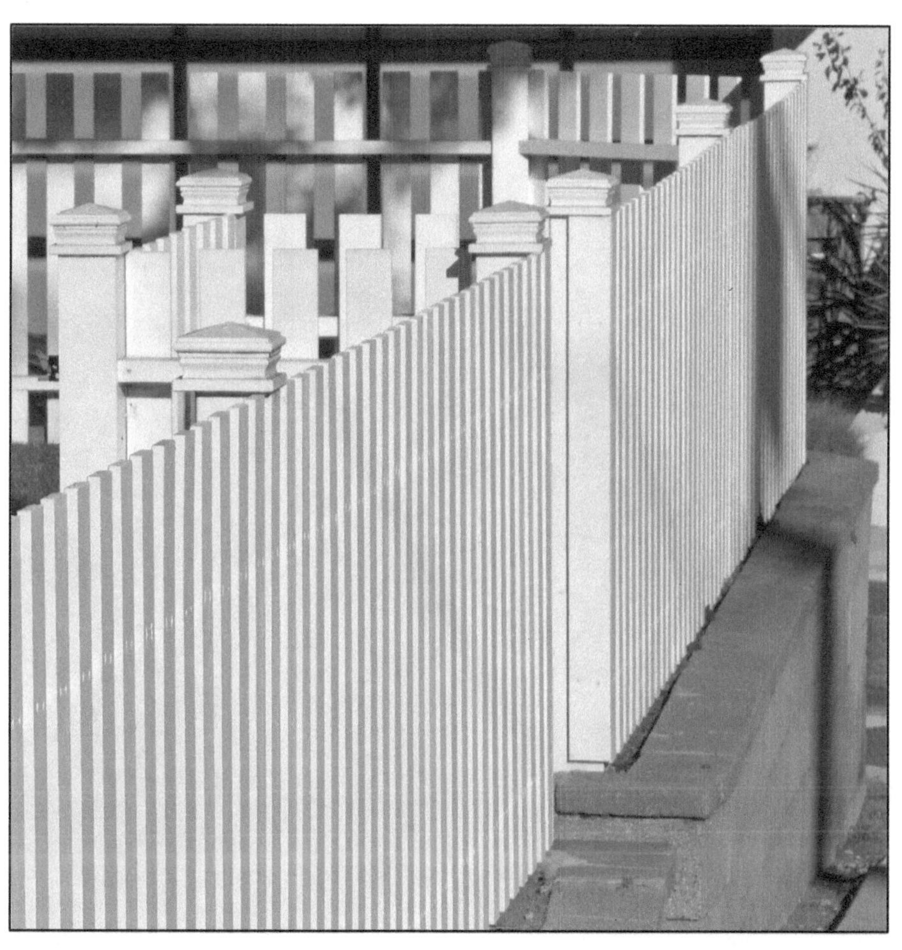

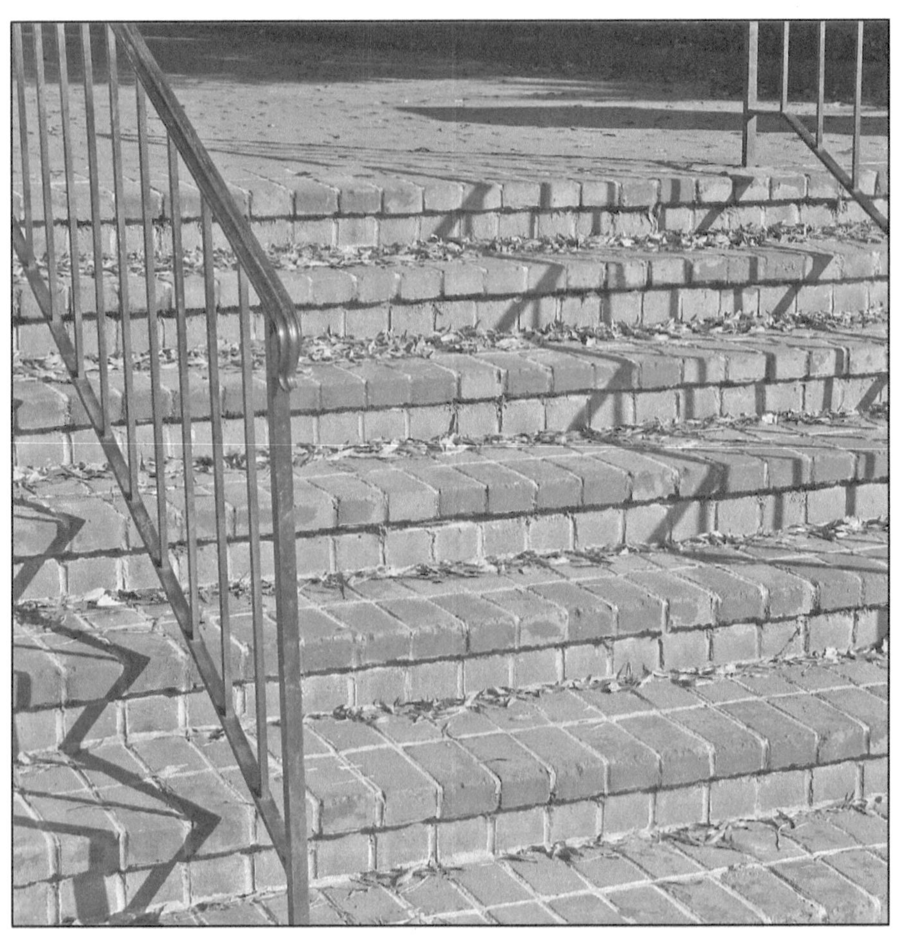

The art of teaching

Ascertain the season
turn the soil
plant the seed
provide water
ever so gently pull the weeds
pray for sunshine
wait for growth
enjoy the fruit when it ripens

§

Teachers are the ones

Teachers are the ones who make your stomach hurt
when you can't finish before the bell

Teachers are the ones who give you new visions
by asking you questions without answers

Teachers are the ones who scold you
for the mistakes they think you make
instead of the ones you really do

Teachers are the ones who lend you their knife
just long enough to scar yourself in new places
while they hold up a mirror for you to reflect on the result

Teachers are the ones who give you balsa in plain blocks
then step back as you carve a glider of your own design
that soars across the plaza and gets stuck in a treetop

Teachers are the ones who stand beside you
turning the pages of book after book
through the remaining years of your life
and smile while you write one of your own

§

More than one way

There's more than one way to see things
I say to Teacher in the first course

You got the answer wrong and that's that
says Teacher

There's more than one way to see things
I say to Teacher in the second course

You got a good grade stop complaining
says Teacher

I'm beginning to understand now
I say to Teacher in the third course

There's more than one way to see things
says Teacher

§

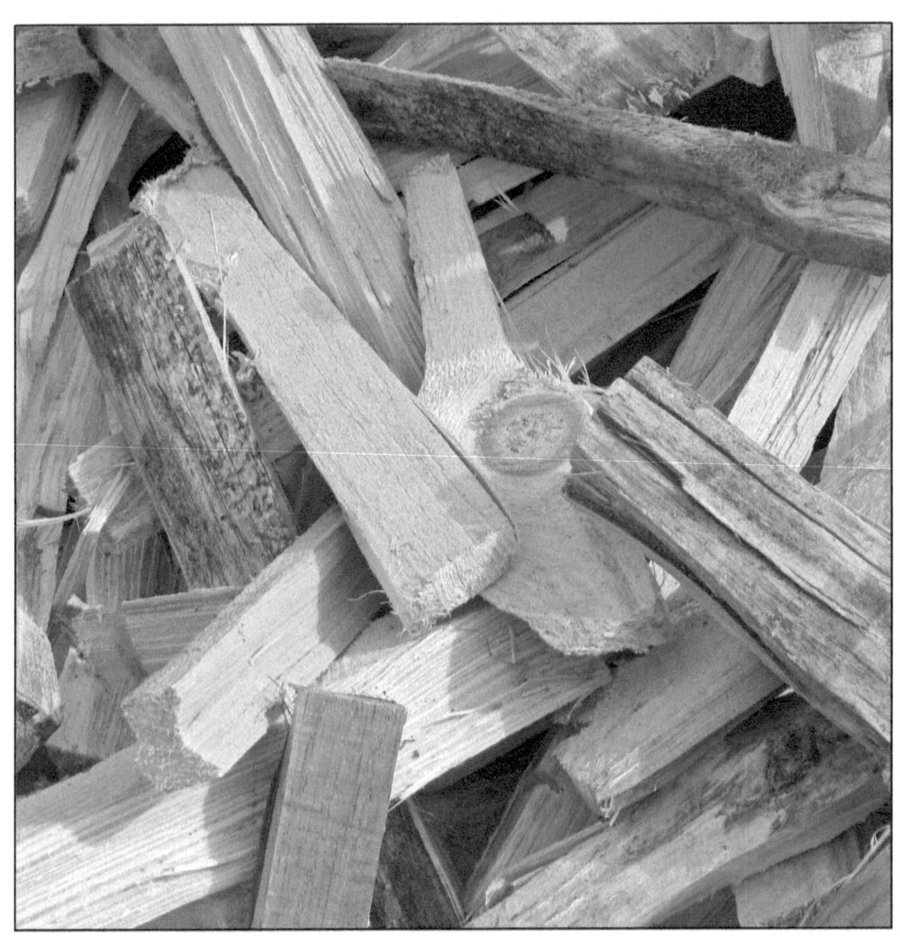

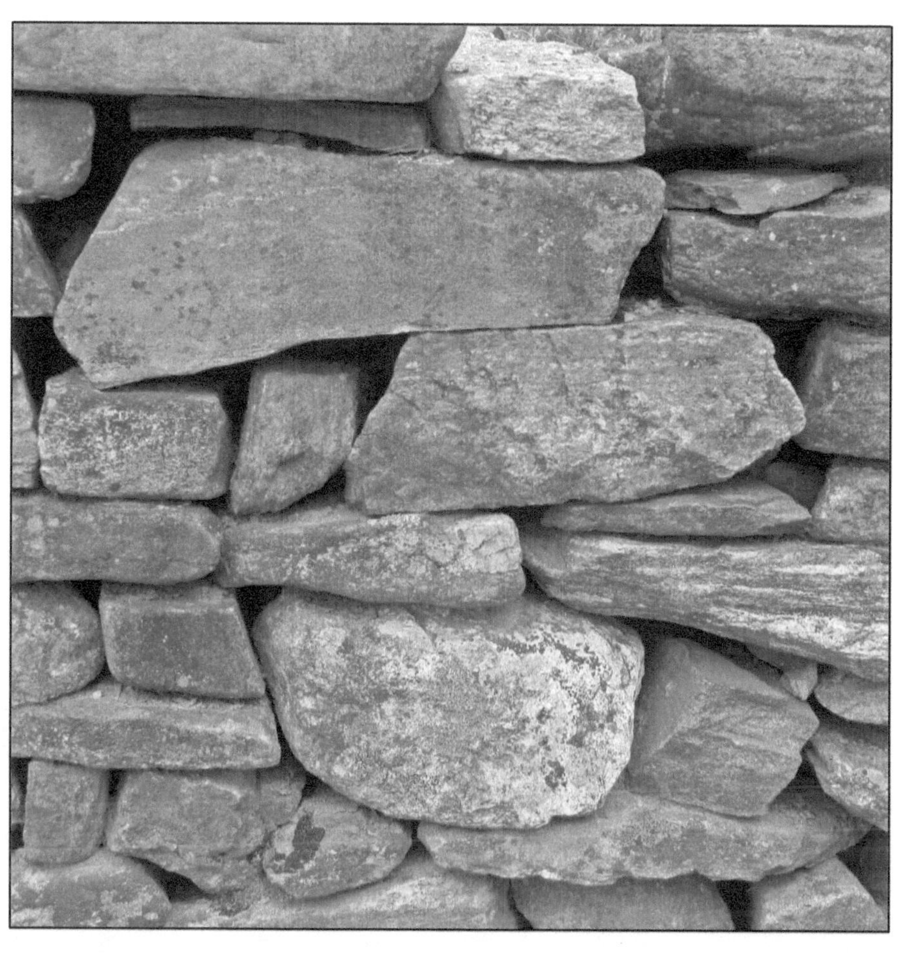

Birthdays

Every year turns over a century
and every day a year
every breath a birthday party
and every blink a tear
the calendar says celebrate
an arbitrary will
some holiday may be too late
this one is here still

We wait too long to show we care
until beyond recall
to live right now and love and share
what matters after all
how much of life does it consume
to give one more caress
what awaits do not presume
just one day we possess

The one farewell we can truly give
belongs to those who live
the only memorial we can ever know
comes before we go

§

Pleasures

Windblown fingers of quiet snow
ducks paddling into a calm brook's flow
electric touch of a lover's eyes
shouts of players as a live ball flies
fire of a rose in alpenglow
evening star hanging in purple skies
those pleasures are greatest which tease and go
and come again in sudden surprise

§

Coins

Perhaps we could measure our age by the coin
we find worthwhile to bend over and pick up

As children we gleefully crawl
in the dust on hands and knees
for a dull piece of copper
and count ourselves lucky

In youth with dreams and passions
anything less than a dime is boring

In firm adulthood full of cares
a dropped dime we may leave to beg
but a quarter still justifies an effort

When joints grow stiff from weight of years
we will not take pains for anything less
than a shiny dollar
which isn't very often anyway

But there comes an age if we are spared
when a penny again commands attention
though infirmity requires conscription
of some nearby child
to get down and crawl on our behalf
to retrieve the errant deed

§

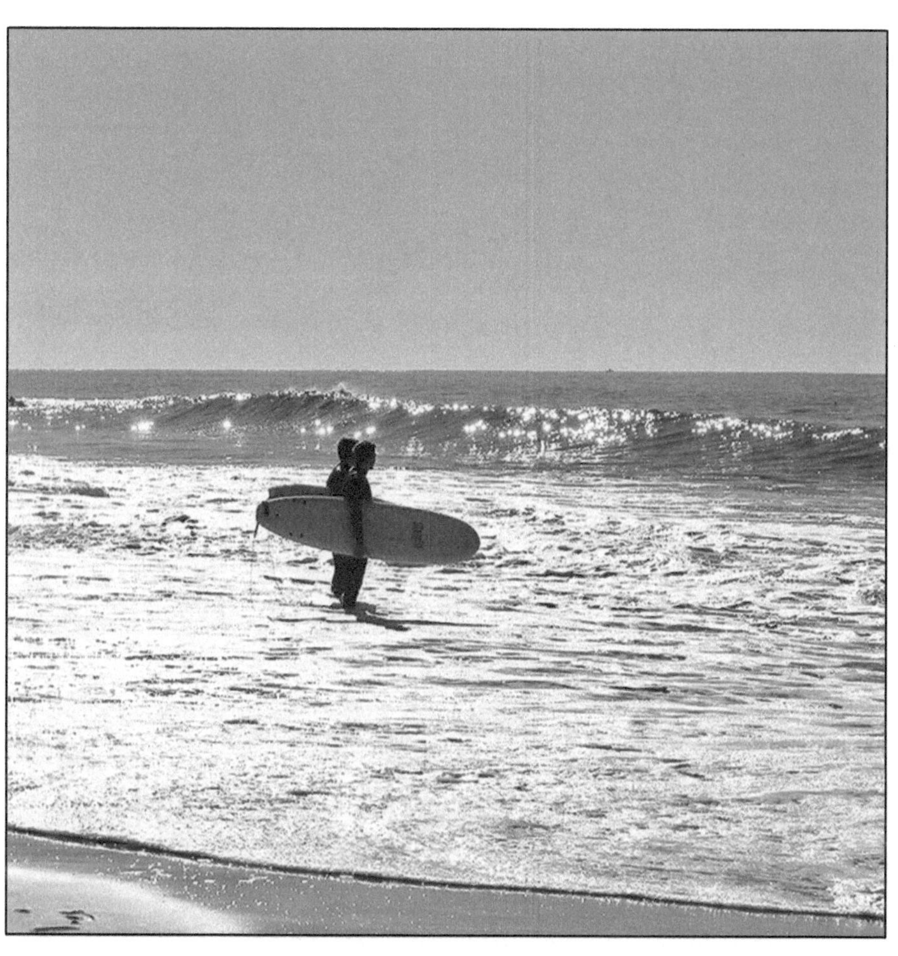

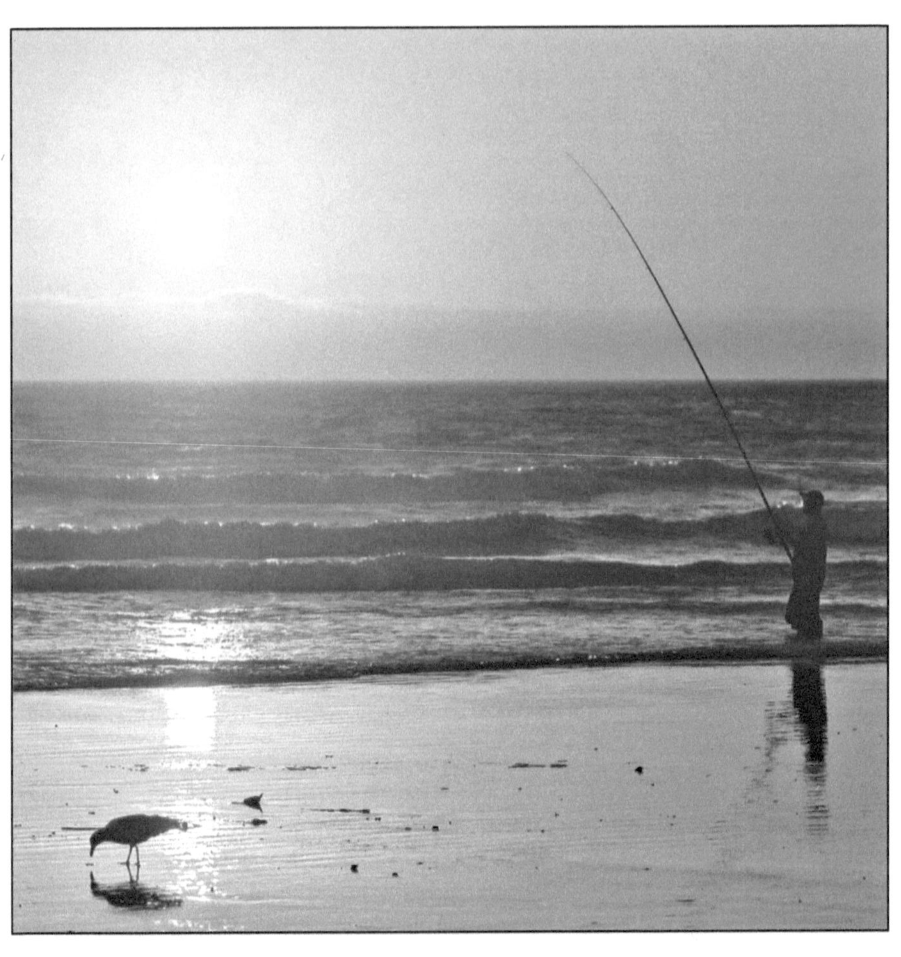

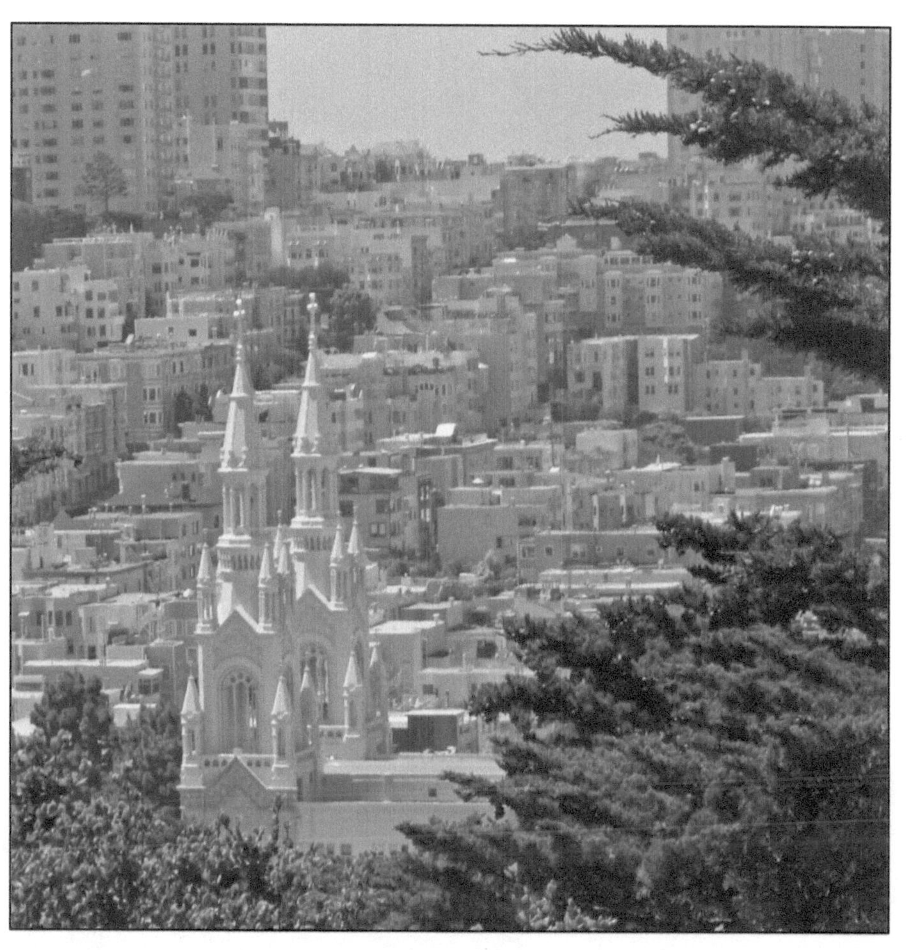

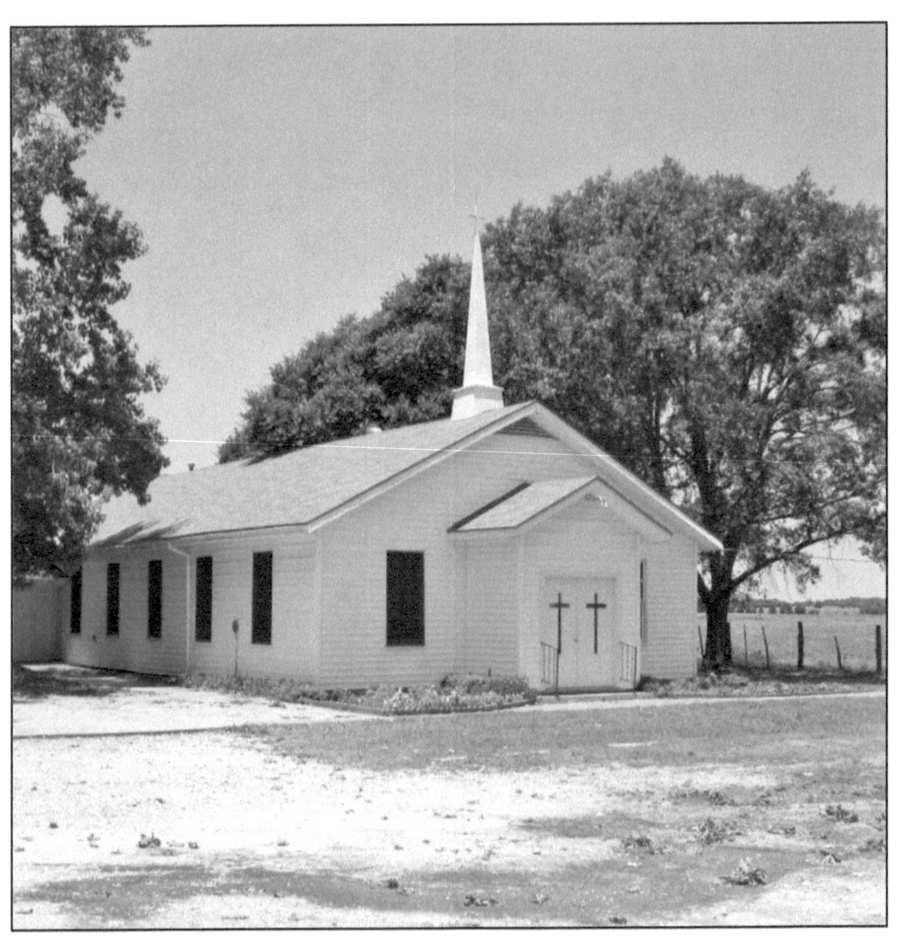

Christmas card

Where shall we find
the king of heaven
if not in a barnyard manger?

Who can give us
the joy of Christmas
unless we carry it through the year?

Where may we discover
the design of the universe
if not in a single falling snowflake?

How shall we build
the city of light
without the stranger in the dark street?

And when shall we ever
find ourselves
if not in the love of a friend?

§

New Year's card

Every new year is a world not yet explored
every new day is a holiday not yet celebrated
may you explore many
celebrate well
and share in peace

§

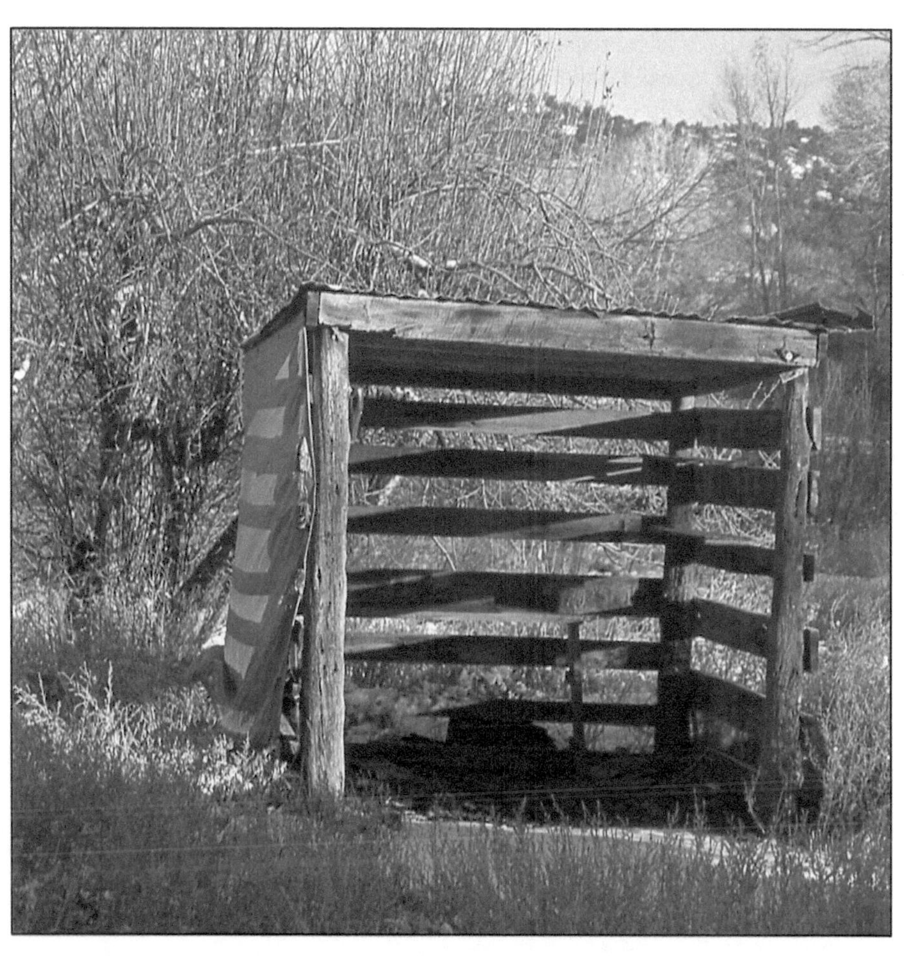

Pointing at the moon

Can a sentence curve up out of still water
like the spoon bow of a schooner at anchor?
can a vowel *elevez* on toes as delicate and strong
as those of a teenage ballerina?
can a pronoun catch and hold the golden fire of dawn
in the towers of an icy town?
can a syllable soar in circles on rising air like a hawk
searching a new-mown hayfield?

What solitary word carries the exhilaration found
at the top of a steep mountain climbed?
what conjoined phrase dances with sudden joy at meeting
a doe and fawn on a misty trail?

Come – teach me again the grammar of the senses
in a material universe
slowly breathe into my ear a childlike lexicon
of concrete delights
read to me again the unpublished scriptures
of unmediated ecstasy
come – heal me of my envy
that the runner's body writes poems
my frail pen cannot

§

Serenity

Not necessary to change what can be changed
not necessary to accept what cannot
not necessary to know the difference
courage patience wisdom serenity not for the asking
not asking not knowing not accepting not changing
by being become serene

§

Mind

The mind that is inattentive is not mind
the mind that goes in a straight line forsakes reality
the mind that goes in circles is not well
the mind that wanders gathers impressions
but achieves no purpose
the mind that becomes entranced
cannot think new thoughts
the mind that is not inquisitive
will never scratch the surface
the mind that is too quickly satisfied
will never sound the depths
the mind that cannot express itself is infertile
the mind that expresses itself too readily invites ridicule
or causes pain

the mind that remains attentive but detached
that softens its lines with wanderings
and stiffens its wanderings with lines
that climbs or descends spirals
when tempted to go in circles
that skips merrily from one entrancement to another
and chooses its path at will
yet follows a difficult path to the end out of respect
that expresses itself thoughtfully when appropriate
knows when to keep silent and when to risk all
and continues to inquire when all around are satisfied

Such a mind is precious
but it too shall perish
only in another mind
may it outlive itself

§

Ones and thousands

A single year of war
can ruin
a thousand years of peace

A single stroke of vandalism
can wipe out
a thousand strokes of genius

A single act of abuse
can crush
a thousand acts of kindness

A single moment of carelessness
can undo
a thousand moments of caution

I am so sorry

§

Limits

A forest doesn't die when a tree falls
but there's a limit

The ocean doesn't die when a reef starves
but there's a limit

A species isn't extinct when one creature dies
but there's a limit

A river doesn't end when it's dammed
but there's a limit

A dream isn't killed when it's cheated of a nickel
but there's a limit

A marriage won't die from a single harsh word
but there's a limit

The truth can't be killed by a solitary lie
well sometimes it can

§

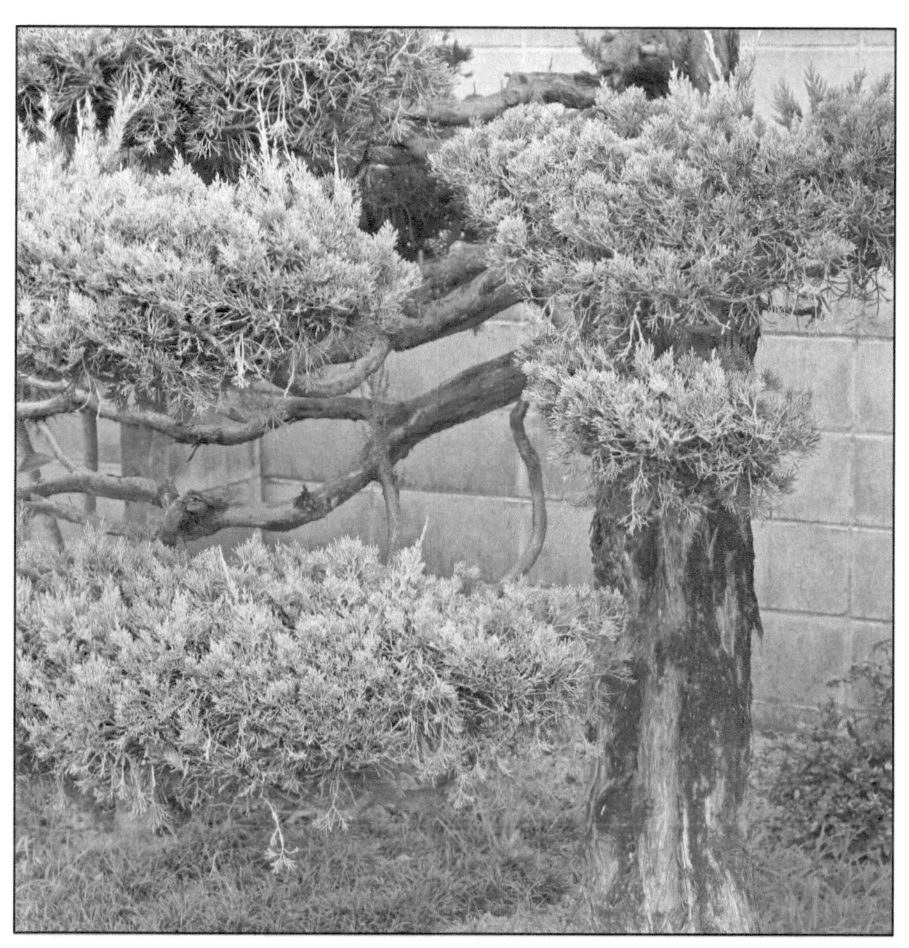

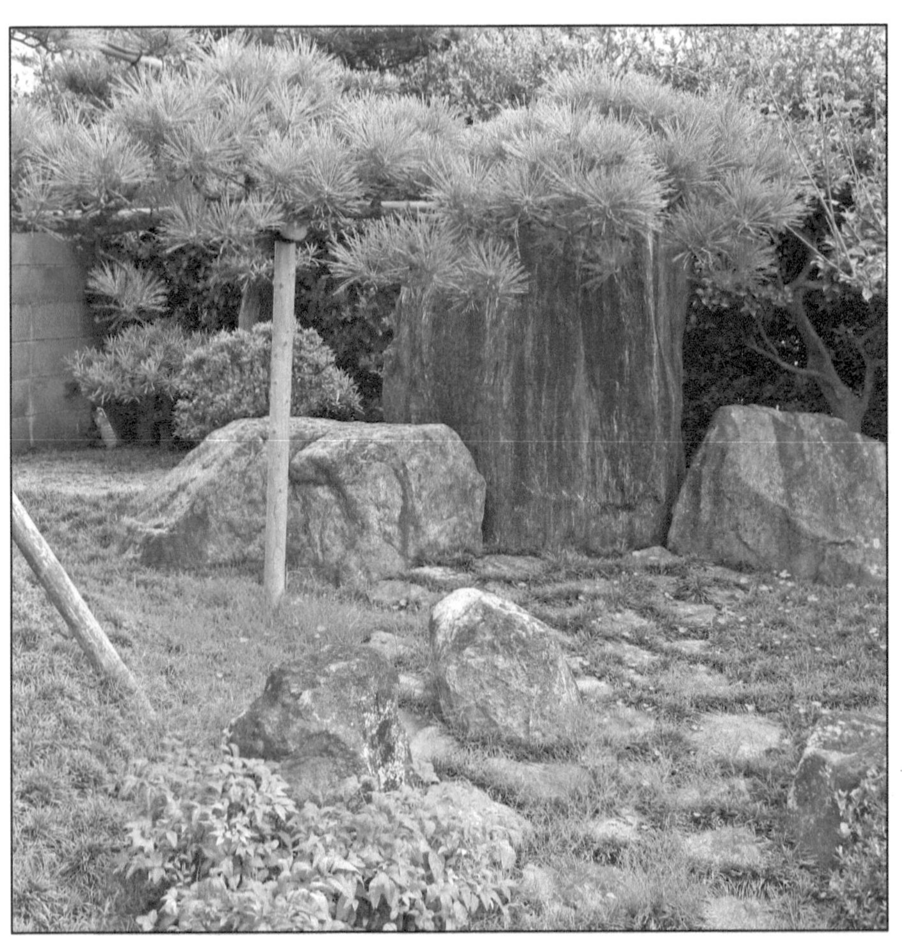

The moment

A moment is forever start to finish
until it happens
it doesn't exist
once passed
it can never change
looking ahead it seems
it might never come
looking back it seems
it had always been inevitable
looking ahead or looking back
is all we can say about it
except there is no
looking ahead or looking back
in the moment
there is no speaking
about the moment
in the moment
there is no knowledge
of the moment
in the moment
there is only the moment
and this one no longer exists

§

The way to no pain

In the moment of pain
nothing makes sense but pain
with its own logic of pain
its grammar of pain
its mythology of pain
its ethic of pain
though I'd rather talk of anything but pain
all that comes to my mind is pain
and all I can do is let it be pain
for the sake of pain

I do all I can to hide the pain
from others who don't want to see pain
since nothing comes between people like pain
because they really can't share the pain
the look they see in my face is pain
the edge they hear in my voice is pain
the pause before I answer is pain
the confusion in my answer is pain
the misunderstanding that comes later is pain
the blaming for fault is pain
the bell that tolls in my ear is pain
the fact that others can't hear it is pain

I wish I could express pain
the eternal music of pain
the melodies and harmonies of pain
the rhythms of pain
the brushstrokes of pain
the colors and shades of pain
the shapes and lines of pain
the spinning and leaping of pain
the whirlwind of pain
the ice needles of pain
the smoke and flame of pain
the red charcoal of pain
the smoldering ashes of pain
the quietness of pain
the stillness of pain

All existence fades but pain
I chant the sutra of pain
over and over till the pain
becomes nothing but pain
no more no less than pain
without beginning or end of pain
a universe empty of all but pain
no life but pain
no worship but pain
no love but pain
no joy but pain
but through that pain
and in that pain
and only because of that pain
do I come to know
all the joy and love and worship and universe I'll ever know
or need to know
or care to know
or know how to know
or not know
or know

§

Joys and sufferings

In all your knowing know this

The greatest sufferings
are knowing and holding on to suffering
and knowing and holding on to joy

The greatest joys
are knowing and letting go of suffering
and knowing and letting go of joy

§

Prayer wheel

All life is born of life
and all will pass away
one self of many selves
one death of many births
one sea of many drops
vapors rise to the sky
snow falls to the ground
rivers flow to their source
all things return

We are connected to each other
incarnations of each other
all past beings are part of us
we are part of all that come
one ever-present past and future self
one tapestry of many threads
one mind of many faces

The wheel of cause and effect
turns upon no single soul
but on the community of all
who live and die and act upon each other
exploiting each other we injure our common self
deceiving each other we misguide our common self
enjoying one another we energize our common self
serving one another we transcend our common self
past and present and future are one

What lives and dies
is no self but an entire world
what is reborn and reborn
is no self but an entire world
what is free from rebirth
is no self but an entire world
what passes into nothingness
is no self but an entire world

§

Today

I am not yesterday
I am not tomorrow
if I am not today I am nothing

When yesterday was today
I was today

If I am nothing today
I will have been nothing
when today becomes yesterday

When tomorrow becomes today
I will be today

If I am nothing today
I will become nothing
when today gives way to tomorrow

Because I am today
I create yesterday
I create tomorrow

§

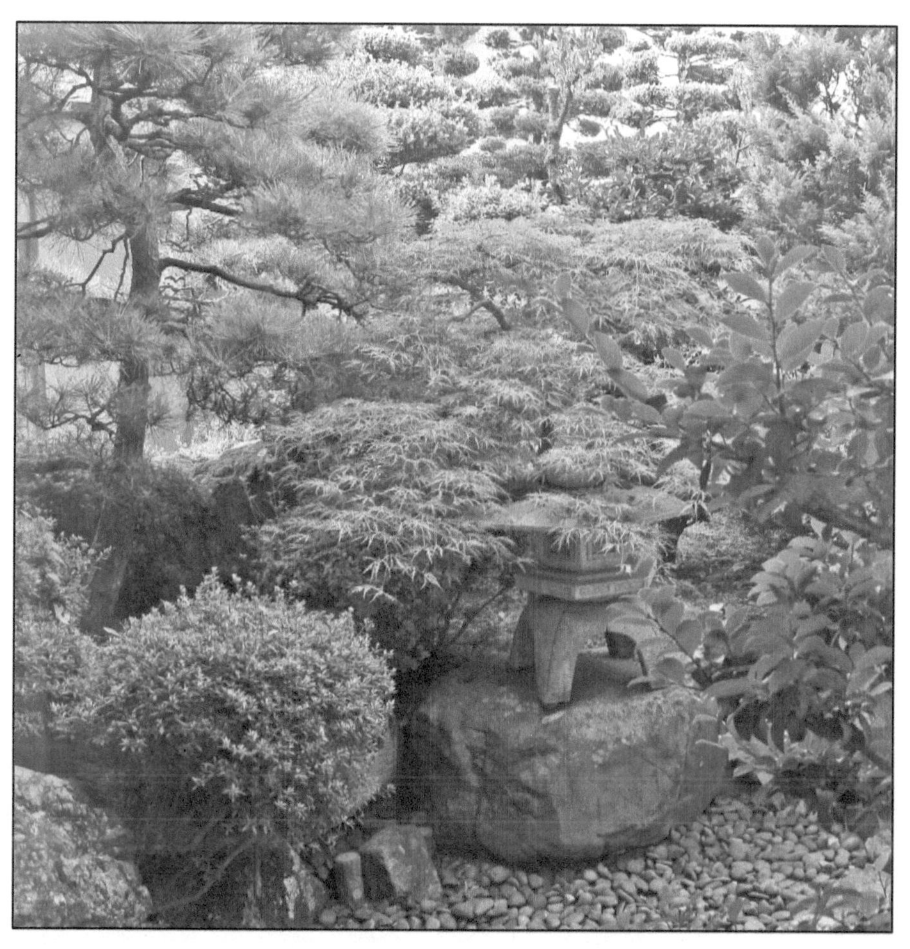

§

But if my reach exceeds my grasp
is Heaven my only comfort?
economic worlds account to task
all overambitious effort

§

What I have truly lost no one can restore
What I have truly gained no one can take

§

There is such a thing as pursuing a dream
too soon
and another such a thing as deferring one
too long
between the two
better too soon
than not at all
is not what I was taught
but what I now teach

§

Compromise
can only be offered
never demanded

§

§

When things go well
sleep is an annoyance
when ill
a friend

§

Enough talk of mind over matter
show me one person
who has achieved mind over mind

§

The terror of our age is to lose our memories
but you can't remember what you didn't experience
and you can't forget what you didn't live

§

There have been times
someone's love for me
was all that kept me alive
and other times
my love for someone
was all that kept me alive

§

§

Three terrifying things have I beheld
and a fourth more fearsome than wild beasts
a seller persuaded that others cannot live
without the product that's for sale
a politician whose positions are ironclad
until needed to trade for favors
an educator in the grip of a curriculum fad
and a religionist convicted of God's will
for everyone else

§

In the refrigerator
macaroni and cheese converts to green mold
green beans grow fuzzy white stuff
milk gets thick and stinks
meat gets hard and black
lettuce turns brown and limp
before it melts into soupy slime
passionate love becomes possessiveness

§

The world is run by fools and villains who profit thereby
while the wise and good suffer thereby
easy for me to say that when I struggle
but how to explain my joy?

§

§

If I'm not hurting
like out-of-work loggers and miners are hurting
am I doing enough
to save the Earth?

If I'm not dying
like children of other colors and clothes are dying
am I doing enough
for justice?

If I'm not living
like survivors of war and cruelty are living
am I doing enough
for peace?

§

Walking on the sidewalk
toward each other
I instinctively step aside
you don't notice or slow your steps
we would have collided if I hadn't bothered
why does that bother me
and not you?

§

Who will mourn for a forest
that grew before they were born?
who will mourn for a child
who is born after they die?
who will rejoice for a star
that explodes when no one is home?

§

§

The wonder is not that we die
but that we stay alive
long enough to celebrate it

§

The length of this journey is as irrelevant
as where it ends
whether the milk run or the express
what matters is getting a window seat
making a friend to talk to
and staying awake

§

The mirror reveals
where I've been
what's chasing me
and what has happened to my face
the windshield offers
only road
horizon
an obstacle or two
a place to stop for breath
and then more road

§

If anything in this world is sacred
the forest is
and the ocean
the stars at night
and every different child

§

§

I can change 'or' to 'and'
with a few pen strokes
but not vice versa

§

Born with nothing but gifts
what else to do but enjoy and give?

§

The meaning of a poem
only becomes apparent
once I forget I painted it

§

Lip service to Whitman and Dickinson
is fine
but don't sound too much like either one
to succeed
and don't even think about combining them
to be original
don't try to avoid them either

§

Dipping a teaspoon
into the waterfall of words
that flows through my mind
over the rocks of nonwords
jump in with me!
have a sip!

§

§

Huckleberry in a pie
half moon across the sky
did you ever wonder why
a baby loves a lullaby?

§

If not for the sea
we would not be
if not for our song
we wouldn't belong
if not for our laughter
we wouldn't have to

§

Call me a riddle
fly me a flute
sing me a puppy
tell me a song
cook me a story
buy me a star
grow me a dream
and bring me your love

§

When things get rough
they may get rougher
life is tough
but I'm tougher

§

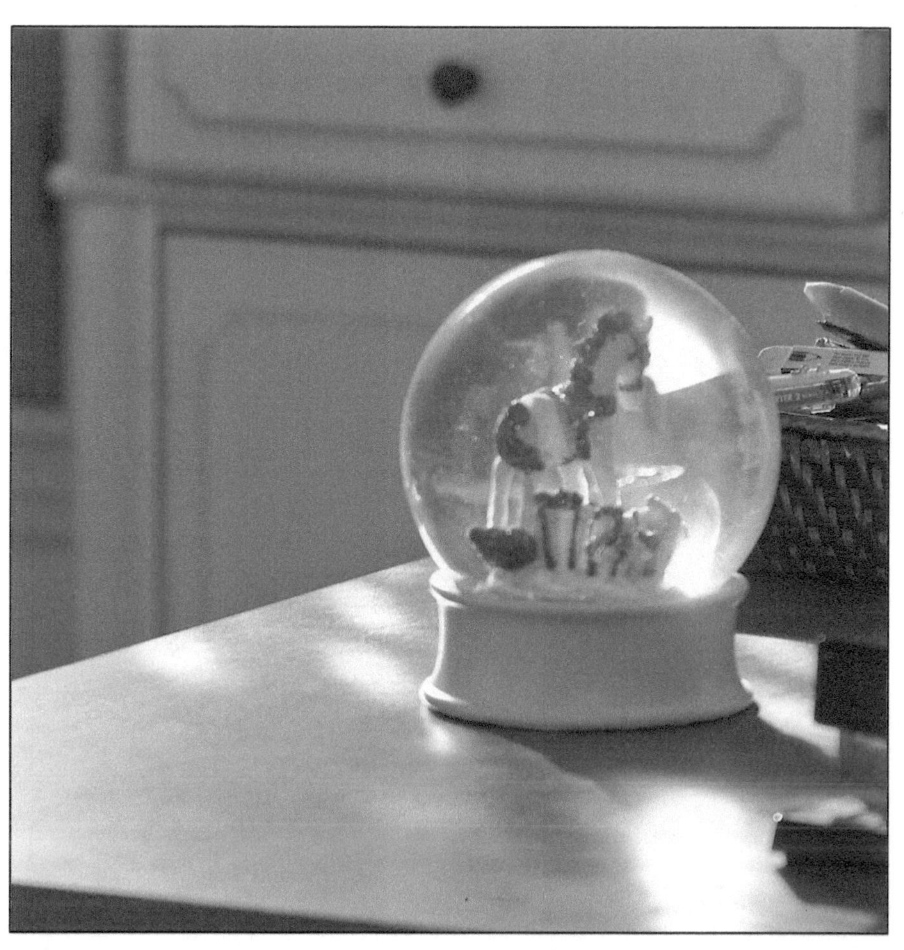

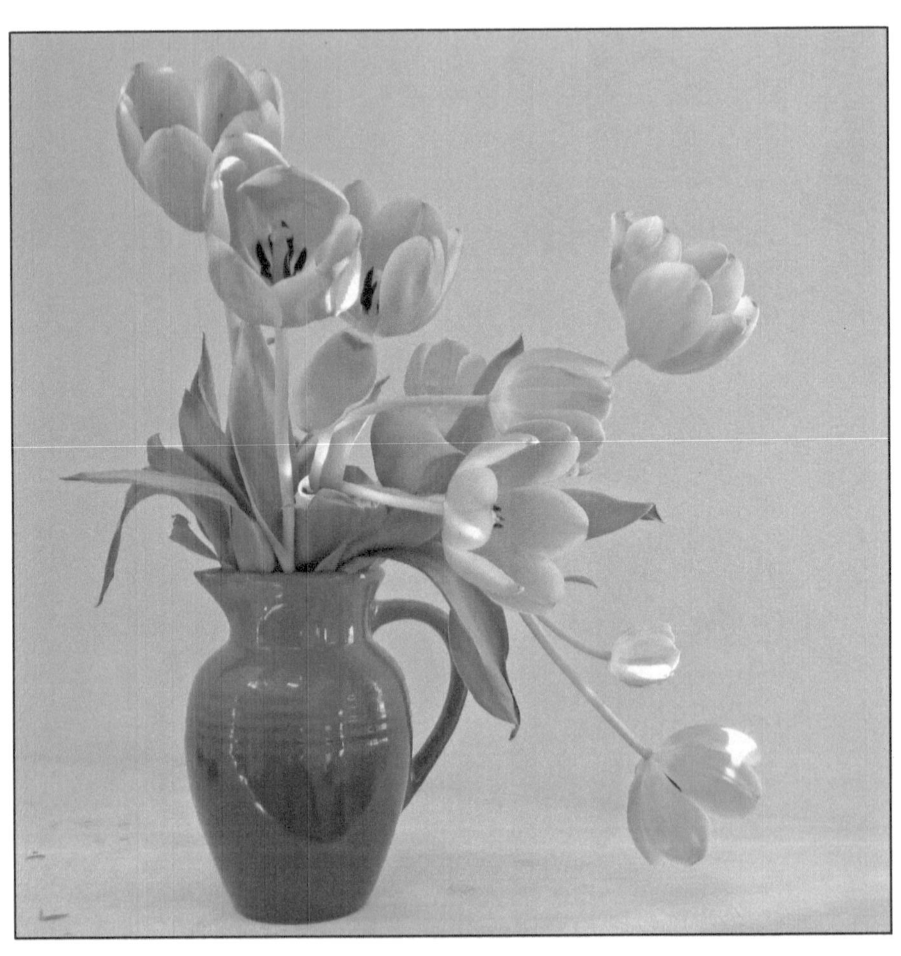

IX.

SCATTERED PIECES

§

Wasted time
a minute lost
to find a marble send another after
so another year

§

Someone rustles papers as I study
a splashing brook

§

In the carrels
between Aquinas and Augustine
someone clips fingernails

§

Silently
on cat's paws
the urge to sleep
stalks me by day
ignores me at night

§

Busy Saturday morning
busily sleeping in

§

§

But is it *haiku* or *senryu*
asks teacher
sparrows chirp outside

§

Five seven five?
I take off my jacket
ah – the fresh air!

§

Project due on Monday
time to write another poem

§

Mozart hangs on my office wall
with a furrowed brow
looking down at the inkjet printer

§

Swirling eddies and vortices
make it impossible to swim upstream
through this crowded hallway

§

§

As I drive I listen to the voices
of dead singers
my depression turns to euphoria
at their sweet sound

§

Potluck dinner with friends
who mock each other at every chance
an ant crawls from behind a bowl
I brush it gently to the floor
when no one is looking
and smile and say nothing

§

Someone comes to me crying
I put my arm around him
now we both cry

§

Sixty candles burn on the cake
I've earned every one
but can't get them all in one breath

§

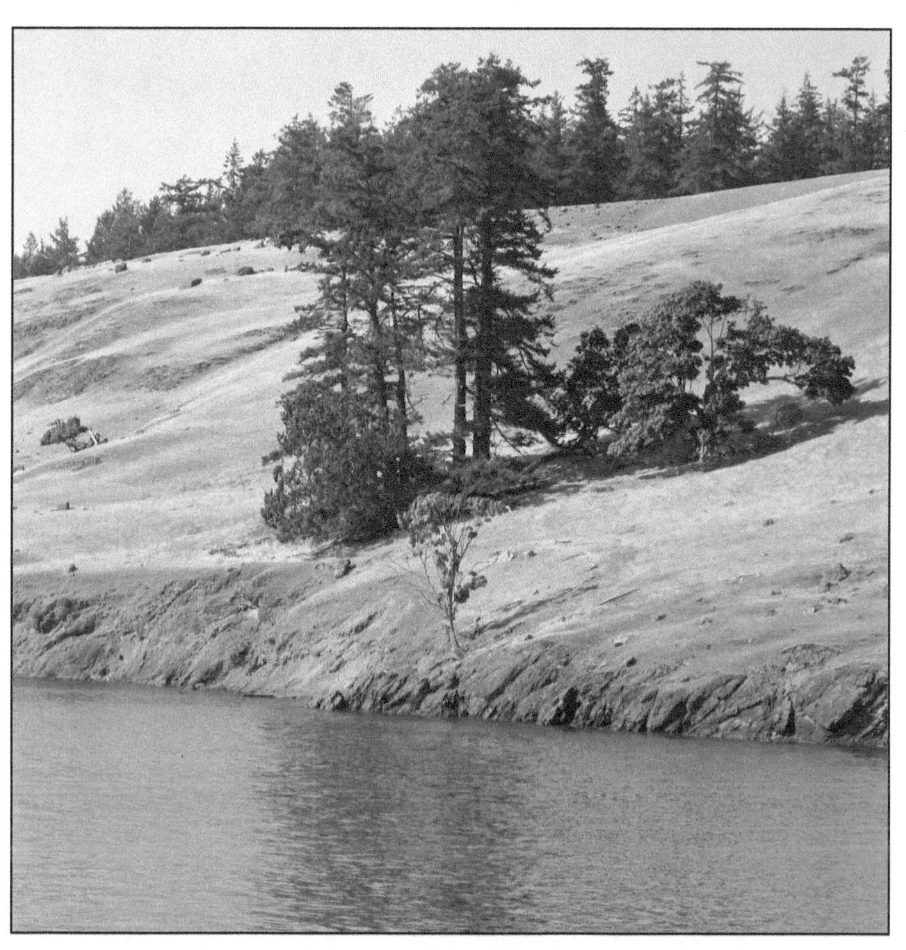

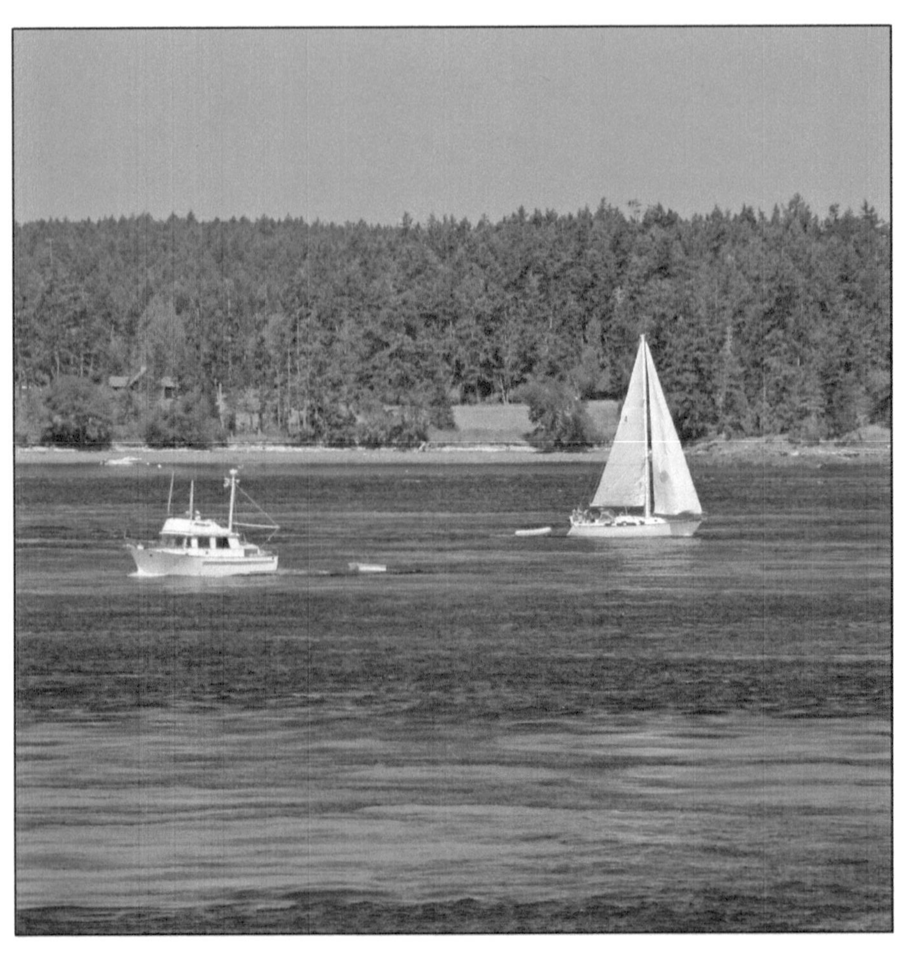

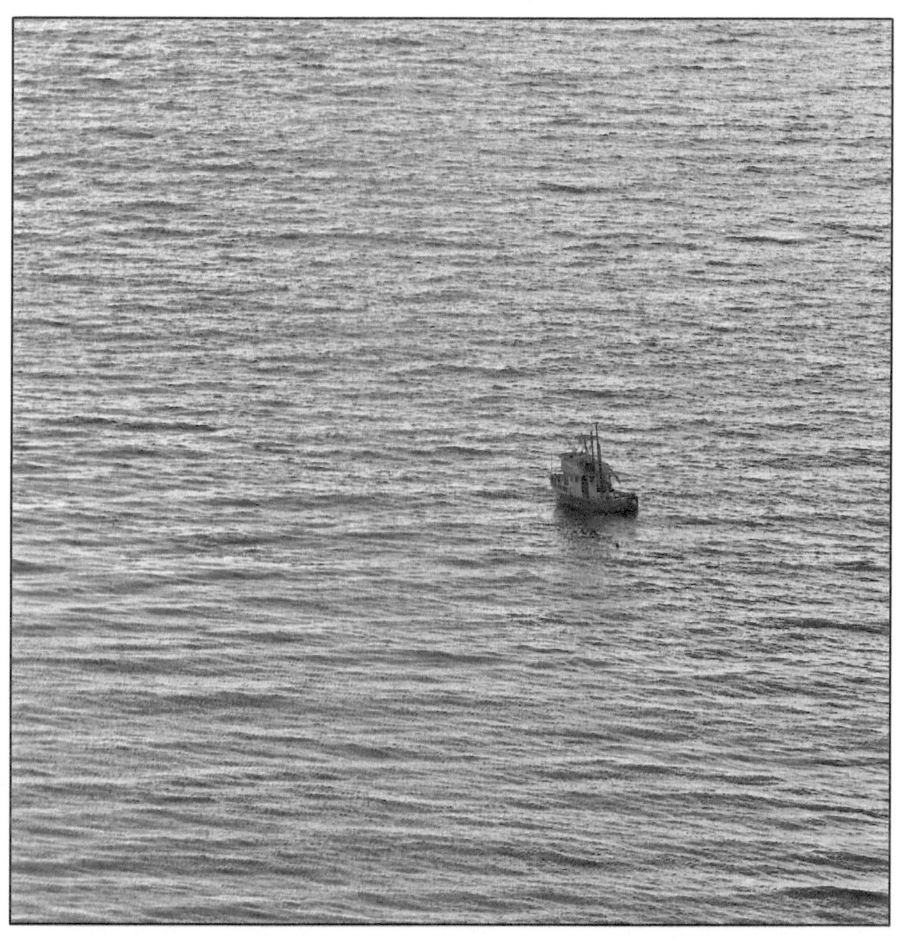

§

Lights slowly waltz
in blackness
come outside!
look up!

§

White tailed intruder among friends
makes the sky strange again

§

Four tiny dewdrops in line
on an invisible web
sparkle purest white on velvet black
hanging from Jove's striped round belly
Galileo's diamonds

§

A wink and a grin
from the cat in the sky
evening star over crescent moon

§

Aphrodite lingers
brilliantly white
in a gown of deepening blue
I am seduced

§

How does the universe know
which stars and planets are Latin
which Greek
and which Arabic?

§

§

Two bright red ovals
the balloon
and the child's grinning face

§

International dinner
flags of many colors
faces of friends

§

Shells on my car floor testify
driving under the influence
of pistachios

§

That funny house
the blue painted walk
outshines the flowers

§

Another dull gray house
with a bright grape
purple painted front door

§

The porcelain white Persian cat
propped in that window
just blinked

§

§

The birds on that wire
watching traffic
carrion eaters

§

In front of the quiet shrine
on a holy day
those drivers are screaming obscenities
at each other

§

Surrounded by cars and trucks
I have trouble breathing
can't wait to get where I'm driving
and eat freshly delivered food

§

A uniform follows me
around the store
blinded by my companion's
dark skin

§

§

At the bus stop
the foreign art student
bumped by hurrying strangers
carefully picks up her scattered portfolio

§

I join crowds behind fire trucks
to see the yacht club burning
the mayoral candidate hands out cards

§

Late at night
the janitors
lean back in leather
rest feet on mahogany
gripe
and laugh

§

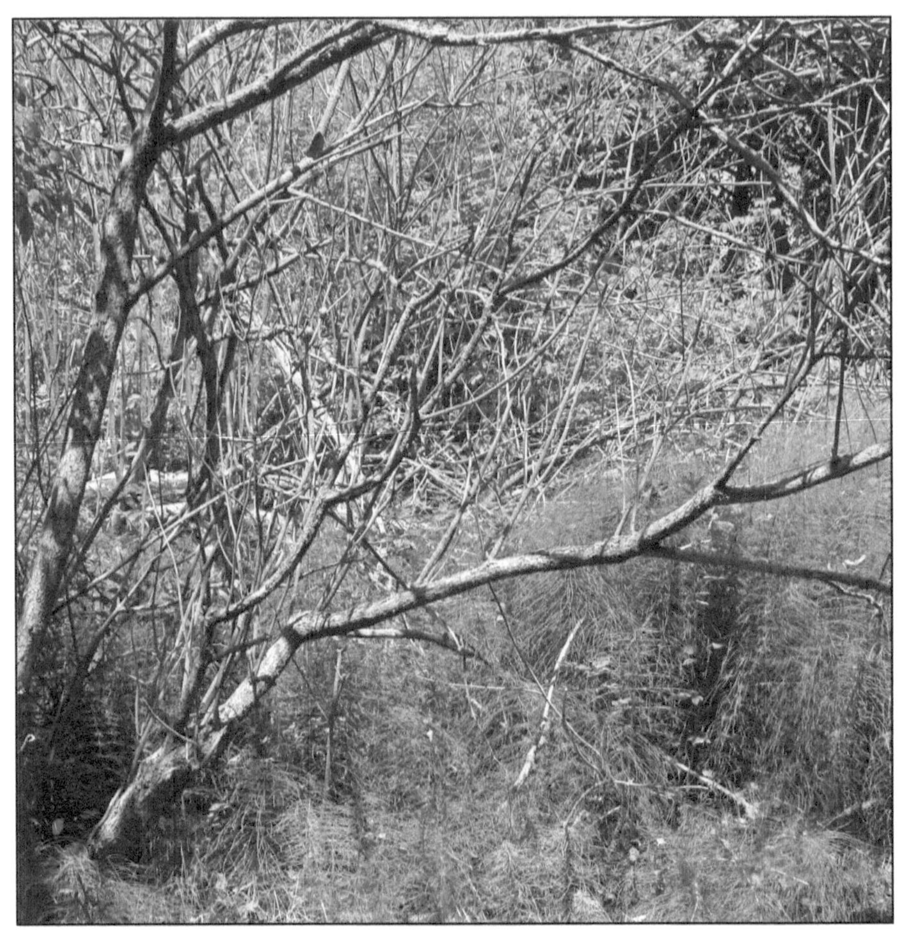

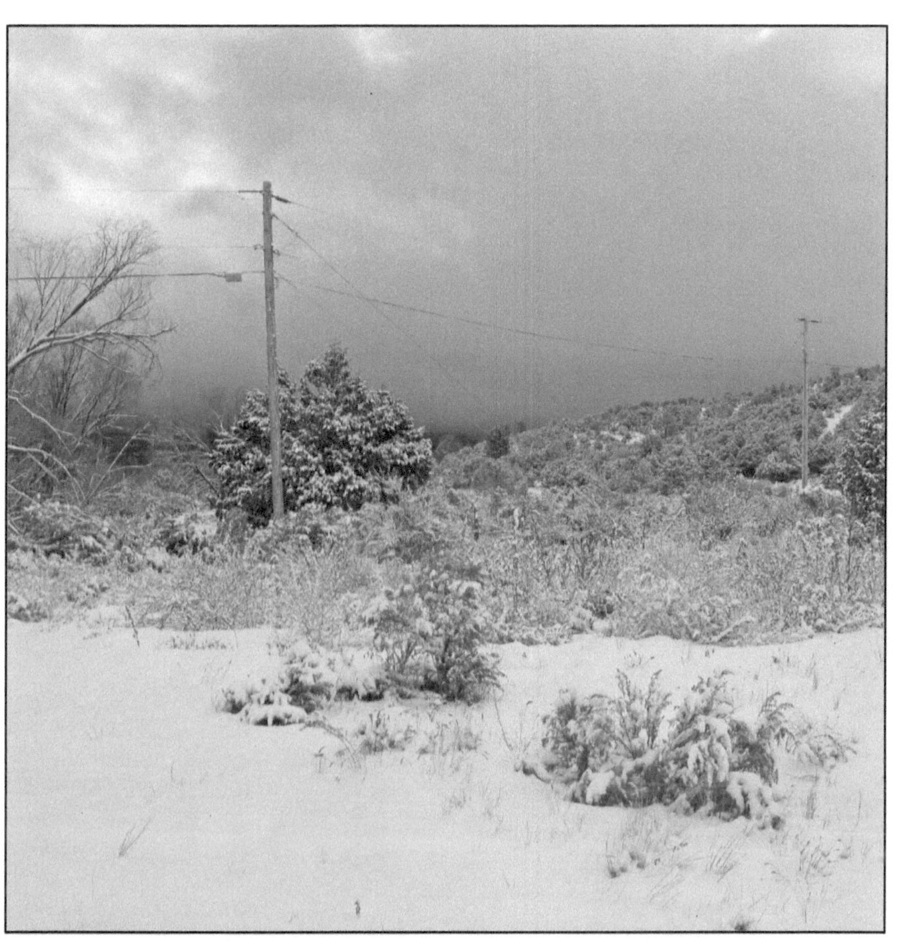

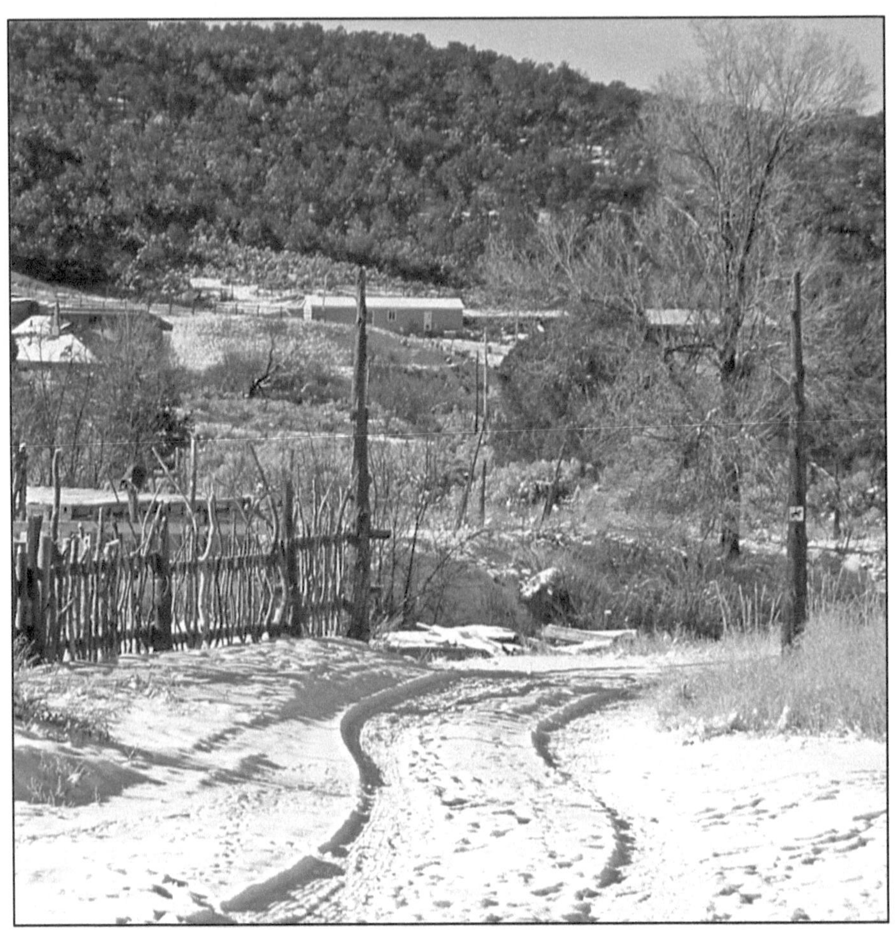

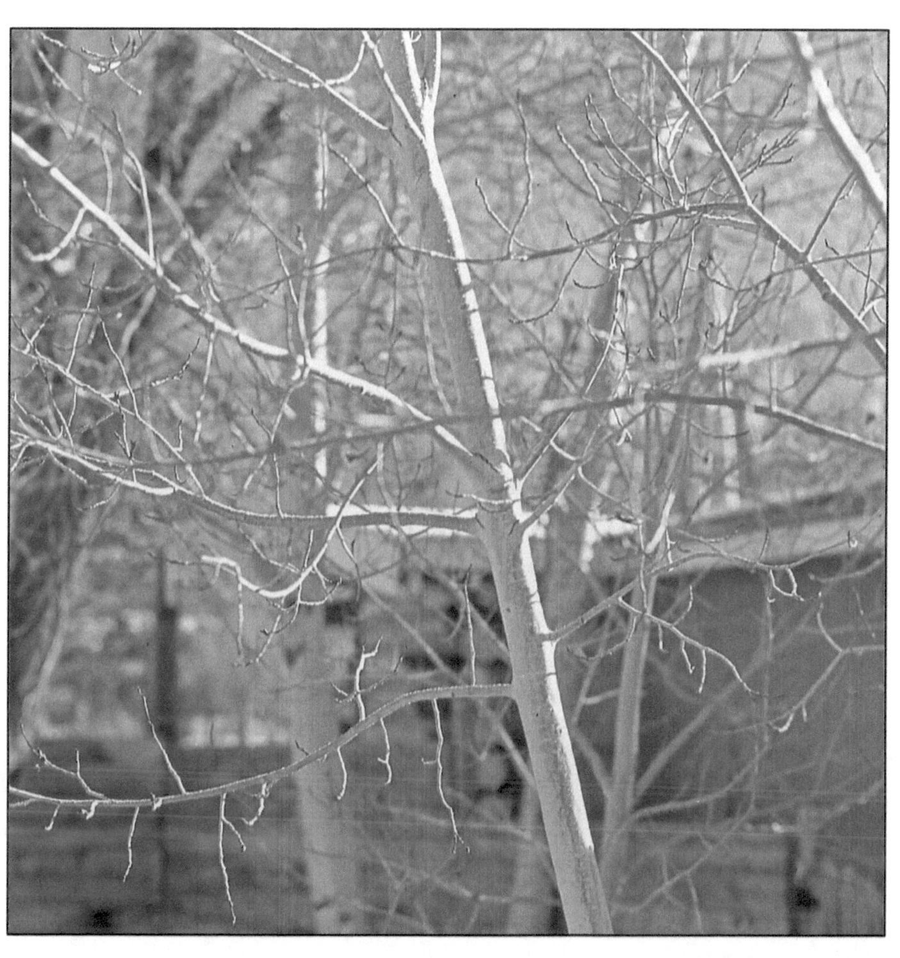

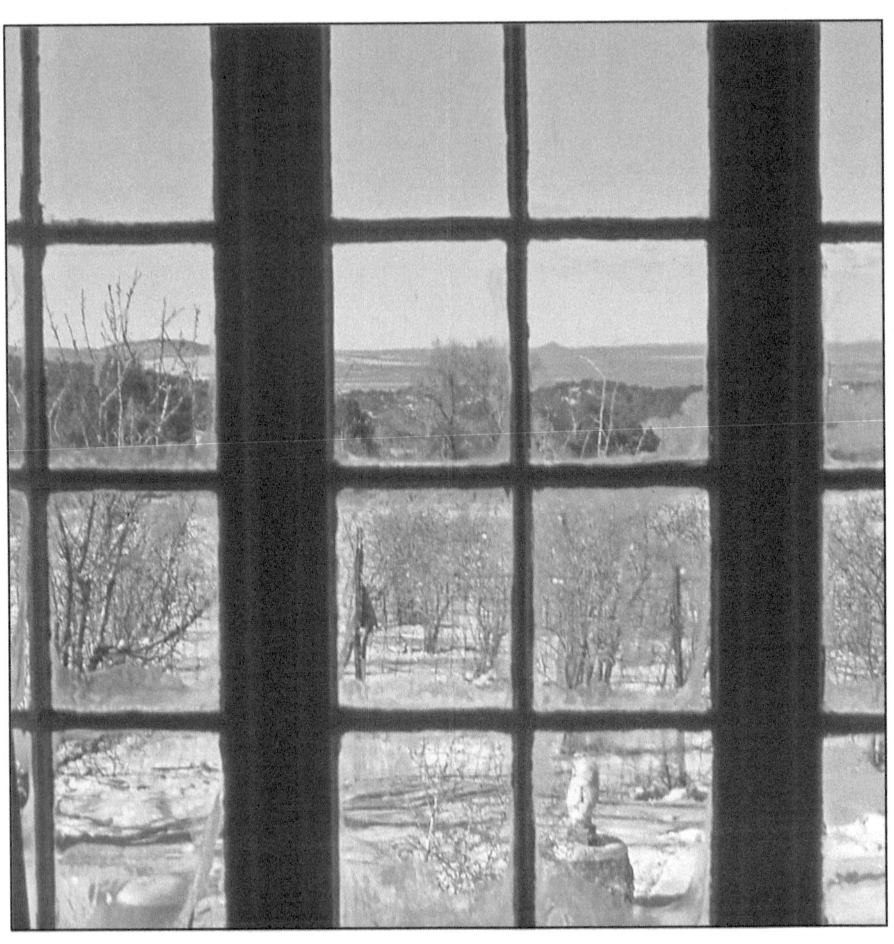

§

Carefully writing Christmas cards
with fountain pen
cat-ambushed

§

Now I must get out of this cozy bed
and fetch the firewood
from its blanket of snow

§

Ancient universe
this tiny newborn snowflake
already melted

§

Someone tapping at the window
just the wind
not just

§

Long after sun emerges
a city bus with snow chains
nags the dry streets

§

§

Arriving home
shedding parka and gloves
ah the familiar smell
of an oil furnace!

§

Water falls
water rises
waterfalls

§

At rush hour
this creek
becomes a river

§

I now live nearer the river
than before
the flood

§

Red-streaked sky
above the sleeping volcano
merely warns of dawn

§

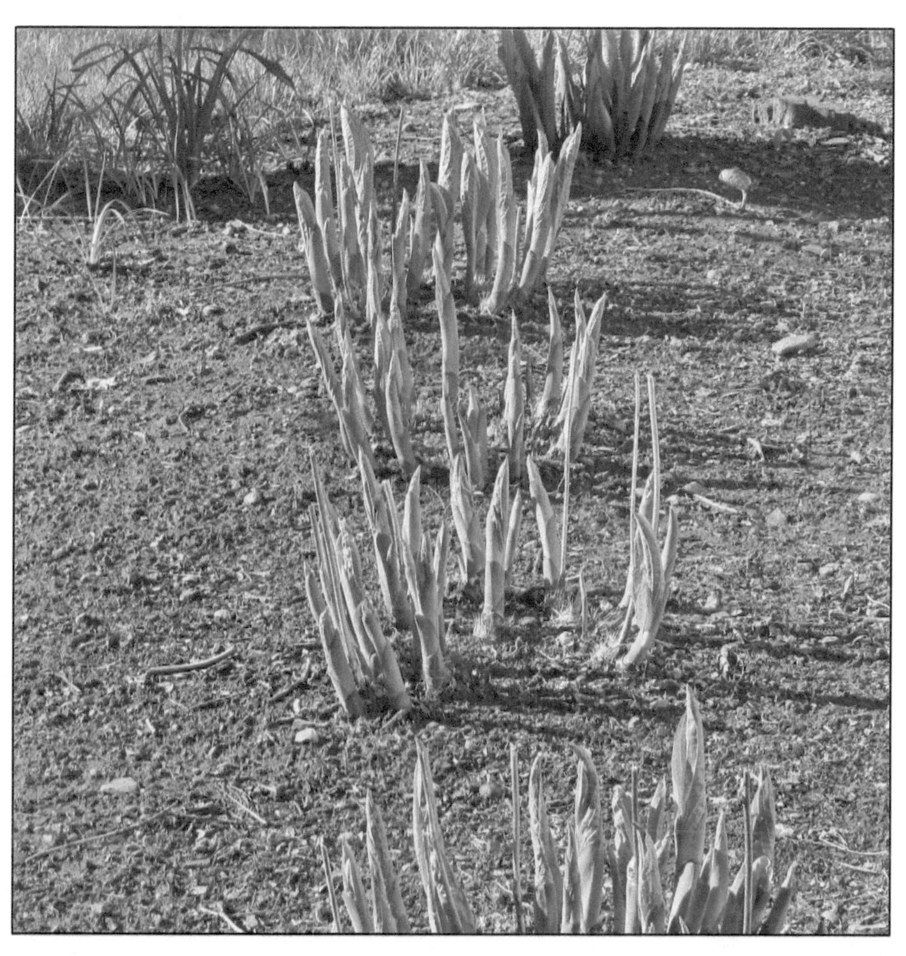

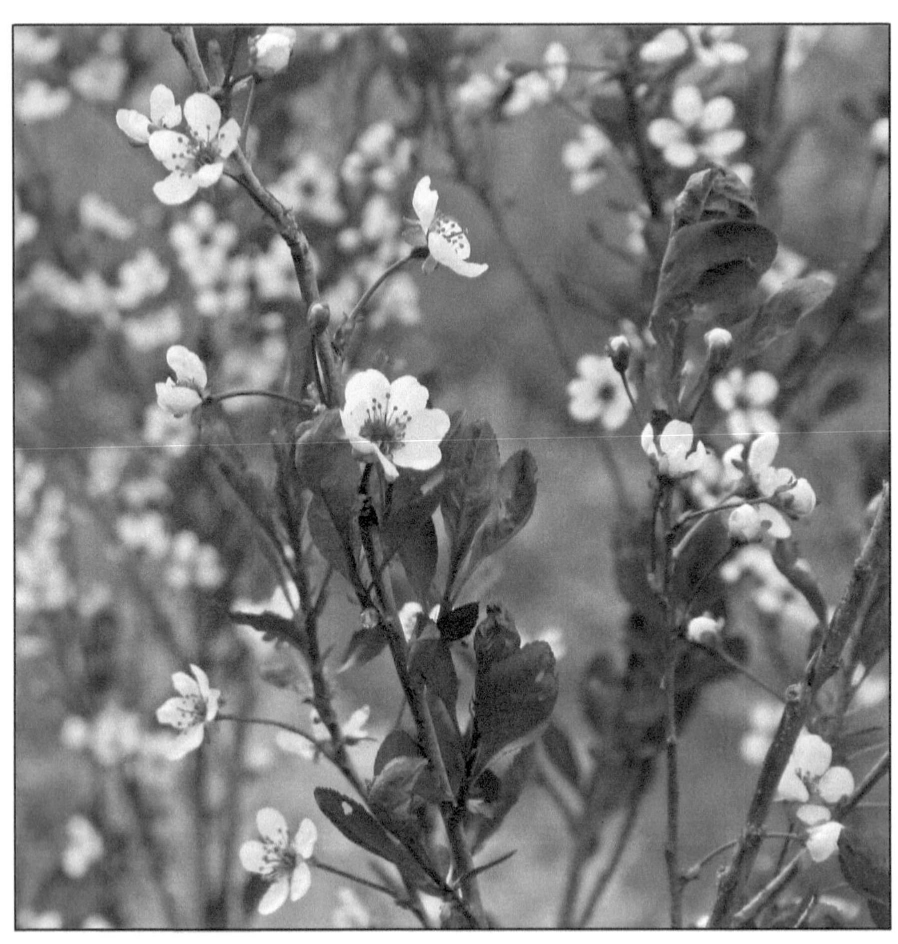

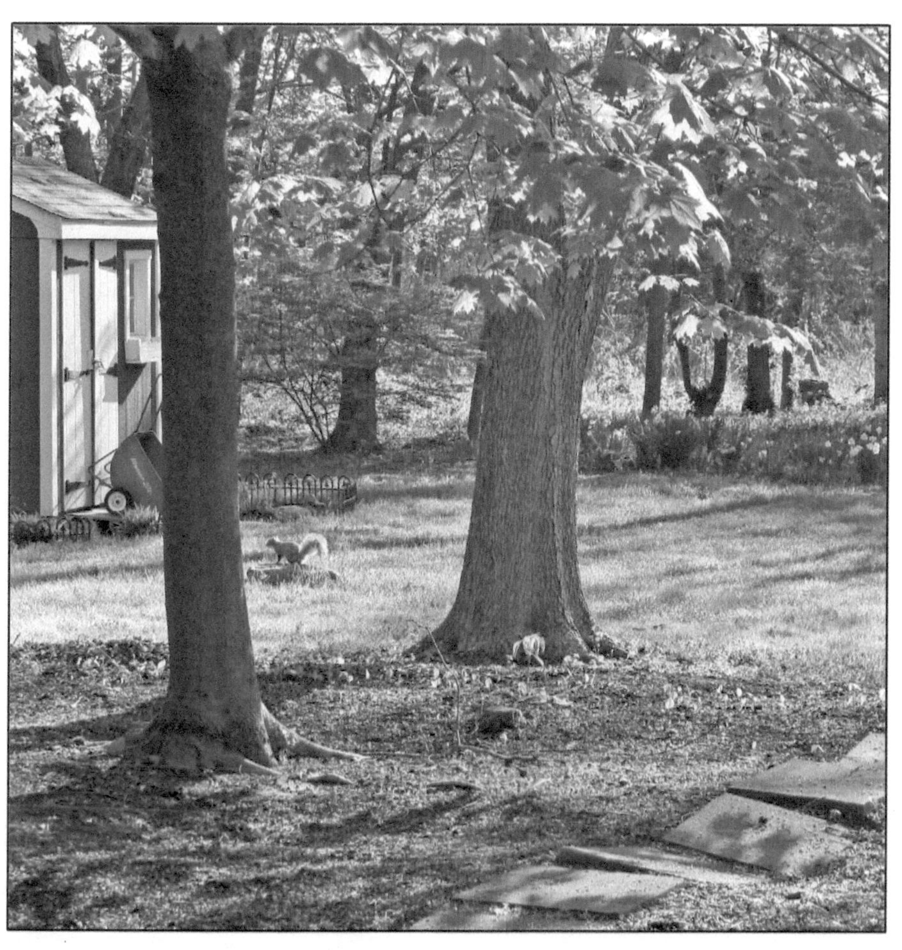

§

Yellow and pink Easter flowers
on a white cross
by the highway

§

That distant fleet of white
hyacinths
sails on the river

§

Hatchlings chirp
outside my open window
when I wake up
hungry

§

The bee in my lemon tree
is helping me
make lemonade

§

How did it get so dusty
under the furniture
since this time last year?

§

§

Unpaid bills
dirty clothes
on my floor
Bougainvillea
green leaves
outside my window
a real dilemma

§

Two squirrels chase each other
around the big firs
and across my solitary path

§

In the afternoon my shadow
leaning away from me
stands alone

§

Green water
transparent in the sunlight
your sand-bottomed eyes

§

The sunlight
catches your face like bright leaves
against the blue sky

§

§

The hummingbird
who lives in my yard
likes my red shirt

§

A small bird
lights on this blossomed branch
shakes off small petals

§

Sky full of white puffs
barely moving
barely breathing

§

Blue sky
white cumulus
yellow sun
hide and seek

§

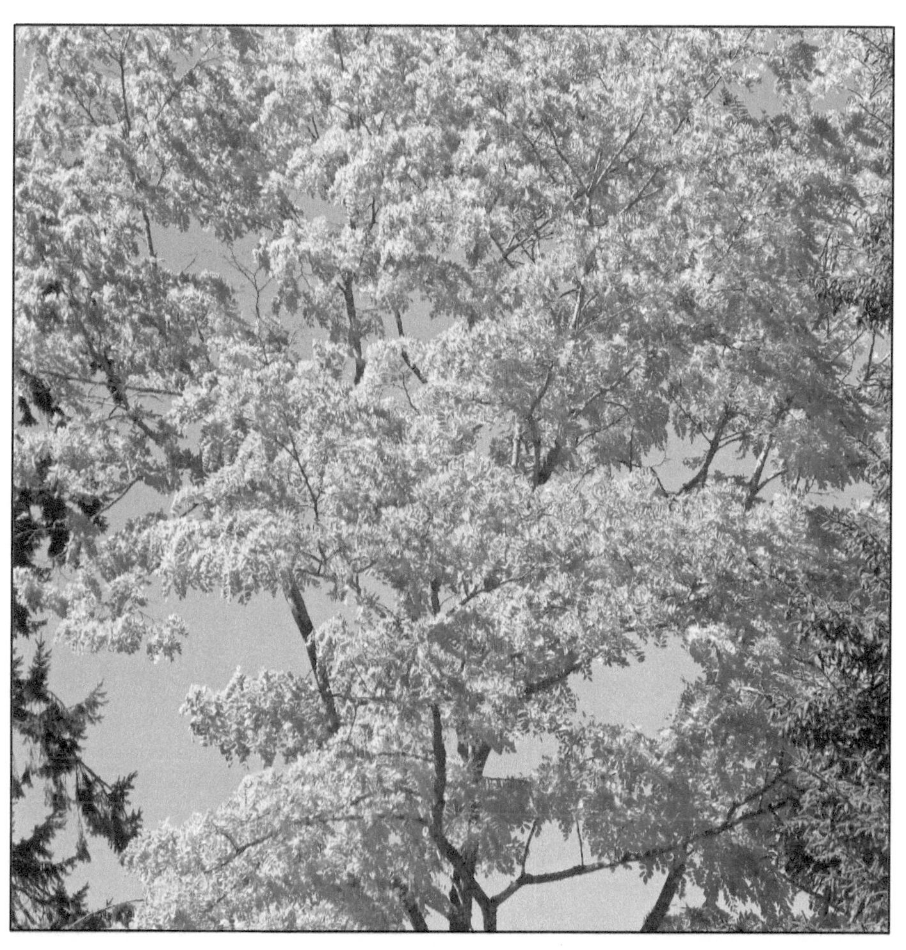

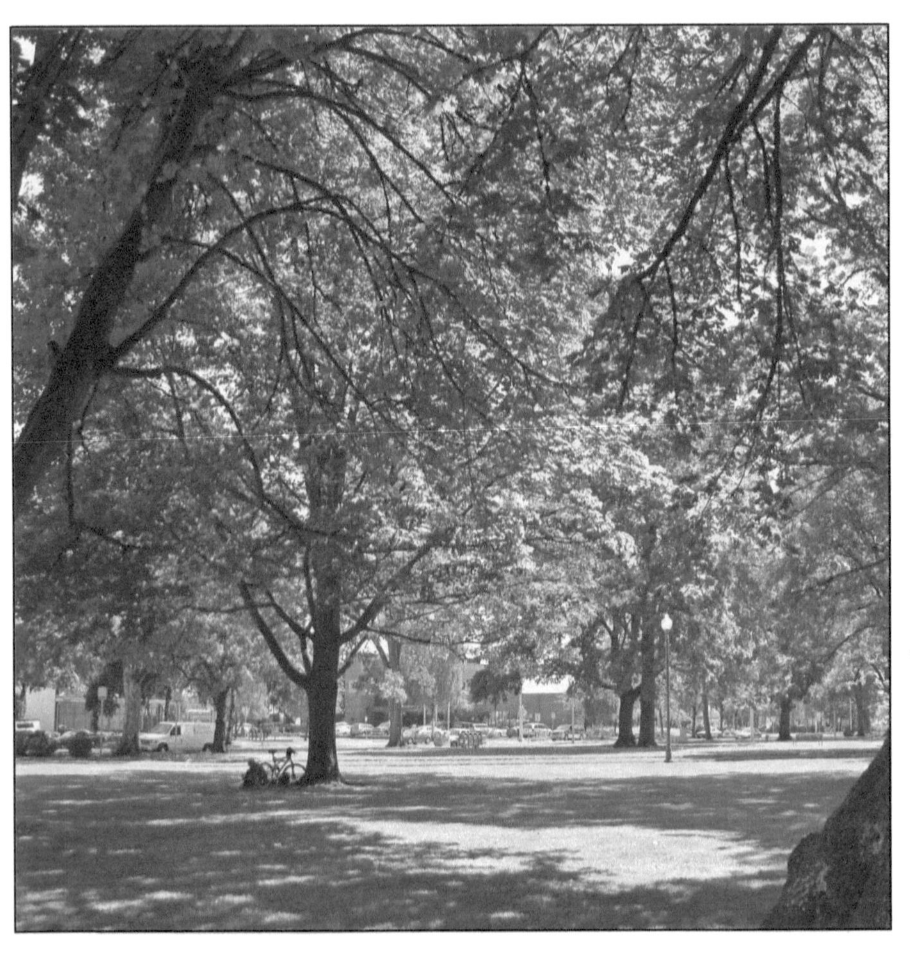

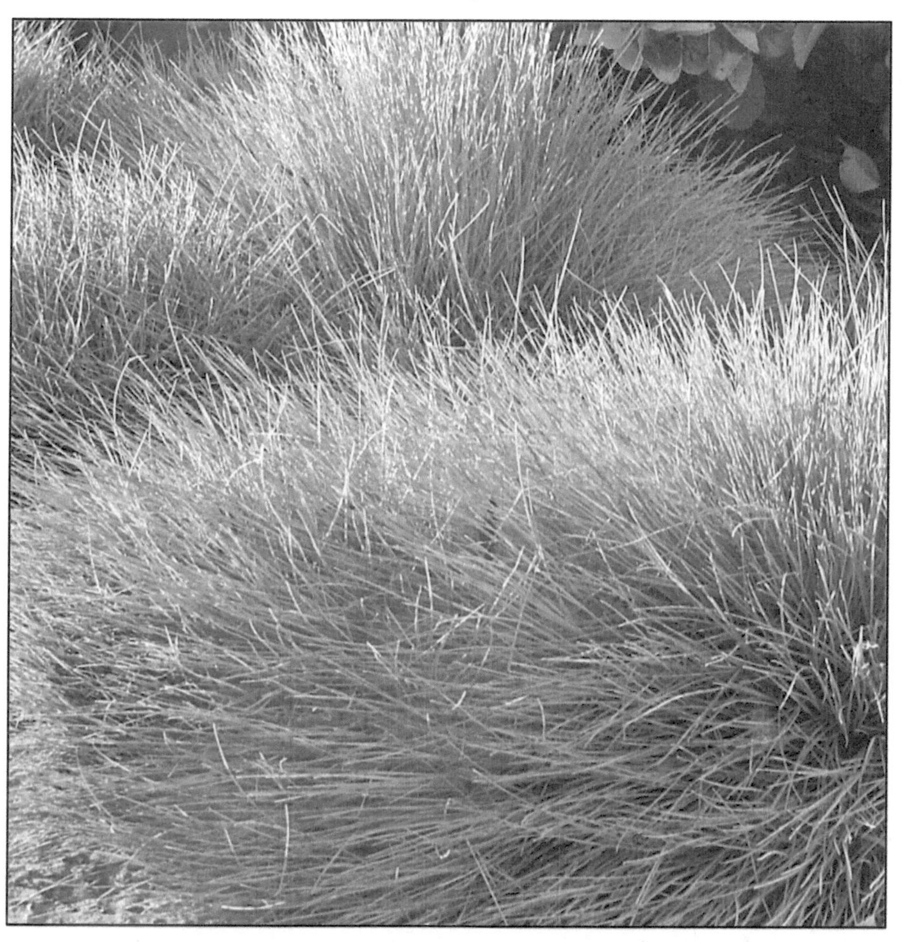

§

Hot and humid in Shiga-ken
visiting my in-laws' graves
ants crawl on the stones

§

Rubbing lotion into my age-ravaged feet
with arthritic hands
so happy after the hike

§

Almost touch
snowy mountains
taste them in a water glass

§

This morning's bright mountain
glowed soft and pink at dusk
bathes in milk under tonight's moon

§

Upthrust fist
through cotton
mountain rock in clouds

§

Sunshine warms my office
awakening I close the blinds
back to work

§

§

Evening sunlight
wanders around
through the same park
I do

§

Warm evening
a billion crickets
a neighbor's power saw

§

The song of the butterfly
silenced forever
by laughing children

§

Sunny afternoon nap
a bug flies into my throat
is this how it ends?

§

Smoky August sunset
fields on fire near Salem
bring back my youth

§

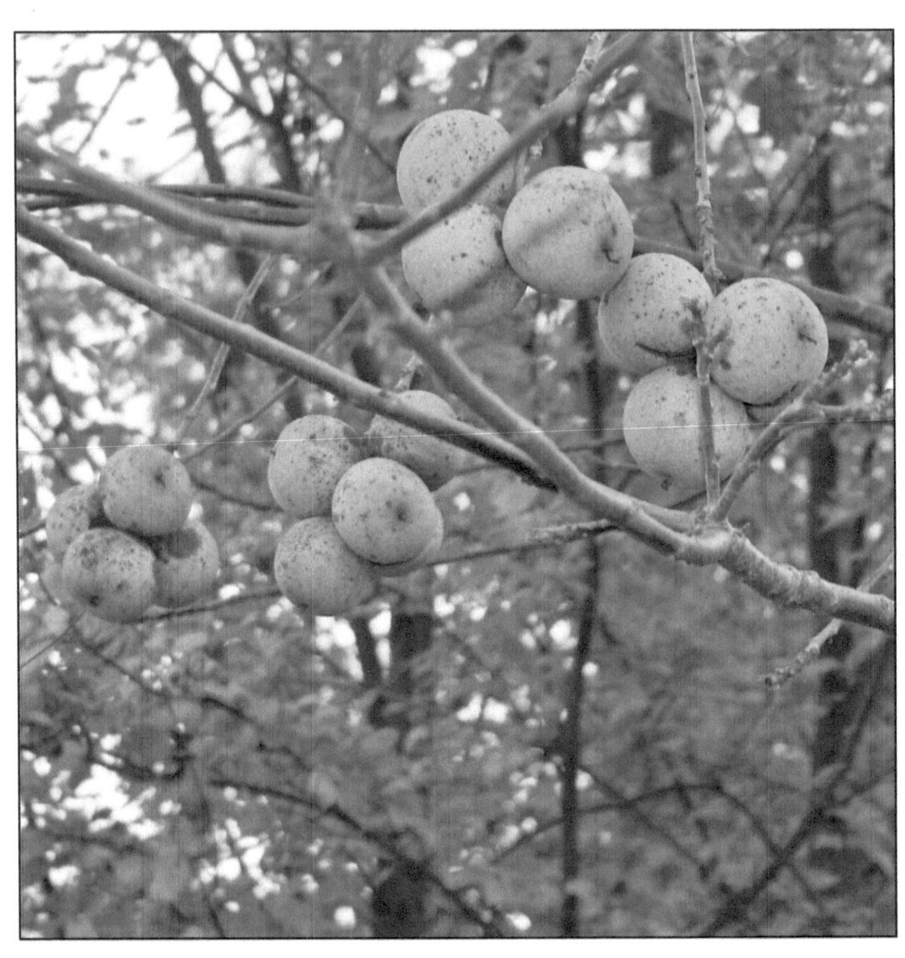

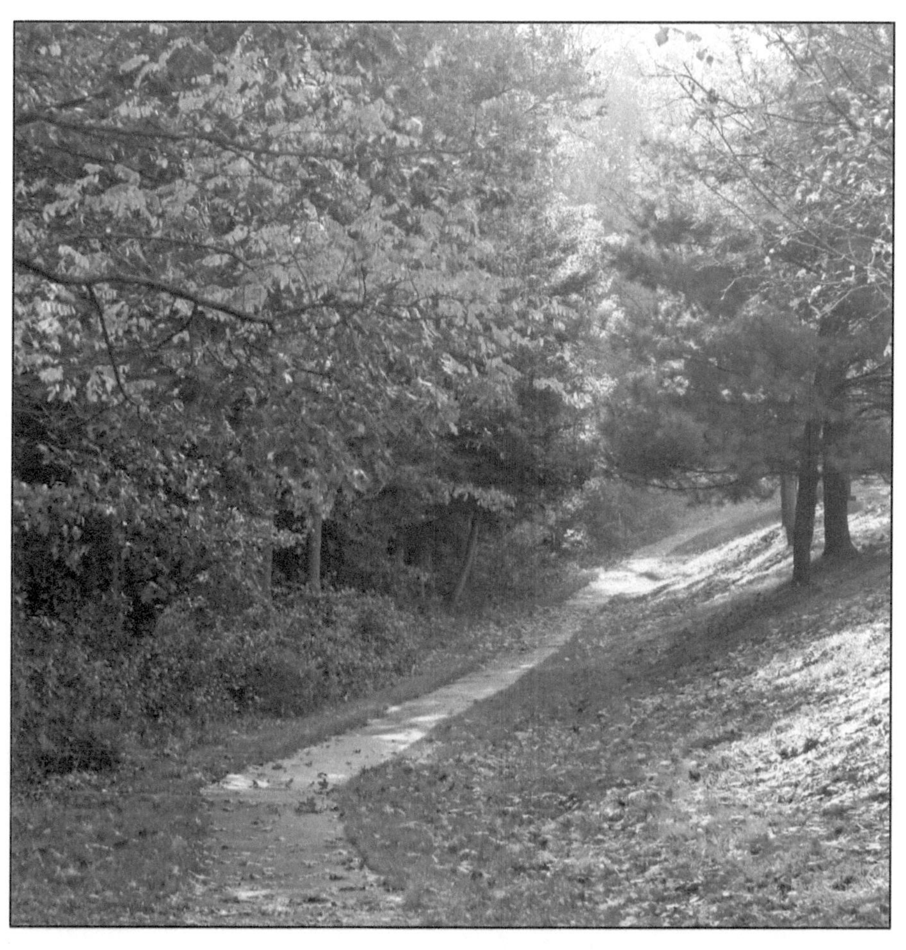

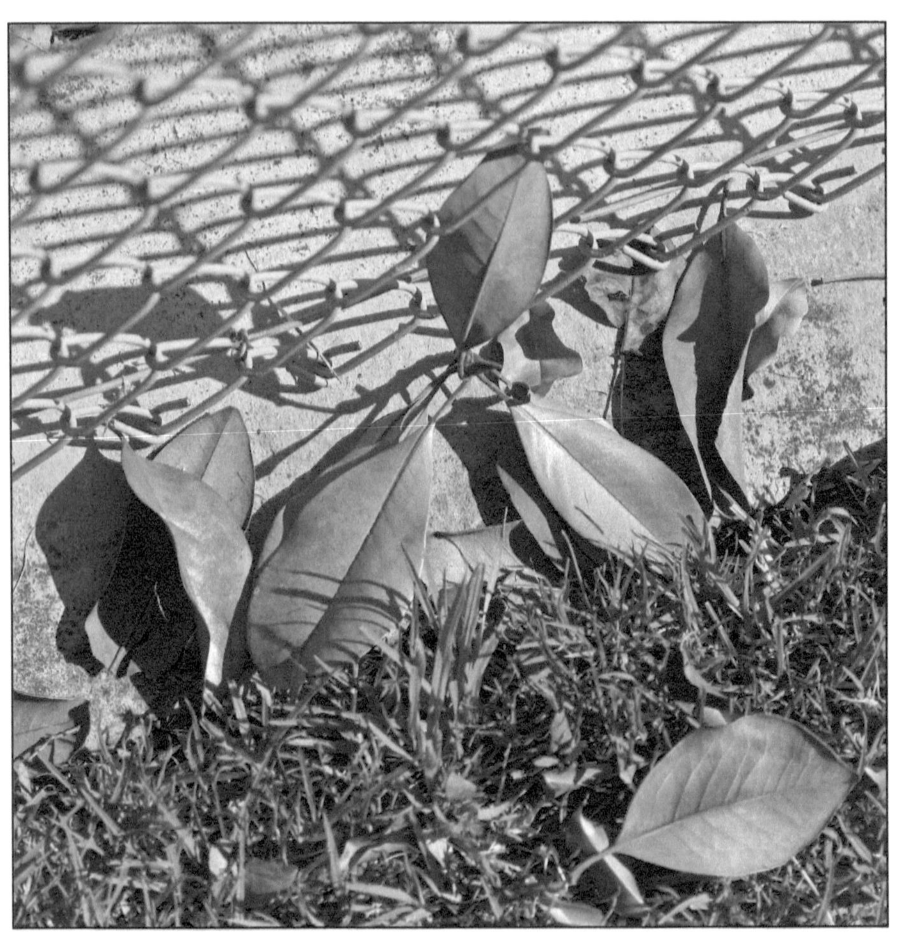

§

A highway of ants
crosses my hardwood floor
I left food out again

§

The spider by my kitchen window
grows fat
like me

§

Sunlight pours over hills
down through fir branches
splashes my face

§

Square fields edged by roads
golden grain
chess board
see the pawns bent over

§

Red and yellow leaves
the air so crisp
yet the geese flee

§

§

Turkey carcass
banging dishes
TV football
twin sleeping kittens

§

Sailboats flutter in kindergarten window
paper announcements
accidental art collaborating
with nature's wind
and someone to see

§

Outside the finance exam
an inch-long cockroach
probes dead leaves

§

Green all my life
I turn red and fall
my work complete

§

Fog in the valley
steaming coffee
a hot bath

§

§

Oh no!
raindrops on my bare head
cool and wet
how wonderful

§

On field no lines
on shirts no numbers
everywhere mud
great game!

§

Sitting in class
struck by a falling leaf
outside the enormous window

§

About the Author

Glenn Alan Daley is an independent scholar and writer living in Southern California. He was born in San Francisco in 1953 and raised as a preacher's kid in Texas, Washington, Idaho, Louisiana, Washington, and Oregon (in that order).

He earned a BA in English and Creative Writing from Stanford University, an MBA from Willamette University, and a MPhil in Policy Analysis from the Pardee RAND Graduate School. However, his three daughters have taught him a substantial fraction of what he knows. Glenn has served in the U.S. Navy, as Director of Research and Evaluation for the Los Angeles Unified School District, and as Associate Adjunct Professor in the USC Price School of Public Policy. He has authored or contributed to numerous public management and education research publications.

Glenn is the founder and president of Empty Rock LLC. *Seasons of a Refractive Mind* is his first book of poetry and photography, gathering pieces from fifty years shared privately with friends but never before published. He is currently working on a biography of his father and a book about economic theory.

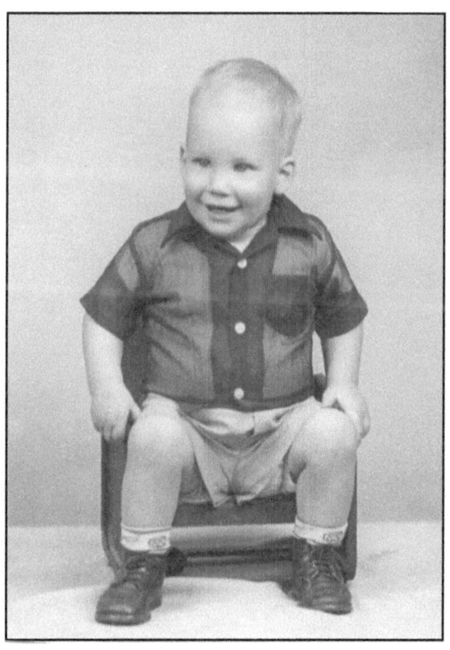

www.ingramcontent.com/pod-product-compliance
Lightning Source LLC
LaVergne TN
LVHW091025080826
845145LV00002B/358
9780692753217